Machine Learning for Hackers

Drew Conway and John Myles White

O'REILLY®

Beijing · Cambridge · Farnham · Köln · Sebastopol · Tokyo

Machine Learning for Hackers
by Drew Conway and John Myles White

Published by O'Reilly Media, Inc., 1005 Gravenstein Highway North, Sebastopol, CA 95472.

O'Reilly books may be purchased for educational, business, or sales promotional use. Online editions are also available for most titles (*http://my.safaribooksonline.com*). For more information, contact our corporate/institutional sales department: (800) 998-9938 or *corporate@oreilly.com*.

Editor: Julie Steele	**Indexer:** Angela Howard
Production Editor: Melanie Yarbrough	**Cover Designer:** Karen Montgomery
Copyeditor: Genevieve d'Entremont	**Interior Designer:** David Futato
Proofreader: Teresa Horton	**Illustrator:** Robert Romano

February 2012:   First Edition.

Revision History for the First Edition:
     2012-02-06   First release
See *http://oreilly.com/catalog/errata.csp?isbn=9781449303716* for release details.

ISBN: 978-1-449-30371-6

[LSI]

1328556641

Table of Contents

Preface vii

1. Using R 1
   R for Machine Learning   2
      Downloading and Installing R   5
      IDEs and Text Editors   8
      Loading and Installing R Packages   9
      R Basics for Machine Learning   12
      Further Reading on R   27

2. Data Exploration 29
   Exploration versus Confirmation   29
   What Is Data?   30
   Inferring the Types of Columns in Your Data   34
   Inferring Meaning   36
   Numeric Summaries   37
   Means, Medians, and Modes   37
   Quantiles   40
   Standard Deviations and Variances   41
   Exploratory Data Visualization   44
   Visualizing the Relationships Between Columns   61

3. Classification: Spam Filtering 73
   This or That: Binary Classification   73
   Moving Gently into Conditional Probability   77
   Writing Our First Bayesian Spam Classifier   78
      Defining the Classifier and Testing It with Hard Ham   85
      Testing the Classifier Against All Email Types   88
      Improving the Results   90

4. Ranking: Priority Inbox **93**

How Do You Sort Something When You Don't Know the Order?   93
Ordering Email Messages by Priority   95
     Priority Features of Email   95
Writing a Priority Inbox   99
     Functions for Extracting the Feature Set   100
     Creating a Weighting Scheme for Ranking   108
     Weighting from Email Thread Activity   113
     Training and Testing the Ranker   117

5. Regression: Predicting Page Views **127**

Introducing Regression   127
     The Baseline Model   127
     Regression Using Dummy Variables   132
     Linear Regression in a Nutshell   133
Predicting Web Traffic   141
Defining Correlation   152

6. Regularization: Text Regression **155**

Nonlinear Relationships Between Columns: Beyond Straight Lines   155
     Introducing Polynomial Regression   158
Methods for Preventing Overfitting   165
     Preventing Overfitting with Regularization   169
Text Regression   174
     Logistic Regression to the Rescue   178

7. Optimization: Breaking Codes **183**

Introduction to Optimization   183
Ridge Regression   190
Code Breaking as Optimization   193

8. PCA: Building a Market Index **205**

Unsupervised Learning   205

9. MDS: Visually Exploring US Senator Similarity **215**

Clustering Based on Similarity   215
     A Brief Introduction to Distance Metrics and Multidirectional Scaling   216
How Do US Senators Cluster?   222
     Analyzing US Senator Roll Call Data (101st–111th Congresses)   223

10. kNN: Recommendation Systems **233**

The *k*-Nearest Neighbors Algorithm   233

R Package Installation Data   239

11. Analyzing Social Graphs **243**
     Social Network Analysis   243
         Thinking Graphically   246
     Hacking Twitter Social Graph Data   248
         Working with the Google SocialGraph API   250
     Analyzing Twitter Networks   256
         Local Community Structure   257
         Visualizing the Clustered Twitter Network with Gephi   261
         Building Your Own "Who to Follow" Engine   267

12. Model Comparison **275**
     SVMs: The Support Vector Machine   275
     Comparing Algorithms   284

Works Cited **293**

Index **295**

Preface

Machine Learning for Hackers

To explain the perspective from which this book was written, it will be helpful to define the terms *machine learning* and *hackers*.

What is machine learning? At the highest level of abstraction, we can think of machine learning as a set of tools and methods that attempt to infer patterns and extract insight from a record of the observable world. For example, if we are trying to teach a computer to recognize the zip codes written on the fronts of envelopes, our data may consist of photographs of the envelopes along with a record of the zip code that each envelope was addressed to. That is, within some context we can take a record of the actions of our subjects, learn from this record, and then create a model of these activities that will inform our understanding of this context going forward. In practice, this requires data, and in contemporary applications this often means a lot of data (perhaps several terabytes). Most machine learning techniques take the availability of such data as given, which means new opportunities for their application in light of the quantities of data that are produced as a product of running modern companies.

What is a hacker? Far from the stylized depictions of nefarious teenagers or Gibsonian cyber-punks portrayed in pop culture, we believe a hacker is someone who likes to solve problems and experiment with new technologies. If you've ever sat down with the latest O'Reilly book on a new computer language and knuckled out code until you were well past "Hello, World," then you're a hacker. Or if you've dismantled a new gadget until you understood the entire machinery's architecture, then we probably mean you, too. These pursuits are often undertaken for no other reason than to have gone through the process and gained some knowledge about the *how* and the *why* of an unknown technology.

Along with an innate curiosity for how things work and a desire to build, a computer hacker (as opposed to a car hacker, life hacker, food hacker, etc.) has experience with software design and development. This is someone who has written programs before, likely in many different languages. To a hacker, Unix is not a four-letter word, and command-line navigation and bash operations may come as naturally as working with GUIs. Using regular expressions and tools such as `sed`, `awk`, and `grep` are a hacker's first line of defense when dealing with text. In the chapters contained in this book, we will assume a relatively high level of this sort of knowledge.

How This Book Is Organized

Machine learning blends concepts and techniques from many different traditional fields, such as mathematics, statistics, and computer science. As such, there are many ways to learn the discipline. Considering its theoretical foundations in mathematics and statistics, newcomers would do well to attain some degree of mastery of the formal specifications of basic machine learning techniques. There are many excellent books that focus on the fundamentals, the classic work being Hastie, Tibshirani, and Friedman's *The Elements of Statistical Learning* ([HTF09]; full references can be found in the Works Cited).[1] But another important part of the hacker mantra is to learn by doing. Many hackers may be more comfortable thinking of problems in terms of the *process* by which a solution is attained, rather than the *theoretical foundation* from which the solution is derived.

From this perspective, an alternative approach to teaching machine learning would be to use "cookbook"-style examples. To understand how a recommendation system works, for example, we might provide sample training data and a version of the model, and show how the latter uses the former. There are many useful texts of this kind as well, and Segaran's *Programming Collective Intelligence* is one recent example [Seg07]. Such a discussion would certainly address the *how* of a hacker's method of learning, but perhaps less of the *why*. Along with understanding the mechanics of a method, we may also want to learn why it is used in a certain context or to address a specific problem.

To provide a more complete reference on machine learning for hackers, therefore, we need to compromise between providing a deep review of the theoretical foundations of the discipline and a broad exploration of its applications. To accomplish this, we have decided to teach machine learning through selected case studies.

We believe the best way to learn is by first having a problem in mind, then focusing on learning the tools used to solve that problem. This is effectively the mechanism through which case studies work. The difference being, rather than having some problem for which there may be no known solution, we can focus on well-understood and studied problems in machine learning and present specific examples of cases where some solutions excelled while others failed spectacularly.

For that reason, each chapter of this book is a self-contained case study focusing on a specific problem in machine learning. The organization of the early cases moves from classification to regression (discussed further in Chapter 1). We then examine topics

---

1. *The Elements of Statistical Learning* can now be downloaded free of charge at *http://www-stat.stanford .edu/~tibs/ElemStatLearn/*.

such as clustering, dimensionality reduction, and optimization. It is important to note that not all problems fit neatly into either the classification or regression categories, and some of the case studies reviewed in this book will include aspects of both (sometimes explicitly, but also in more subtle ways that we will review). Following are brief descriptions of all the case studies reviewed in this book in the order they appear:

Text classification: spam detection

> In this chapter we introduce the idea of binary classification, which is motivated through the use of email text data. Here we tackle the classic problem in machine learning of classifying some input as one of two types, which in this case is either ham (legitimate email) or spam (unwanted email).

Ranking items: priority inbox

> Using the same email text data as in the previous case study, here we move beyond a binary classification to a discrete set of types. Specifically, we need to identify the appropriate features to extract from the email that can best inform its "priority" rank among all emails.

Regression models: predicting page views

> We now introduce the second primary tool in machine learning, linear regression. Here we explore data whose relationship roughly approximates a straight line. In this case study, we are interested in predicting the number of page views for the top 1,000 websites on the Internet as of 2011.

Regularization: text regression

> Sometimes the relationships in our data are not well described by a straight line. To describe the relationship, we may need to fit a different function; however, we also must be cautious not to overfit. Here we introduce the concept of regularization to overcome this problem, and motivate it through a case study, focusing on understanding the relationship among words in the text from O'Reilly book descriptions.

Optimization: code breaking

> Moving beyond regression models, almost every algorithm in machine learning can be viewed as an optimization problem in which we try to minimize some measure of prediction error. Here we introduce classic algorithms for performing this optimization and attempt to break a simple letter cipher with these techniques.

Unsupervised learned: building a stock market index

> Up to this point we have discussed only supervised learning techniques. Here we introduce its methodological counterpart: unsupervised learning. The important difference is that in supervised learning, we wish to use the structure of our data to make predictions, whereas in unsupervised learning, we wish to discover structure in our data for structure's sake. In this case we will use stock market data to create an index that describes how well the overall market is doing.

Spatial similarity: clustering US Senators by the voting records
> Here we introduce the concept of spatial distances among observations. To do so, we define measures of distance and describe methods for clustering observations basing on their spatial distances. We use data from US Senator roll call voting to cluster those legislators based on their votes.

Recommendation system: suggesting R packages to users
> To further the discussion of spatial similarities, we discuss how to build a recommendation system based on the closeness of observations in space. Here we introduce the *k*-nearest neighbors algorithm and use it to suggest R packages to programmers based on their currently installed packages.

Social network analysis: who to follow on Twitter
> Here we attempt to combine many of the concepts previously discussed, as well as introduce a few new ones, to design and build a "who to follow" recommendation system from Twitter data. In this case we build a system for downloading Twitter network data, discover communities within the structure, and recommend new users to follow using basic social network analysis techniques.

Model comparison: finding the best algorithm for your problem
> In the final chapter, we discuss techniques for choosing which machine learning algorithm to use to solve your problem. We introduce our final algorithm, the support vector machine, and compare its performance on the spam data from Chapter 3 with the performance of the other algorithms we introduce earlier in the book.

The primary tool we use to explore these case studies is the R statistical programming language (*http://www.r-project.org/*). R is particularly well suited for machine learning case studies because it is a high-level, functional scripting language designed for data analysis. Much of the underlying algorithmic scaffolding required is already built into the language or has been implemented as one of the thousands of R packages available on the Comprehensive R Archive Network (CRAN).[2] This will allow us to focus on the *how* and the *why* of these problems, rather than review and rewrite the foundational code for each case.

Conventions Used in This Book

The following typographical conventions are used in this book:

Italic
> Indicates new terms, URLs, email addresses, filenames, and file extensions.

---

2. For more information on CRAN, see *http://cran.r-project.org/*.

Constant width

Used for program listings, as well as within paragraphs to refer to program elements such as variable or function names, databases, data types, environment variables, statements, and keywords.

Constant width bold

Shows commands or other text that should be typed literally by the user.

Constant width italic

Shows text that should be replaced with user-supplied values or by values determined by context.

This icon signifies a tip, suggestion, or general note.

This icon indicates a warning or caution.

Using Code Examples

This book is here to help you get your job done. In general, you may use the code in this book in your programs and documentation. You do not need to contact us for permission unless you're reproducing a significant portion of the code. For example, writing a program that uses several chunks of code from this book does not require permission. Selling or distributing a CD-ROM of examples from O'Reilly books does require permission. Answering a question by citing this book and quoting example code does not require permission. Incorporating a significant amount of example code from this book into your product's documentation does require permission.

We appreciate, but do not require, attribution. An attribution usually includes the title, author, publisher, and ISBN. For example: "*Machine Learning for Hackers* by Drew Conway and John Myles White (O'Reilly). Copyright 2012 Drew Conway and John Myles White, 978-1-449-30371-6."

If you feel your use of code examples falls outside fair use or the permission given above, feel free to contact us at *permissions@oreilly.com*.

Safari® Books Online

Safari Books Online is an on-demand digital library that lets you easily search over 7,500 technology and creative reference books and videos to find the answers you need quickly.

With a subscription, you can read any page and watch any video from our library online. Read books on your cell phone and mobile devices. Access new titles before they are available for print, and get exclusive access to manuscripts in development and post feedback for the authors. Copy and paste code samples, organize your favorites, download chapters, bookmark key sections, create notes, print out pages, and benefit from tons of other time-saving features.

O'Reilly Media has uploaded this book to the Safari Books Online service. To have full digital access to this book and others on similar topics from O'Reilly and other publishers, sign up for free at *http://my.safaribooksonline.com*.

How to Contact Us

Please address comments and questions concerning this book to the publisher:

O'Reilly Media, Inc.
1005 Gravenstein Highway North
Sebastopol, CA 95472
800-998-9938 (in the United States or Canada)
707-829-0515 (international or local)
707-829-0104 (fax)

We have a web page for this book, where we list errata, examples, and any additional information. You can access this page at:

http://shop.oreilly.com/product/0636920018483.do

To comment or ask technical questions about this book, send email to:

bookquestions@oreilly.com

For more information about our books, courses, conferences, and news, see our website at *http://www.oreilly.com*.

Find us on Facebook: *http://facebook.com/oreilly*

Follow us on Twitter: *http://twitter.com/oreillymedia*

Watch us on YouTube: *http://www.youtube.com/oreillymedia*

Acknowledgements

From the Authors

First off, we'd like to thank our editor, Julie Steele, for helping us through the entire process of publishing our first book. We'd also like to thank Melanie Yarbrough and Genevieve d'Entremont for their remarkably thorough work in cleaning the book up for publication. We'd also like to thank the other people at O'Reilly who've helped to improve the book, but whose work was done in the background.

In addition to the kind folks at O'Reilly, we'd like to thank our technical reviewers: Mike Dewar, Max Shron, Matt Canning, Paul Dix, and Maxim Khesin. Their comments improved the book greatly and as the saying goes, the errors that remain are entirely our own responsibility.

We'd also like to thank the members of the NYC Data Brunch for originally inspiring us to write this book and for giving us a place to refine our ideas about teaching machine learning. In particular, thanks to Hilary Mason for originally introducing us to several people at O'Reilly.

Finally, we'd like to thank the many friends of ours in the data science community who've been so supportive and encouraging while we've worked on this book. Knowing that people wanted to read our book helped us keep up pace during the long haul that writing a full-length book entails.

From Drew Conway

I would like to thank Julie Steele, our editor, for appreciating our motivation for this book and giving us the ability to produce it. I would like to thank all of those who provided feedback, both during and after writing; but especially Mike Dewar, Max Shron and Max Khesin. I would like to thank Kristen, my wife, who has always inspired me and was there throughout the entire process with me. Finally, I would like to thank my co-author, John, for having the idea to write a book like this and then the vision to see it to completion.

From John Myles White

First off, I'd like to thank my co-author, Drew, for writing this book with me. Having someone to collaborate with makes the enormous task of writing an entire book manageable and even fun. In addition, I'd like to thank my parents for having always encouraged me to explore any and every topic that interested me. I'd also like to thank Jennifer Mitchel and Jeffrey Achter for inspiring me to focus on mathematics as an undergraduate. My college years shaped my vision of the world and I'm very grateful for the role you two played in that. As well, I'd like to thank my friend Harek for continually inspiring me to push my limits and to work more. On a less personal note, thanks are due to the band La Dispute for providing the soundtrack to which I've done almost all of the writing of this book. And finally I want to thank the many people who've given me space to work in, whether it's the friends whose couches I've sat on or the owners of the Boutique Hotel Steinerwirt 1493 and the Linger Cafe where I finished the rough and final drafts of this book respectively.

## CHAPTER 1

Using R

Machine learning exists at the intersection of traditional mathematics and statistics with software engineering and computer science. In this book, we will describe several tools from traditional statistics that allow you to make sense of the world. Statistics has almost always been concerned with learning something interpretable from data, whereas machine learning has been concerned with turning data into something practical and usable. This contrast makes it easier to understand the term *machine learning*: Machine learning is concerned with teaching *computers* something about the world, so that they can use that knowledge to perform other tasks. In contrast, statistics is more concerned with developing tools for teaching *humans* something about the world, so that they can think more clearly about the world in order to make better decisions.

In machine learning, the *learning* occurs by extracting as much information from the data as possible (or reasonable) through algorithms that parse the basic structure of the data and distinguish the signal from the noise. After they have found the signal, or *pattern*, the algorithms simply decide that everything else that's left over is noise. For that reason, machine learning techniques are also referred to as *pattern recognition algorithms*. We can "train" our machines to learn about how data is generated in a given context, which allows us to use these algorithms to automate many useful tasks. This is where the term *training set* comes from, referring to the set of data used to build a machine learning process. The notion of observing data, learning from it, and then automating some process of recognition is at the heart of machine learning and forms the primary arc of this book. Two particularly important types of patterns constitute the core problems we'll provide you with tools to solve: the problem of classification and the problem of regression, which will be introduced over the course of this book.

In this book, we assume a relatively high degree of knowledge in basic programming techniques and algorithmic paradigms. That said, R remains a relatively niche language, even among experienced programmers. In an effort to establish the same starting point for everyone, this chapter provides some basic information on how to get started using the R language. Later in the chapter we will provide an extended case study for working with data in R.

This chapter does not provide a complete introduction to the R programming language. As you might expect, no such introduction could fit into a single book chapter. Instead, this chapter is meant to prepare the reader for the tasks associated with doing machine learning in R, specifically the process of loading, exploring, cleaning, and analyzing data. There are many excellent resources on R that discuss language fundamentals such as data types, arithmetic concepts, and coding best practices. In so far as those topics are relevant to the case studies presented here, we will touch on all of these issues; however, there will be no explicit discussion of these topics. For those interested in reviewing these topics, many of these resources are listed in Table 1-3.

If you have never seen the R language and its syntax before, we highly recommend going through this introduction to get some exposure. Unlike other high-level scripting languages, such as Python or Ruby, R has a unique and somewhat prickly syntax and tends to have a steeper learning curve than other languages. If you have used R before but not in the context of machine learning, there is still value in taking the time to go through this review before moving on to the case studies.

R for Machine Learning

R is a language and environment for statistical computing and graphics....R provides a wide variety of statistical (linear and nonlinear modeling, classical statistical tests, time-series analysis, classification, clustering, ...) and graphical techniques, and is highly extensible. The S language is often the vehicle of choice for research in statistical methodology, and R provides an Open Source route to participation in that activity.

—The R Project for Statistical Computing, *http://www.r-project.org/*

The best thing about R is that it was developed by statisticians. The worst thing about R is that...it was developed by statisticians.

—Bo Cowgill, Google, Inc.

R is an extremely powerful language for manipulating and analyzing data. Its meteoric rise in popularity within the data science and machine learning communities has made it the de facto *lingua franca* for analytics. R's success in the data analysis community stems from two factors described in the preceding epitaphs: R provides most of the technical power that statisticians require built into the default language, and R has been supported by a community of statisticians who are also open source devotees.

There are many technical advantages afforded by a language designed specifically for statistical computing. As the description from the R Project notes, the language provides an open source bridge to S, which contains many highly specialized statistical operations as base functions. For example, to perform a basic linear regression in R, one must simply pass the data to the 1m function, which then returns an object containing detailed information about the regression (coefficients, standard errors, residual values, etc.). This data can then be visualized by passing the results to the `plot` function, which is designed to visualize the results of this analysis.

In other languages with large scientific computing communities, such as Python, duplicating the functionality of `lm` requires the use of several third-party libraries to represent the data (NumPy), perform the analysis (SciPy), and visualize the results (matplotlib). As we will see in the following chapters, such sophisticated analyses can be performed with a single line of code in R.

In addition, as in other scientific computing environments, the fundamental data type in R is a vector. Vectors can be aggregated and organized in various ways, but at the core, all data is represented this way. This relatively rigid perspective on data structures can be limiting, but is also logical given the application of the language. The most frequently used data structure in R is the *data frame*, which can be thought of as a matrix with attributes, an internally defined "spreadsheet" structure, or relational database-like structure in the core of the language. Fundamentally, a data frame is simply a column-wise aggregation of vectors that R affords specific functionality to, which makes it ideal for working with any manner of data.

 For all of its power, R also has its disadvantages. R does not scale well with large data, and although there have been many efforts to address this problem, it remains a serious issue. For the purposes of the case studies we will review, however, this will not be an issue. The data sets we will use are relatively small, and all of the systems we will build are prototypes or proof-of-concept models. This distinction is important because if your intention is to build enterprise-level machine learning systems at the Google or Facebook scale, then R is not the right solution. In fact, companies like Google and Facebook often use R as their "data sandbox" to play with data and experiment with new machine learning methods. If one of those experiments bears fruit, then the engineers will attempt to replicate the functionality designed in R in a more appropriate language, such as C.

This ethos of experimentation has also engendered a great sense of community around the language. The social advantages of R hinge on this large and growing community of experts using and contributing to the language. As Bo Cowgill alludes to, R was borne out of statisticians' desire to have a computing environment that met their specific needs. Many R users, therefore, are experts in their various fields. This includes an extremely diverse set of disciplines, including mathematics, statistics, biology, chemistry, physics, psychology, economics, and political science, to name a few. This community of experts has built a massive collection of packages on top of the extensive base functions in R. At the time of writing, CRAN, the R repository for packages, contained over 2,800 packages. In the case studies that follow, we will use many of the most popular packages, but this will only scratch the surface of what is possible with R.

Finally, although the latter portion of Cowgill's statement may seem a bit menacing, it further highlights the strength of the R community. As we will see, the R language has a particularly odd syntax that is rife with coding "gotchas" that can drive away even experienced developers. But all grammatical grievances with a language can eventually be overcome, especially for persistent hackers. What is more difficult for nonstatisticians is the liberal assumption of familiarity with statistical and mathematical methods built into R functions. Using the lm function as an example, if you had never performed a linear regression, you would not know to look for coefficients, standard errors, or residual values in the results. Nor would you know how to interpret those results.

But because the language is open source, you are always able to look at the code of a function to see exactly what it is doing. Part of what we will attempt to accomplish with this book is to explore many of these functions in the context of machine learning, but that exploration will ultimately address only a tiny subset of what you can do in R. Fortunately, the R community is full of people willing to help you understand not only the language, but also the methods implemented in it. Table 1-1 lists some of the best places to start.

Table 1-1. Community resources for R help

Resource	Location	Description
RSeek	http://rseek.org/	When the core development team decided to create an open source version of S and call it R, they had not considered how hard it would be to search for documents related to a single-letter language on the Web. This specialized search tool attempts to alleviate this problem by providing a focused portal to R documentation and information.
Official R mailing lists	http://www.r-project.org/mail.html	There are several mailing lists dedicated to the R language, including announcements, packages, development, and—of course—help. Many of the language's core developers frequent these lists, and responses are often quick and terse.
StackOverflow	http://stackoverflow.com/questions/tagged/r	Hackers will know StackOverflow.com as one of the premier web resources for coding tips in any language, and the R tag is no exception. Thanks to the efforts of several prominent R community members, there is an active and vibrant collection of experts adding and answering R questions on StackOverflow.
#rstats Twitter hashtag	http://search.twitter.com/search?q=%23rstats	There is also a very active community of R users on Twitter, and they have designated the #rstats hash tag as their signifier. The thread is a great place to find links to useful resources, find experts in the language, and post questions—as long as they can fit into 140 characters!
R-Bloggers	http://www.r-bloggers.com/	There are hundreds of people blogging about how they use R in their research, work, or just for fun. R-bloggers.com aggregates these blogs and provides a single source for all things related to R in the blogosphere, and it is a great place to learn by example.
Video Rchive	http://www.vcasmo.com/user/drewconway	As the R community grows, so too do the number of regional meetups and gatherings related to the language. The Rchive attempts to document the presentations and tutorials given at these meetings by posting videos and slides, and now contains presentations from community members all over the world.

The remainder of this chapter focuses on getting you set up with R and using it. This includes downloading and installing R, as well as installing R packages. We conclude with a miniature case study that will serve as an introduction to some of the R idioms we'll use in later chapters. This includes issues of loading, cleaning, organizing, and analyzing data.

Downloading and Installing R

Like many open source projects, R is distributed by a series of regional mirrors. If you do not have R already installed on your machine, the first step is to download it. Go to *http://cran.r-project.org/mirrors.html* and select the CRAN mirror closest to you. Once you have selected a mirror, you will need to download the appropriate distribution of R for whichever operating system you are running.

R relies on several legacy libraries compiled from C and Fortran. As such, depending on your operating system and your familiarity with installing software from source code, you may choose to install R from either a compiled binary distribution or the source. Next, we present instructions for installing R on Windows, Mac OS X, and Linux distributions, with notes on installing from either source or binaries when available.

Finally, R is available in both 32- and 64-bit versions. Depending on your hardware and operating system combination, you should install the appropriate version.

Windows

For Windows operating systems, there are two subdirectories available to install R: *base* and *contrib*. The latter is a directory of compiled Windows binary versions of all of the contributed R packages in CRAN, whereas the former is the basic installation. Select the *base* installation, and download the latest compiled binary. Installing contributed packages is easy to do from R itself and is not language-specific; therefore, it is not necessary to to install anything from the *contrib* directory. Follow the on-screen instructions for the installation.

Once the installation has successfully completed, you will have an R application in your Start menu, which will open the RGui and R Console, as pictured in Figure 1-1.

For most standard Windows installations, this process should proceed without any issues. If you have a customized installation or encounter errors during the installation, consult the *R for Windows FAQ* at your mirror of choice.

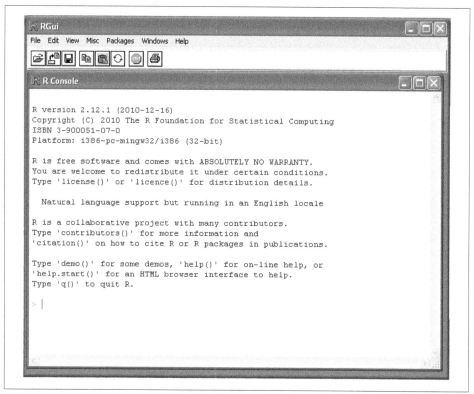

Figure 1-1. The RGui and R Console on a Windows installation

Mac OS X

Fortunately for Mac OS X users, R comes preinstalled with the operating system. You can check this by opening *Terminal.app* and simply typing **R** at the command line. You are now ready to begin! For some users, however, it will be useful to have a GUI application to interact with the R Console. For this you will need to install separate software. With Mac OS X, you have the option of installing from either a compiled binary or the source. To install from a binary—recommended for users with no experience using a Linux command line—simply download the latest version at your mirror of choice at *http://cran.r-project.org/mirrors.html*, and follow the on-screen instructions. Once the installation is complete, you will have both *R.app* (32-bit) and *R64.app* (64-bit) available in your *Applications* folder. Depending on your version of Mac OS X and your machine's hardware, you may choose which version you wish to work with.

As with the Windows installation, if you are installing from a binary, this process should proceed without any problems. When you open your new R application, you will see a console similar to the one pictured in Figure 1-2.

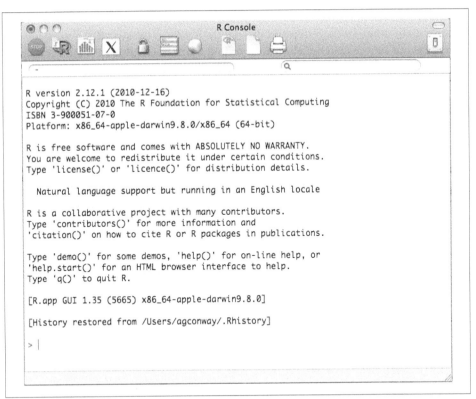

Figure 1-2. The R Console on a 64-bit version of the Mac OS X installation

If you have a custom installation of Mac OS X or wish to customize the installation of R for your particular configuration, we recommend that you install from the source code. Installing R from source on Mac OS X requires both the C and Fortran compilers, which are not included in the standard installation of the operating system. You can install these compilers using the Mac OS X Developers Tools DVD included with your original Mac OS X installation package, or you can install the necessary compilers from the *tools* directory at the mirror of your choice.

Once you have all of the necessary compilers to install from source, the process is the typical configure, make, and install procedure used to install most software at the command line. Using *Terminal.app*, navigate to the folder with the source code and execute the following commands:

```
$ ./configure
$ make
$ make install
```

Depending on your permission settings, you may have to invoke the sudo command as a prefix to the configuration step and provide your system password. If you encounter any errors during the installation, using either the compiled binary distribution or the source code, consult the *R for Mac OS X FAQ* at the mirror of your choice.

Linux

As with Mac OS X, R comes preinstalled on many Linux distributions. Simply type R at the command line, and the R console will be loaded. You can now begin programming! The CRAN mirror also includes installations specific to several Linux distributions, with instructions for installing R on Debian, RedHat, SUSE, and Ubuntu. If you use one of these installations, we recommend that you consult the instructions for your operating system because there is considerable variance in the best practices among Linux distributions.

IDEs and Text Editors

R is a scripting language, and therefore the majority of the work done in the case studies that follow will be done within an IDE or text editor, rather than directly inputted into the R console. As we show in the next section, some tasks are well suited for the console, such as package installation, but primarily you will want to work within the IDE or text editor of your choice.

For those running the GUI in either Windows or Mac OS X, there is a basic text editor available from that application. By either navigating to *File→New Document* from the menu bar or clicking on the blank document icon in the header of the window (highlighted in Figure 1-3), you will open a blank document in the text editor. As a hacker, you likely already have an IDE or text editor of choice, and we recommend that you use whichever environment you are most comfortable in for the case studies. There are simply too many options to enumerate here, and we have no intention of inserting ourselves in the infamous Emacs versus Vim debate.

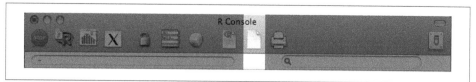

Figure 1-3. Text editor icon in R GUI

Loading and Installing R Packages

There are many well-designed, -maintained, and -supported R packages related to machine learning. With respect to the case studies we will describe, there are packages for dealing with spatial data, text analysis, network structures, and interacting with web-based APIs, among many others. As such, we will be relying heavily on the functionality built into several of these packages.

Loading packages in R is very straightforward. There are two functions to perform this: `library` and `require`. There are some subtle differences between the two, but for the purposes of this book, the primary difference is that `require` will return a Boolean (TRUE or FALSE) value, indicating whether the package is installed on the machine after attempting to load it. For example, in Chapter 6 we will use the `tm` package to tokenize text. To load these packages, we can use either the `library` or `require` functions. In the following example, we use `library` to load `tm` but use `require` for XML. By using the `print` function, we can see that we have XML installed because a Boolean value of TRUE was returned after the package was loaded:

```
library(tm)
print(require(XML))
#[1] TRUE
```

If we did not have XML installed—i.e., if `require` returned FALSE—then we would need to install that package before proceeding.

 If you are working with a fresh installation of R, then you will have to install a number of packages to complete all of the case studies in this book.

There are two ways to install packages in R: either with the GUI or with the `install.packages` function from the console. Given the intended audience for this book, we will be interacting with R exclusively from the console during the case studies, but it is worth pointing out how to use the GUI to install packages. From the menu bar in the application, navigate to Packages & Data→Package Installer, and a window will appear, as displayed in Figure 1-4. From the Package Repository drop-down, select either "CRAN (binaries)"or "CRAN (sources)", and click the Get List button to load all of the packages available for installation. The most recent version of packages will be available in the "CRAN (sources)" repository, and if you have the necessary compilers installed on your machine, we recommend using this sources repository. You can now select the package you wish to install and click Install Selected to install the packages.

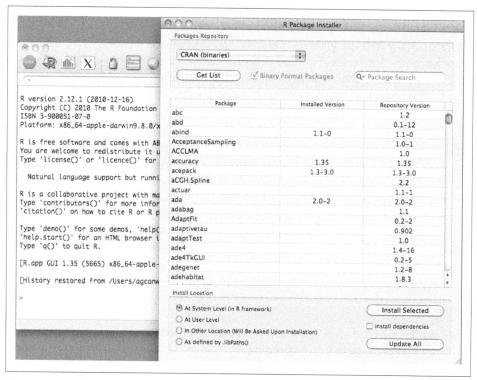

Figure 1-4. Installing R packages using the GUI

The `install.packages` function is the preferred way to install packages because it provides greater flexibility in how and where packages get installed. One of the primary advantages of using `install.packages` is that it allows you to install from local source code as well as from CRAN. Though uncommon, occasionally you may want to install a package that is not yet available on CRAN—for example, if you're updating to an experimental version of a package. In these cases you will need to install from source:

```
install.packages("tm", dependencies=TRUE)
setwd("~/Downloads/")
install.packages("RCurl_1.5-0.tar.gz", repos=NULL, type="source")
```

In the first example, we use the default settings to install the `tm` package from CRAN. The `tm` provides a function used to do text mining, and we will use it in Chapter 3 to perform classifications on email text. One useful parameter in the `install.packages` function is **suggests**, which by default is set to **FALSE**, but if activated will instruct the function to download and install any secondary packages used by the primary installation. As a best practice, we recommend always setting this to **TRUE**, especially if you are working with a clean installation of R.

Alternatively, we can also install directly from compressed source files. In the previous example, we installed the `RCurl` package from the source code available on the author's website. Using the `setwd` function to make sure the R working directory is set to the directory where the source file has been saved, we can simply execute the command shown earlier to install directly from the source code. Note the two parameters that have been altered in this case. First, we must tell the function not to use one of the CRAN repositories by setting `repos=NULL`, and we also specify the type of installation using `type="source"`.

Table 1-2. R packages used in Machine Learning for Hackers

Name	Location	Author(s)	Description and use
arm	*http://cran.r-project.org/web/packages/arm/*	Andrew Gelman, et al.	Package for doing multilevel/hierarchical regression models.
ggplot2	*http://cran.r-project.org/web/packages/glmnet/index.html*	Hadley Wickham	An implementation of the grammar of graphics in R. The premier package for creating high-quality graphics.
glmnet	*http://had.co.nz/ggplot2/*	Jerome Friedman, Trevor Hastie, and Rob Tibshirani	Lasso and elastic-net regularized generalized linear models.
igraph	*http://igraph.sourceforge.net/*	Gabor Csardi	Routines for simple graphs and network analysis. Used for representing social networks.
lme4	*http://cran.r-project.org/web/packages/lme4/*	Douglas Bates, Martin Maechler, and Ben Bolker	Provides functions for creating linear and generalized mixed-effects models.
lubridate	*https://github.com/hadley/lubridate*	Hadley Wickham	Provides convenience function to making working with dates in R easier.
RCurl	*http://www.omegahat.org/RCurl/*	Duncan Temple Lang	Provides an R interface to the `libcurl` library for interacting with the HTTP protocol. Used to import raw data from the Web.
reshape	*http://had.co.nz/plyr/*	Hadley Wickham	A set of tools used to manipulate, aggregate, and manage data in R.
RJSONIO	*http://www.omegahat.org/RJSONIO/*	Duncan Temple Lang	Provides functions for reading and writing JavaScript Object Notation (JSON). Used to parse data from web-based APIs.
tm	*http://www.spatstat.org/spatstat/*	Ingo Feinerer	A collection of functions for performing text mining in R. Used to work with unstructured text data.
XML	*http://www.omegahat.org/RSXML/*	Duncan Temple Lang	Provides the facility to parse XML and HTML documents. Used to extract structured data from the Web.

As mentioned, we will use several packages through the course of this book. Table 1-2 lists all of the packages used in the case studies and includes a brief description of their purpose, along with a link to additional information about each. Given the number of prerequisite packages, to expedite the installation process we have created a short script that will check whether each required package is installed and, if it is not, will attempt to install it from CRAN. To run the script, use the `setwd` function to set the *Working Directory* to the *code* folder for this chapter, and execute the `source` command as shown here:

```
source("package_installer.R")
```

If you have not yet done so, you may be asked to select a CRAN repository. Once set, the script will run, and you will see the progress of any required package installation that you did not yet have. We are now ready to begin exploring machine learning with R! Before we proceed to the case studies, however, we will review some R functions and operations that we will use frequently.

R Basics for Machine Learning

As we stated at the outset, we believe that the best way to learn a new technical skill is to start with a problem you wish to solve or a question you wish to answer. Being excited about the higher-level vision of your work makes learning from case studies effective. In this review of basic concepts in the R language, we will not be addressing a machine learning problem, but we will encounter several issues related to working with data and managing it in R. As we will see in the case studies, quite often we will spend the bulk of our time getting the data formatted and organized in a way that suits the analysis. Usually very little time, in terms of coding, is spent running the analysis.

For this case we will address a question with pure entertainment value. Recently, the data service Infochimps.com released a data set with over 60,000 documented reports of unidentified flying object (UFO) sightings. The data spans hundreds of years and has reports from all over the world. Though it is international, the majority of sightings in the data come from the United States. With the time and spatial dimensions of the data, we might ask the following questions: are there seasonal trends in UFO sightings; and what, if any, variation is there among UFO sightings across the different states in the US?

This is a great data set to start exploring because it is rich, well-structured, and fun to work with. It is also useful for this exercise because it is a large text file, which is typically the type of data we will deal with in this book. In such text files there are often messy parts, and we will use base functions in R and some external libraries to clean and organize the raw data. This section will bring you through, step by step, an entire simple analysis that tries to answer the questions we posed earlier. You will find the code for this section in the *code* folder for this chapter in the file *ufo_sightings.R*. We begin by loading the data and required libraries for the analysis.

Loading libraries and the data

First, we will load the `ggplot2` package, which we will use in the final steps of our visual analysis:

```
library(ggplot2)
```

While loading ggplot2, you will notice that this package also loads two other required packages: plyr and reshape. Both of these packages are used for manipulating and organizing data in R, and we will use plyr in this example to aggregate and organize the data.

The next step is to load the data into R from the text file *ufo_awesome.tsv*, which is located in the *data/ufo/* directory for this chapter. Note that the file is tab-delimited (hence the *.tsv* file extension), which means we will need to use the read.delim function to load the data. Because R exploits defaults very heavily, we have to be particularly conscientious of the default parameter settings for the functions we use in our scripts. To see how we can learn about parameters in R, suppose that we had never used the read.delim function before and needed to read the help files. Alternatively, assume that we do not know that read.delim exists and need to find a function to read delimited data into a data frame. R offers several useful functions for searching for help:

```
?read.delim                  # Access a function's help file
??base::delim                # Search for 'delim' in all help files for functions
                             #  in 'base'
help.search("delimited")     # Search for 'delimited' in all help files
RSiteSearch("parsing text")  # Search for the term 'parsing text' on the R site.
```

In the first example, we append a question mark to the beginning of the function. This will open the help file for the given function, and it's an extremely useful R shortcut. We can also search for specific terms inside of packages by using a combination of ?? and ::. The double question marks indicate a search for a specific term. In the example, we are searching for occurrences of the term "delim" in all base functions, using the double colon. R also allows you to perform less structured help searches with help.search and RSiteSearch. The help.search function will search all help files in your installed packages for some term, which in the preceding example is "delimited". Alternatively, you can search the R website, which includes help files and the mailing lists archive, using the RSiteSearch function. Please note that this is by no means meant to be an exhaustive review of R or the functions used in this section. As such, we *highly recommend* using these search functions to explore R's base functions on your own.

For the UFO data there are several parameters in read.delim that we will need to set by hand in order to read in the data properly. First, we need to tell the function how the data is delimited. We know this is a tab-delimited file, so we set sep to the Tab character. Next, when read.delim is reading in data, it attempts to convert each column of data into an R data type using several heuristics. In our case, all of the columns are strings, but the default setting for all read.* functions is to convert strings to factor types. This class is meant for categorical variables, but we do not want this. As such, we have to set stringsAsFactors=FALSE to prevent this. In fact, it is always a good practice to switch off this default, especially when working with unfamiliar data. Also, this data does not include a column header as its first row, so we will need to switch off that default as well to force R to not use the first row in the data as a header. Finally, there are many empty elements in the data, and we want to set those to the special R value NA.

To do this, we explicitly define the empty string as the na.string:

```
ufo<-read.delim("data/ufo/ufo_awesome.tsv", sep="\t", stringsAsFactors=FALSE,
            header=FALSE, na.strings="")
```

 The term "categorical variable" refers to a type of data that denotes an observation's membership in category. In statistics, categorical variables are very important because we may be interested in what makes certain observations of a certain type. In R we represent categorical variables as factor types, which essentially assigns numeric references to string labels. In this case, we convert certain strings—such as state abbreviations —into categorical variables using as.factor, which assigns a unique numeric ID to each state abbreviation in the data set. We will repeat this process many times.

We now have a data frame containing all of the UFO data! Whenever you are working with data frames, especially when they are from external data sources, it is always a good idea to inspect the data by hand. Two great functions for doing this are head and tail. These functions will print the first and last six entries in a data frame:

```
head(ufo)
       V1        V2                       V3   V4      V5  V6
1 19951009 19951009         Iowa City, IA <NA>    <NA>  Man repts. witnessing "flash..
2 19951010 19951011         Milwaukee, WI <NA>  2 min.  Man  on Hwy 43 SW of Milwauk..
3 19950101 19950103           Shelton, WA <NA>    <NA>  Telephoned Report:CA woman v..
4 19950510 19950510          Columbia, MO <NA>  2 min.  Man repts. son's bizarre sig..
5 19950611 19950614           Seattle, WA <NA>    <NA>  Anonymous caller repts. sigh..
6 19951025 19951024 Brunswick County, ND <NA> 30 min.  Sheriff's office calls to re..
```

The first obvious issue with the data frame is that the column names are generic. Using the documentation for this data set as a reference, we can assign more meaningful labels to the columns. Having meaningful column names for data frames is an important best practice. It makes your code and output easier to understand, both for you and other audiences. We will use the names function, which can either access the column labels for a data structure or assign them. From the data documentation, we construct a character vector that corresponds to the appropriate column names and pass it to the names functions with the data frame as its only argument:

```
names(ufo)<-c("DateOccurred","DateReported","Location","ShortDescription",
        "Duration","LongDescription")
```

From the head output and the documentation used to create column headings, we know that the first two columns of data are dates. As in other languages, R treats dates as a special type, and we will want to convert the date strings to actual date types. To do this, we will use the as.Date function, which will take the date string and attempt to convert it to a Date object. With this data, the strings have an uncommon date format of the form *YYYMMDD*. As such, we will also have to specify a format string in as.Date so the function knows how to convert the strings. We begin by converting the DateOccurred column:

```
ufo$DateOccurred<-as.Date(ufo$DateOccurred, format="%Y%m%d")
Error in strptime(x, format, tz = "GMT") : input string is too long
```

We've just come upon our first error! Though a bit cryptic, the error message contains the substring "input string too long", which indicates that some of the entries in the `DateOccurred` column are too long to match the format string we provided. Why might this be the case? We are dealing with a large text file, so perhaps some of the data was malformed in the original set. Assuming this is the case, those data points will not be parsed correctly when loaded by `read.delim`, and that would cause this sort of error. Because we are dealing with real-world data, we'll need to do some cleaning by hand.

Converting date strings and dealing with malformed data

To address this problem, we first need to locate the rows with defective date strings, then decide what to do with them. We are fortunate in this case because we know from the error that the errant entries are "too long." Properly parsed strings will always be eight characters long, i.e., "YYYYMMDD". To find the problem rows, therefore, we simply need to find those that have strings with more than eight characters. As a best practice, we first inspect the data to see what the malformed data looks like, in order to get a better understanding of what has gone wrong. In this case, we will use the `head` function as before to examine the data returned by our logical statement.

Later, to remove these errant rows, we will use the `ifelse` function to construct a vector of TRUE and FALSE values to identify the entries that are eight characters long (TRUE) and those that are not (FALSE). This function is a vectorized version of the typical if-else logical switch for some Boolean test. We will see many examples of vectorized operations in R. They are the preferred mechanism for iterating over data because they are often—but not always—more efficient than explicitly iterating over a vector:[1]

```
head(ufo[which(nchar(ufo$DateOccurred)!=8 | nchar(ufo$DateReported)!=8),1])
[1] "ler@gnv.ifas.ufl.edu"
[2] "0000"
[3] "Callers report sighting a number of soft white  balls of lights headingin
an easterly directing then changing direction to the west beforespeeding off to
the north west."
[4] "0000"
[5] "0000"
[6] "0000"

good.rows<-ifelse(nchar(ufo$DateOccurred)>!=8 | nchar(ufo$DateReported)!=8,FALSE,
                  TRUE)
length(which(!good.rows))
[1] 371
ufo<-ufo[good.rows,]
```

We use several useful R functions to perform this search. We need to know the length of the string in each entry of `DateOccurred` and `DateReported`, so we use the `nchar`

---

1. For a brief introduction to vectorized operations in R, see R help desk: How can I avoid this loop or make it faster? [LF08].

function to compute this. If that length is not equal to eight, then we return FALSE. Once we have the vectors of Booleans, we want to see how many entries in the data frame have been malformed. To do this, we use the which command to return a vector of vector indices that are FALSE. Next, we compute the length of that vector to find the number of bad entries. With only 371 rows not conforming, the best option is to simply remove these entries and ignore them. At first, we might worry that losing 371 rows of data is a bad idea, but there are over 60,000 total rows, and so we will simply ignore those malformed rows and continue with the conversion to Date types:

```
ufo$DateOccurred<-as.Date(ufo$DateOccurred, format="%Y%m%d")
ufo$DateReported<-as.Date(ufo$DateReported, format="%Y%m%d")
```

Next, we will need to clean and organize the location data. Recall from the previous head call that the entries for UFO sightings in the United States take the form "City, State". We can use R's regular expression integration to split these strings into separate columns and identify those entries that do not conform. The latter portion, identifying those that do not conform, is particularly important because we are only interested in sighting variation in the United States and will use this information to isolate those entries.

Organizing location data

To manipulate the data in this way, we will first construct a function that takes a string as input and performs the data cleaning. Then we will run this function over the location data using one of the vectorized apply functions:

```
get.location<-function(l) {
  split.location<-tryCatch(strsplit(l,",")[[1]], error= function(e) return(c(NA, NA)))
  clean.location<-gsub("^ ","",split.location)
  if (length(clean.location)>2) {
    return(c(NA,NA))
  }
  else {
    return(clean.location)
  }
}
```

There are several subtle things happening in this function. First, notice that we are wrapping the strsplit command in R's error-handling function, tryCatch. Again, not all of the entries are of the proper "City, State" form, and in fact, some do not even contain a comma. The strsplit function will throw an error if the split character is not matched; therefore, we have to catch this error. In our case, when there is no comma to split, we will return a vector of NA to indicate that this entry is not valid. Next, the original data included leading whitespace, so we will use the gsub function (part of R's suite of functions for working with regular expressions) to remove the leading white-space from each character. Finally, we add an additional check to ensure that only those location vectors of length two are returned. Many non-US entries have multiple commas, creating larger vectors from the strsplit function. In this case, we will again return an NA vector.

With the function defined, we will use the lapply function, short for "list-apply," to iterate this function over all strings in the Location column. As mentioned, members of the apply family of functions in R are extremely useful. They are constructed of the form apply(vector, function) and return results of the vectorized application of the function to the vector in a specific form. In our case, we are using lapply, which always returns a list:

```
city.state<-lapply(ufo$Location, get.location)
head(city.state)
[[1]]
[1] "Iowa City" "IA"

[[2]]
[1] "Milwaukee" "WI"

[[3]]
[1] "Shelton" "WA"

[[4]]
[1] "Columbia" "MO"

[[5]]
[1] "Seattle" "WA"

[[6]]
[1] "Brunswick County" "ND"
```

As you can see in this example, a list in R is a key-value-style data structure, wherein the keys are indexed by the double bracket and values are contained in the single bracket. In our case the keys are simply integers, but lists can also have strings as keys.[2] Though convenient, having the data stored in a list is not desirable, because we would like to add the city and state information to the data frame as separate columns. To do this, we will need to convert this long list into a two-column matrix, with the city data as the leading column:

```
location.matrix<-do.call(rbind, city.state)
ufo<-transform(ufo, USCity=location.matrix[,1], USState=tolower(location.matrix[,2]),
    stringsAsFactors=FALSE)
```

To construct a matrix from the list, we use the do.call function. Similar to the apply functions, do.call executes a function call over a list. We will often use the combination of lapply and do.call to manipulate data. In the preceding example we pass the rbind function, which will "row-bind" all of the vectors in the city.state list to create a matrix. To get this into the data frame, we use the transform function. We create two new columns: USCity and USState from the first and second columns of location.matrix, respectively. Finally, the state abbreviations are inconsistent, with some uppercase and others lowercase, so we use the tolower function to make them all lowercase.

---

2. For a thorough introduction to lists, see Chapter 1 of Data Manipulation with R [Spe08].

Dealing with data outside our scope

The final issue related to data cleaning that we must consider are entries that meet the "City, State" form, but are not from the US. Specifically, the data includes several UFO sightings from Canada, which also take this form. Fortunately, none of the Canadian province abbreviations match US state abbreviations. We can use this information to identify non-US entries by constructing a vector of US state abbreviations and keeping only those entries in the USState column that match an entry in this vector:

```
us.states<-c("ak","al","ar","az","ca","co","ct","de","fl","ga","hi","ia","id","il",
    "in","ks","ky","la","ma","md","me","mi","mn","mo","ms","mt","nc","nd","ne","nh",
    "nj","nm","nv","ny","oh","ok","or","pa","ri","sc","sd","tn","tx","ut","va","vt",
    "wa","wi","wv","wy")
ufo$USState<-us.states[match(ufo$USState,us.states)]
ufo$USCity[is.na(ufo$USState)]<-NA
```

To find the entries in the USState column that do not match a US state abbreviation, we use the match function. This function takes two arguments: first, the values to be matched, and second, those to be matched against. The function returns a vector of the same length as the first argument in which the values are the index of entries in that vector that match some value in the second vector. If no match is found, the function returns NA by default. In our case, we are only interested in which entries are NA, as these are the entries that do not match a US state. We then use the is.na function to find which entries are not US states and reset them to NA in the USState column. Finally, we also set those indices in the USCity column to NA for consistency.

Our original data frame now has been manipulated to the point that we can extract from it only the data we are interested in. Specifically, we want a subset that includes only US incidents of UFO sightings. By replacing entries that did not meet this criteria in the previous steps, we can use the subset command to create a new data frame of only US incidents:

```
ufo.us<-subset(ufo, !is.na(USState))
head(ufo.us)
  DateOccurred DateReported               Location ShortDescription Duration
1   1995-10-09   1995-10-09          Iowa City, IA             <NA>     <NA>
2   1995-10-10   1995-10-11          Milwaukee, WI             <NA>   2 min.
3   1995-01-01   1995-01-03            Shelton, WA             <NA>     <NA>
4   1995-05-10   1995-05-10           Columbia, MO             <NA>   2 min.
5   1995-06-11   1995-06-14            Seattle, WA             <NA>     <NA>
6   1995-10-25   1995-10-24  Brunswick County, ND             <NA>  30 min.

  LongDescription                    USCity           USState
1 Man repts. witnessing "flash...    Iowa City         ia
2 Man  on Hwy 43 SW of Milwauk...    Milwaukee         wi
3 Telephoned Report:CA woman v...    Shelton           wa
4 Man repts. son's bizarre sig...    Columbia          mo
5 Anonymous caller repts. sigh...    Seattle           wa
6 Sheriff's office calls to re...    Brunswick County  nd
```

Aggregating and organizing the data

We now have our data organized to the point where we can begin analyzing it! In the previous section we spent a lot of time getting the data properly formatted and identifying the relevant entries for our analysis. In this section we will explore the data to further narrow our focus. This data has two primary dimensions: space (where the sighting happened) and time (when a sighting occurred). We focused on the former in the previous section, but here we will focus on the latter. First, we use the `summary` function on the `DateOccurred` column to get a sense of this chronological range of the data:

```
summary(ufo.us$DateOccurred)
   Min.      1st Qu.      Median       Mean      3rd Qu.       Max.
"1400-06-30" "1999-09-06" "2004-01-10" "2001-02-13" "2007-07-26" "2010-08-30"
```

Surprisingly, this data goes back quite a long time; the oldest UFO sighting comes from 1400! Given this outlier, the next question is: how is this data distributed over time? And is it worth analyzing the entire time series? A quick way to look at this visually is to construct a histogram. We will discuss histograms in more detail in the next chapter, but for now you should know that histograms allow you to bin your data by a given dimension and observe the frequency with which your data falls into those bins. The dimension of interest here is time, so we construct a histogram that bins the data over time:

```
quick.hist<-ggplot(ufo.us, aes(x=DateOccurred))+geom_histogram()+
scale_x_date(major="50 years")
ggsave(plot=quick.hist, filename="../images/quick_hist.png", height=6, width=8)
stat_bin: binwidth defaulted to range/30. Use 'binwidth = x' to adjust this.
```

There are several things to note here. This is our first use of the ggplot2 package, which we use throughout this book for all of our data visualizations. In this case, we are constructing a very simple histogram that requires only a single line of code. First, we create a `ggplot` object and pass it the UFO data frame as its initial argument. Next, we set the x-axis aesthetic to the `DateOccurred` column, as this is the frequency we are interested in examining. With ggplot2 we must always work with data frames, and the first argument to create a `ggplot` object must always be a data frame. ggplot2 is an R implementation of Leland Wilkinson's *Grammar of Graphics* [Wil05]. This means the package adheres to this particular philosophy for data visualization, and all visualizations will be built up as a series of layers. For this histogram, shown in Figure 1-5, the initial layer is the x-axis data, namely the UFO sighting dates. Next, we add a histogram layer with the `geom_histogram` function. In this case, we will use the default settings for this function, but as we will see later, this default often is not a good choice. Finally, because this data spans such a long time period, we will rescale the x-axis labels to occur every 50 years with the `scale_x_date` function.

Once the `ggplot` object has been constructed, we use the `ggsave` function to output the visualization to a file. We also could have used > `print(quick.hist)` to print the visualization to the screen. Note the warning message that is printed when you draw the visualization. There are many ways to bin data in a histogram, and we will discuss this in detail in the next chapter, but this warning is provided to let you know exactly how ggplot2 does the binning by default.

We are now ready to explore the data with this visualization.

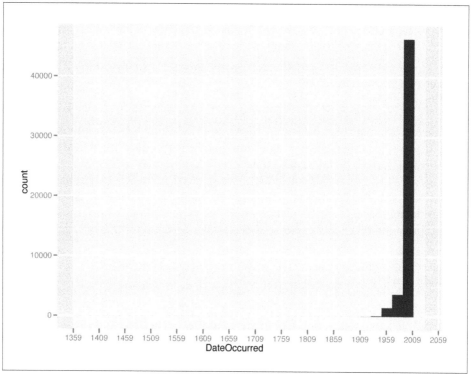

Figure 1-5. Exploratory histogram of UFO data over time

The results of this analysis are stark. The vast majority of the data occur between 1960 and 2010, with the majority of UFO sightings occurring within the last two decades. For our purposes, therefore, we will focus on only those sightings that occurred between 1990 and 2010. This will allow us to exclude the outliers and compare relatively similar units during the analysis. As before, we will use the subset function to create a new data frame that meets this criteria:

```
ufo.us<-subset(ufo.us, DateOccurred>=as.Date("1990-01-01"))
nrow(ufo.us)
#[1] 46347
```

Although this removes many more entries than we eliminated while cleaning the data, it still leaves us with over 46,000 observations to analyze. To see the difference, we regenerate the histogram of the subset data in Figure 1-6. We see that there is much more variation when looking at this sample. Next, we must begin organizing the data such that it can be used to address our central question: what, if any, seasonal variation exists for UFO sightings in US states? To address this, we must first ask: what do we mean by "seasonal?" There are many ways to aggregate time series data with respect to seasons: by week, month, quarter, year, etc. But which way of aggregating our data is most appropriate here? The DateOccurred column provides UFO sighting information by the day, but there is considerable inconsistency in terms of the coverage throughout the entire set. We need to aggregate the data in a way that puts the amount of data for each state on relatively level planes. In this case, doing so by year-month is the best option. This aggregation also best addresses the core of our question, as monthly aggregation will give good insight into seasonal variations.

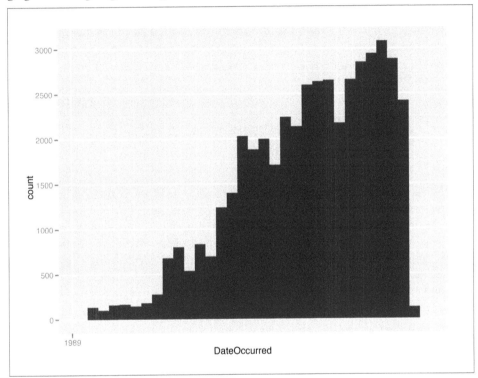

Figure 1-6. Histogram of subset UFO data over time (1990–2010)

We need to count the number of UFO sightings that occurred in each state by all year-month combinations from 1990–2010. First, we will need to create a new column in the data that corresponds to the years and months present in the data. We will use the strftime function to convert the Date objects to a string of the "YYYY-MM" format. As before, we will set the format parameter accordingly to get the strings:

```
ufo.us$YearMonth<-strftime(ufo.us$DateOccurred, format="%Y-%m")
```

Notice that in this case we did not use the transform function to add a new column to the data frame. Rather, we simply referenced a column name that did not exist, and R automatically added it. Both methods for adding new columns to a data frame are useful, and we will switch between them depending on the particular task. Next, we want to count the number of times each state and year-month combination occurs in the data. For the first time we will use the `ddply` function, which is part of the extremely useful `plyr` library for manipulating data.

The `plyr` family of functions work a bit like the map-reduce-style data aggregation tools that have risen in popularity over the past several years. They attempt to group data in some specific way that was meaningful to all observations, and then do some calculation on each of these groups and return the results. For this task we want to group the data by state abbreviations and the year-month column we just created. Once the data is grouped as such, we count the number of entries in each group and return that as a new column. Here we will simply use the `nrow` function to reduce the data by the number of rows in each group:

```
sightings.counts<-ddply(ufo.us,.(USState,YearMonth), nrow)
head(sightings.counts)
USState YearMonth V1
1      ak    1990-01  1
2      ak    1990-03  1
3      ak    1990-05  1
4      ak    1993-11  1
5      ak    1994-11  1
6      ak    1995-01  1
```

We now have the number of UFO sightings for each state by the year and month. From the `head` call in the example, however, we can see that there may be a problem with using the data as is because it contains a lot of missing values. For example, we see that there was one UFO sighting in January, March, and May of 1990 in Alaska, but no entries appear for February and April. Presumably, there were no UFO sightings in these months, but the data does not include entries for nonsightings, so we have to go back and add these as zeros.

We need a vector of years and months that spans the entire data set. From this we can check to see whether they are already in the data, and if not, add them as zeros. To do this, we will create a sequence of dates using the `seq.Date` function, and then format them to match the data in our data frame:

```
date.range<-seq.Date(from=as.Date(min(ufo.us$DateOccurred)),
                     to=as.Date(max(ufo.us$DateOccurred)), by="month")
date.strings<-strftime(date.range, "%Y-%m")
```

With the new `date.strings` vector, we need to create a new data frame that has all year-months and states. We will use this to perform the matching with the UFO sighting data. As before, we will use the `lapply` function to create the columns and the `do.call` function to convert this to a matrix and then a data frame:

```
states.dates<-lapply(us.states,function(s) cbind(s,date.strings))
states.dates<-data.frame(do.call(rbind, states.dates), stringsAsFactors=FALSE)
head(states.dates)
s date.strings
```

```
1 ak      1990-01
2 ak      1990-02
3 ak      1990-03
4 ak      1990-04
5 ak      1990-05
6 ak      1990-06
```

The `states.dates` data frame now contains entries for every year, month, and state combination possible in the data. Note that there are now entries from February and March 1990 for Alaska. To add in the missing zeros to the UFO sighting data, we need to merge this data with our original data frame. To do this, we will use the `merge` function, which takes two ordered data frames and attempts to merge them by common columns. In our case, we have two data frames ordered alphabetically by US state abbreviations and chronologically by year and month. We need to tell the function which columns to merge these data frames by. We will set the `by.x` and `by.y` parameters according to the matching column names in each data frame. Finally, we set the `all` parameter to `TRUE`, which instructs the function to include entries that do not match and to fill them with `NA`. Those entries in the `V1` column will be those state, year, and month entries for which no UFOs were sighted:

```
all.sightings<-merge(states.dates,sightings.counts,by.x=c("s","date.strings"),
    by.y=c("USState","YearMonth"),all=TRUE)
head(all.sightings)
   s  date.strings V1
1 ak      1990-01  1
2 ak      1990-02  NA
3 ak      1990-03  1
4 ak      1990-04  NA
5 ak      1990-05  1
6 ak      1990-06  NA
```

The final steps for data aggregation are simple housekeeping. First, we will set the column names in the new `all.sightings` data frame to something meaningful. This is done in exactly the same way as we did it at the outset. Next, we will convert the `NA` entries to zeros, again using the `is.na` function. Finally, we will convert the `YearMonth` and `State` columns to the appropriate types. Using the `date.range` vector we created in the previous step and the `rep` function to create a new vector that repeats a given vector, we replace the year and month strings with the appropriate `Date` object. Again, it is better to keep dates as `Date` objects rather than strings because we can compare `Date` objects mathematically, but we can't do that easily with strings. Likewise, the state abbreviations are better represented as categorical variables than strings, so we convert these to `factor` types. We will describe `factors` and other R data types in more detail in the next chapter:

```
names(all.sightings)<-c("State","YearMonth","Sightings")
all.sightings$Sightings[is.na(all.sightings$Sightings)]<-0
all.sightings$YearMonth<-as.Date(rep(date.range,length(us.states)))
all.sightings$State<-as.factor(toupper(all.sightings$State))
```

We are now ready to analyze the data visually!

Analyzing the data

For this data, we will address the core question only by analyzing it visually. For the remainder of the book, we will combine both numeric and visual analyses, but as this example is only meant to introduce core R programming paradigms, we will stop at the visual component. Unlike the previous histogram visualization, however, we will take greater care with `ggplot2` to build the visual layers explicitly. This will allow us to create a visualization that directly addresses the question of seasonal variation among states over time and produce a more professional-looking visualization.

We will construct the visualization all at once in the following example, then explain each layer individually:

```
state.plot<-ggplot(all.sightings, aes(x=YearMonth,y=Sightings))+
    geom_line(aes(color="darkblue"))+
    facet_wrap(~State,nrow=10,ncol=5)+
    theme_bw()+
    scale_color_manual(values=c("darkblue"="darkblue"),legend=FALSE)+
    scale_x_date(major="5 years", format="%Y")+
    xlab("Time")+ylab("Number of Sightings")+
    opts(title="Number of UFO sightings by Month-Year and U.S. State (1990-2010)")
ggsave(plot=state.plot, filename="../images/ufo_sightings.pdf",width=14,height=8.5)
```

As always, the first step is to create a `ggplot` object with a data frame as its first argument. Here we are using the `all.sightings` data frame we created in the previous step. Again, we need to build an aesthetic layer of data to plot, and in this case the x-axis is the `YearMonth` column and the y-axis is the `Sightings` data. Next, to show seasonal variation among states, we will plot a line for each state. This will allow us to observe any spikes, lulls, or oscillation in the number of UFO sightings for each state over time. To do this, we will use the `geom_line` function and set the `color` to `"darkblue"` to make the visualization easier to read.

As we have seen throughout this case, the UFO data is fairly rich and includes many sightings across the United States over a long period of time. Knowing this, we need to think of a way to break up this visualization such that we can observe the data for each state, but also compare it to the other states. If we plot all of the data in a single panel, it will be very difficult to discern variation. To check this, run the first line of code from the preceding block, but replace `color="darkblue"` with `color=State` and enter `> print(state.plot)` at the console. A better approach would be to plot the data for each state individually and order them in a grid for easy comparison.

To create a multifaceted plot, we use the `facet_wrap` function and specify that the panels be created by the `State` variable, which is already a `factor` type, i.e., categorical. We also explicitly define the number of rows and columns in the grid, which is easier in our case because we know we are creating 50 different plots.

The `ggplot2` package has many plotting themes. The default theme is the one we used in the first example and has a gray background with dark gray gridlines. Although it is strictly a matter of taste, we prefer using a white background for this plot because that will make it easier to see slight differences among data points in our visualization. We add the `theme_bw` layer, which will produce a plot with a white background and black gridlines. Once you become more comfortable with `ggplot2`, we recommend experimenting with different defaults to find the one you prefer.[3]

The remaining layers are done as housekeeping to make sure the visualization has a professional look and feel. Though not formally required, paying attention to these details is what can separate amateurish plots from professional-looking data visualizations. The `scale_color_manual` function is used to specify that the string "darkblue" corresponds to the web-safe color "darkblue." Although this may seem repetitive, it is at the core of `ggplot2`'s design, which requires explicit definition of details such as color. In fact, `ggplot2` tends to think of colors as a way of distinguishing among different types or categories of data and, as such, prefers to have a `factor` type used to specify color. In our case we are defining a color explicitly using a string and therefore have to define the value of that string with the `scale_color_manual` function.

As we did before, we use the `scale_x_date` to specify the major gridlines in the visualization. Because this data spans 20 years, we will set these to be at regular five-year intervals. Then we set the tick labels to be the year in a full four-digit format. Next, we set the x-axis label to "Time" and the y-axis label to "Number of Sightings" by using the `xlab` and `ylab` functions, respectively. Finally, we use the `opts` function to give the plot a title. There are many more options available in the `opts` function, and we will see some of them in later chapters, but there are many more that are beyond the scope of this book.

With all of the layers built, we are now ready to render the image with `ggsave` and analyze the data.

There are many interesting observations that fall out of this analysis (see Figure 1-7). We see that California and Washington are large outliers in terms of the number of UFO sightings in these states compared to the others. Between these outliers, there are also interesting differences. In California, the number of reported UFO sightings seems to be somewhat random over time, but steadily increasing since 1995, whereas in Washington, the seasonal variation seems to be very consistent over time, with regular peaks and valleys in UFO sightings starting from about 1995.

We can also notice that many states experience sudden spikes in the number of UFO sightings reported. For example, Arizona, Florida, Illinois, and Montana seem to have experienced spikes around mid-1997, and Michigan, Ohio, and Oregon experienced similar spikes in late-1999. Only Michigan and Ohio are geographically close among these groups. If we do not believe that these are actually the result of extraterrestrial visitors, what are some alternative explanations? Perhaps there was increased vigilance

---

3. For more information on `ggplot2` themes, see Chapter 8 of *ggplot2: Elegant Graphics for Data Analysis* [Wic09].

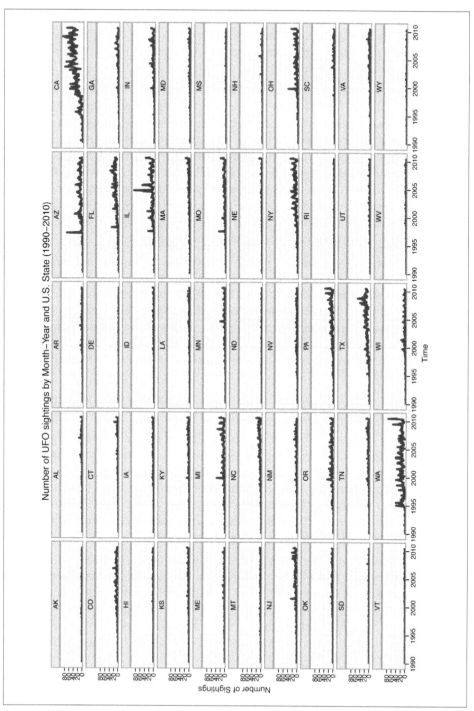

Figure 1-7. Number of UFO sightings by year-month and US state (1990-2010)

among citizens to look to the sky as the millennium came to a close, causing heavier reporting of false sightings.

If, however, you are sympathetic to the notion that we may be regularly hosting visitors from outer space, there is also evidence to pique your curiosity. In fact, there is surprising regularity of these sightings in many states in the US, with evidence of regional clustering as well. It is almost as if the sightings really contain a meaningful pattern.

Further Reading on R

This introductory case is by no means meant to be an exhaustive review of the language. Rather, we used this data set to introduce several R paradigms related to loading, cleaning, organizing, and analyzing data. We will revisit many of these functions and processes in the following chapters, along with many others. For those readers interested in gaining more practice and familiarity with R before proceeding, there are many excellent resources. These resources can roughly be divided into either reference books and texts or online resources, as shown in Table 1-3.

In the next chapter, we review exploratory data analysis. Much of the case study in this chapter involved exploring data, but we moved through these steps rather quickly. In the next chapter we will consider the process of data exploration much more deliberately.

Table 1-3. R references

Title	Author	Reference	Description
Text references			
Data Manipulation with R	Phil Spector	[Spe08]	A deeper review of many of the data manipulation topics covered in the previous section, and an introduction to several techniques not covered.
R in a Nutshell	Joseph Adler	[Adl10]	A detailed exploration of all of R's base functions. This book takes the R manual and adds several practical examples.
Introduction to Scientific Programming and Simulation Using R	Owen Jones, Robert Maillardet, and Andrew Robinson	[JMR09]	Unlike other introductory texts to R, this book focuses on the primacy of learning the language first, then creating simulations.
Data Analysis Using Regression and Multilevel/ Hierarchical Models	Andrew Gelman and Jennifer Hill	[GH06]	This text is heavily focused on doing statistical analyses, but all of the examples are in R, and it is an excellent resource for learning both the language and methods.

Title	Author	Reference	Description
ggplot2: Elegant Graphics for Data Analysis	Hadley Wickham	[Wic09]	The definitive guide to creating data visualizations with `ggplot2`.

Online references

Title	Author	Reference	Description
An Introduction to R	Bill Venables and David Smith	*http://cran.r-project.org/doc/manuals/R-intro.html*	An extensive and ever-changing introduction to the language from the R Core Team.
The R Inferno	Patrick Burns	*http://lib.stat.cmu.edu/S/Spoetry/Tutor/R_inferno.pdf (http://lib.stat.cmu.edu/S/Spoetry/Tutor/R_inferno.pdf)*	An excellent introduction to R for the experienced programmer. The abstract says it best: "If you are using R and you think you're in hell, this is a map for you."
R for Programmers	Norman Matloff	*http://heather.cs.ucdavis.edu/~matloff/R/RProg.pdf*	Similar to *The R Inferno*, this introduction is geared toward programmers with experience in other languages.
"The Split-Apply-Combine Strategy for Data Analysis"	Hadley Wickham	*http://www.jstatsoft.org/v40/i01/paper (http://www.jstatsoft.org/v40/i01/paper)*	The author of `plyr` provides an excellent introduction to the map-reduce paradigm in the context of his tools, with many examples.
"R Data Analysis Examples"	UCLA Academic Technology Services	*http://www.ats.ucla.edu/stat/r/dae/default.htm*	A great "Rosetta Stone"-style introduction for those with experience in other statistical programming platforms, such as SAS, SPSS, and Stata.

## CHAPTER 2

Data Exploration

Exploration versus Confirmation

Whenever you work with data, it's helpful to imagine breaking up your analysis into two completely separate parts: exploration and confirmation. The distinction between exploratory data analysis and confirmatory data analysis comes down to us from the famous John Tukey,[1] who emphasized the importance of designing simple tools for practical data analysis. In Tukey's mind, the exploratory steps in data analysis involve using summary tables and basic visualizations to search for hidden patterns in your data. In this chapter, we describe some of the basic tools that R provides for summarizing your data numerically, and then we teach you how to make sense of the results. After that, we show you some of the tools that exist in R for visualizing your data, and at the same time, we give you a whirlwind tour of the basic visual patterns that you should keep an eye out for in any gization.

But before you start searching through your first data set, we should warn you about a real danger that's present whenever you explore data: you're likely to find patterns that aren't really there. The human mind is designed to find patterns in the world and will do so even when those patterns are just quirks of chance. You don't need a degree in statistics to know that we human beings will easily find shapes in clouds after looking at them for only a few seconds. And plenty of people have convinced themselves that they've discovered hidden messages in run-of-the-mill texts like Shakespeare's plays. Because humans are vulnerable to discovering patterns that won't stand up to careful scrutiny, the exploratory step in data analysis can't exist in isolation; it needs to be accompanied by a confirmatory step. Think of confirmatory data analysis as a sort of mental hygiene routine that we use to clean off our beliefs about the world after we've gone slogging through the messy —and sometimes lawless— world of exploratory data visualization.

---

1. The same person who invented the word "bit."

Confirmatory data analysis usually employs two tools:

- Testing a formal model of the pattern that you think you've found on a new data set that you didn't use to find the pattern.
- Using probability theory to test whether the patterns you've found in your original data set could reasonably have been produced by chance.

Because confirmatory data analysis requires more math than exploratory data analysis, this chapter is exclusively concerned with exploratory tools. In practice, that means we'll focus on numeric summaries of your data and some standard visualization tools. The numerical summaries we describe are the stuff of introductory statistics courses: means and modes, percentiles and medians, and standard deviations and variances. The visualization tools we use are also some of the most basic tools that you would learn about in an "Intro to Stats" course: histograms, kernel density estimates, and scatterplots. We think simple visualizations are often underappreciated, and we hope we can convince you that you can often learn a lot about your data using only these basic tools. Much more sophisticated techniques will come up in the later chapters of this book, but the intuitions for analyzing data are best built up while working with the simplest of tools.

What Is Data?

Before we start to describe some of the basic tools that you can use to explore your data, we should agree on what we mean when we use the word "data." It would be easy to write an entire book about the possible definitions of the word "data," because there are so many important questions you might want to ask about any so-called data set. For example, you often want to know how the data you have was generated and whether the data can reasonably be expected to be representative of the population you truly want to study. Although you could learn a lot about the social structure of the Amazonian Indians by studying records of their marriages, it's not clear that you'd learn something that applied very well to other cultures in the process. The interpretation of data requires that you know something about the source of your data. Often the only way to separate causation from correlation is to know whether the data you're working with was generated experimentally or was only observationally recorded because experimental data wasn't available.

Although these sorts of concerns are interesting issues that we hope you'll want to learn about some day,[2] we're going to completely avoid issues of data collection in this book. For our purposes, the subtler philosophical issues of data analysis are going to be treated as if they were perfectly separable from the sorts of prediction problems for which we're going to use machine learning techniques. In the interest of pragmatism, we're therefore going to use the following definition throughout the rest of this book: a "data set" is

---

2. When you're interested, we'd recommend reading Judea Pearl's *Causality* [Pea09].

nothing more than a big table of numbers and strings in which every row describes a single observation of the real world and every column describes a single attribute that was measured for each of the observations represented by the rows. If you're at all familiar with databases, this definition of data should match your intuitions about the structure of database tables pretty closely. If you're worried that your data set isn't really a single table, let's just pretend that you've used R's merge, SQL's JOIN family of operations, or some of the other tools we described earlier to create a data set that looks like a single table.

We'll call this the "data as rectangles" model. This viewpoint is clearly a substantial simplification, but it will let us motivate many of the big ideas of data analysis visually, which we hope makes what are otherwise very abstract ideas a little more tangible. And the "data as rectangles" model serves another purpose: it lets us freely exploit ideas from database design as well as ideas from pure mathematics. If you're worried that you don't know much about matrices, don't worry; throughout this book, you'll always be able to think of matrices as nothing more than two-dimensional arrays, i.e., a big table. As long as we assume we're working with rectangular arrays, we can use lots of powerful mathematical techniques without having to think very carefully about the actual mathematical operations being performed. For example, we briefly describe matrix multiplication in Chapter 9, even though almost every technique we're going to exploit can be described in terms of matrix multiplications, whether it's the standard linear regression model or the modern matrix factorization techniques that have become so popular lately thanks to the Netflix Prize.

Because we'll treat data rectangles, tables, and matrices interchangeably, we ask for your patience when we switch back and forth between those terms throughout this book. Whatever term we use, you should just remember that we're thinking of something like Table 2-1 when we talk about data.

Table 2-1. Your authors

Name	Age
Drew Conway	28
John Myles White	29

Because data consists of rectangles, we can actually draw pictures of the sorts of operations we'll perform pretty easily. A numerical data summary involves reducing all of the rows from your table into a few numbers—often just a single number for each column in your data set. An example of this type of data summary is shown in Figure 2-1.

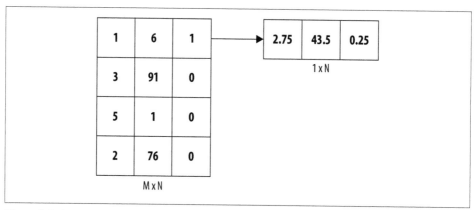

Figure 2-1. Summarizing many columns in one number per column

In contrast to a numerical summary, a visualization of a single column's contents usually involves reducing all of the rows from a single column in your data into one image. An example of a visual summary of a single column is shown in Figure 2-2.

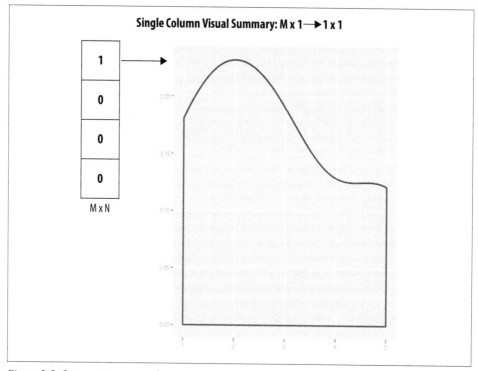

Figure 2-2. Summarizing one column in one image

Beyond the tools you can use for analyzing isolated columns, there are lots of tools you can use to understand the relationships between multiple columns in your data set.

For example, computing the correlation between two columns turns all of the rows from two columns of your table into a single number that summarizes the strength of the relationship between those two columns. An example of this is shown in Figure 2-3.

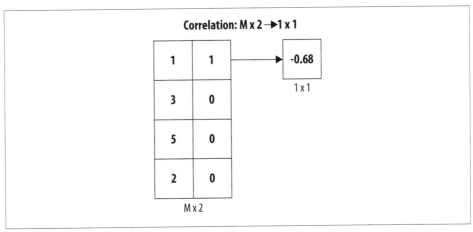

Figure 2-3. Correlation: summarizing two columns in one number

And there are other tools that go further. Beyond relating pairs of columns together, you might want to reduce the number of columns in your data set if you think there's a lot of redundancy. Replacing many columns in your data set with a few columns or even just one is called dimensionality reduction, which we'll describe in Chapter 8. An example of what dimensionality reduction techniques achieve is shown in Figure 2-4.

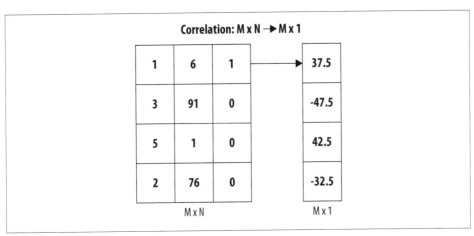

Figure 2-4. Dimensionality reduction: summarizing many columns in one column

As Figures 2-1 through 2-4 suggest, summary statistics and dimensionality reduction move along opposite directions: summary statistics tell you something about how all of the rows in your data set behave when you move along a single column, whereas dimensionality reduction tools let you replace all of the columns in your data with a small number of columns that have a unique value for every row. When you're exploring data, both of these approaches can be helpful because they allow you to turn the mountains of data you sometimes get handed into something that's immediately comprehensible.

Inferring the Types of Columns in Your Data

Before you do anything else with a new data set, you should try to find out what each column in your current table represents. Some people like to call this information a data dictionary, by which they mean that you might be handed a short verbal description of every column in the data set. For example, imagine that you had the unlabeled data set in Table 2-2 given to you.

Table 2-2. Unlabeled data

...	...	...
"1"	73.847017017515	241.893563180437
"0"	58.9107320370127	102.088326367840

Without any identifying information, it's really hard to know what to make of these numbers. Indeed, as a starting point you should figure out the type of each column: is the first column really a string, even though it looks like it contains only 0s and 1s? In the UFO example in the first chapter, we immediately labeled all of the columns of the data set we were given. When we're given a data set without labels, we can use some of the type determination functions built into R. Three of the most important of these functions are shown in Table 2-3.

Table 2-3. Type determination in R

R function	Description
is.numeric	Returns TRUE if the entries of the vector are numbers, which can be either integers or floating points. Returns FALSE otherwise.
is.character	Returns TRUE if the entries of the vector are character strings. R does not provide a single-character data type. Returns FALSE otherwise.
is.factor	Returns TRUE if the entries of the vector are levels of a factor, which is a data type used by R to represent categorical information. If you've used enumerations in SQL, a factor is somewhat analogous. It differs from a character vector in both its hidden internal representation and semantics: most statistical functions in R work on numeric vectors or factor vectors, but not on character vectors. Returns FALSE otherwise.

Having basic type information about each column can be very important as we move forward because a single R function will often do different things depending on the type of its inputs. Those 0s and 1s stored as characters in our current data set need to be translated into numbers before we can use some of the built-in functions in R, but they actually need to be converted into factors if we're going to use some other built-in functions. In part, this tendency to move back and forth between types comes from a general tradition in machine learning for dealing with categorical distinctions. Many variables that really work like labels or categories are encoded mathematically as 0 and 1. You can think of these numbers as if they were Boolean values: 0 might indicate that an email is *not* spam, a 1 might indicate that the email *is* spam. This specific use of 0s and 1s to describe qualitative properties of an object is often called dummy coding in machine learning and statistics. The dummy coding system should be distinguished from R's factors, which express qualitative properties using explicit labels.

 Factors in R can be thought of as labels, but the labels are actually encoded numerically in the background: when the programmer accesses the label, the numeric values are translated into the character labels specified in an indexed array of character strings. Because R uses a numeric coding in the background, naive attempts to convert the labels for an R factor into numbers will produce strange results because you'll be given the actual encoding scheme's numbers rather than the numbers associated with the labels for the factor.

Tables 2-4 through 2-6 show the same data, but the data has been described with three different encoding schemes.

Table 2-4. Factor coding

MessageID	IsSpam
1	"Yes"
2	"No"

Table 2-5. Dummy coding

MessageID	IsSpam
1	1
2	0

Table 2-6. Physicists' coding

MessageID	IsSpam
1	1
2	-1

In Table 2-4, IsSpam is meant to be treated directly as a factor in R, which is one way to express qualitative distinctions. In practice, it might be loaded as a factor or as a string, depending on the data loading function you use (see the stringsAsFactors parameter that was described in Chapter 1 for details). With every new data set, you'll need to figure out whether the values are being loaded properly as factors or as strings after you've decided how you would like each column to be treated by R.

 If you are unsure, it is often better to begin by loading things as strings. You can always convert a string column to a factor column later.

In Table 2-5, IsSpam is still a qualitative concept, but it's being encoded using numeric values that represent a Boolean distinction: 1 means IsSpam is true, whereas 0 means IsSpam is false. This style of numeric coding is actually required by some machine learning algorithms. For example, glm, the default function in R for using logistic regression and a classification algorithm we'll describe in the next chapter, assumes that your variables are dummy coded.

Finally, in Table 2-6, we show another type of numeric encoding for the same qualitative concept. In this encoding system, people use +1 and –1 instead of 1 and 0. This style of encoding qualitative distinctions is very popular with physicists, so you will eventually see it as you read more about machine learning. In this book, though, we completely avoid using this style of notation because we think it's a needless source of confusion to move back and forth between different ways of expressing the same distinctions.

Inferring Meaning

Even after you've figured out the type of each column, you still may not know what a column means. Determining what an unlabeled table of numbers describes can be surprisingly difficult. Let's return to the table that we saw earlier, shown again in Table 2-7.

Table 2-7. Unlabeled data

...	...	...
"1"	73.847017017515	241.893563180437
"0"	58.9107320370127	102.088326367840

How much more sense does this table make if we tell you that a) the rows describe individual people, b) the first column is a dummy code indicating whether the person is male (written as a 1) or female (written as 0), c) the second column is the person's height in inches, and d) the third column is the person's weight in pounds? The numbers suddenly have meaning when they're put into proper context, and that will shape how you think about them.

But, sadly, sometimes you will not be given this sort of interpretative information. In those cases, human intuition, aided by liberally by searching through Google, is often the only tool that we can suggest to you. Thankfully, your intuition can be substantially improved after you've looked at some numerical and visual summaries of the columns whose meaning you don't understand.

Numeric Summaries

One of the best ways to start making sense of a new data set is to compute simple numeric summaries of all of the columns. R is very well suited to doing this. If you have just one column from a data set as a vector, summary will spit out the most obvious values you should look at first:

```
data.file <- file.path('data', '01_heights_weights_genders.csv')
heights.weights <- read.csv(data.file, header = TRUE, sep = ',')
heights <- with(heights.weights, Height)
summary(heights)

# Min. 1st Qu.  Median    Mean 3rd Qu.    Max.
#54.26   63.51   66.32   66.37   69.17   79.00
```

Asking for the summary of a vector of numbers from R will give you the numbers you see in the example:

1. The minimum value in the vector
2. The first quartile (which is also called the 25th percentile and is the smallest number that's bigger than 25% of your data)
3. The median (aka the 50th percentile)
4. The mean
5. The 3rd quartile (aka the 75th percentile)
6. The maximum value

This is close to everything you should ask for when you want a quick numeric summary of a data set. All that's really missing is the standard deviation of the column entries, a numeric summary we'll define later in this chapter. In the following pages, we'll describe how to compute each of the numbers that summary produces separately, and then we'll show you how to interpret them.

Means, Medians, and Modes

Learning to tell means and medians apart is one of the most tedious parts of the typical "Intro to Stats" class. It can take a little while to become familiar with those concepts, but we really do believe that you'll need to be able to tell them apart if you want to seriously work with data. In the interests of better pedagogy, we'll try to hammer home the meaning of those terms in two pretty different ways. First, we'll show you how to compute the mean and the median algorithmically. For most hackers, code is a more natural language to express ideas than mathematical symbols, so we think that rolling your own functions to compute means and medians will probably make more sense than showing you the defining equations for those two statistics. And later in this chapter, we'll show you how you can tell when the mean and median are different by looking at the shape of your data in histograms and density plots.

Computing the mean is incredibly easy. In R, you would normally use the mean function. Of course, telling you to use a black-box function doesn't convey much of the intuition for what a mean is, so let's implement our own version of mean, which we'll call my.mean. It's just one line of R code because the relevant concepts are already available as two other functions in R: sum and length.

```
my.mean <- function(x) {
  return(sum(x) / length(x))
}
```

That single line of code is all there is to a mean: you just add up all the numbers in your vector and then divide the sum by the length of the vector. As you'd expect, this function produces the average value of the numbers in your vector, x. The mean is so easy to compute in part because it doesn't have anything to do with the sorted positions of the numbers in your list.

The median is just the opposite: it entirely depends upon the relative position of the numbers in your list. In R, you would normally compute the median using median, but let's write our version, which we'll call my.median:

```
my.median <- function(x) {
  sorted.x <- sort(x)

  if (length(x) %% 2 == 0)
  {
    indices <- c(length(x) / 2, length(x) / 2 + 1)
    return(mean(sorted.x[indices]))
  }
  else
  {
    index <- ceiling(length(x) / 2)
    return(sorted.x[index])
  }
}
```

Just counting lines of code should tell you that the median takes a little bit more work to compute than the mean. As a first step, we had to sort the vector, because the median is essentially the number that's in the middle of your sorted vector. That's why the median is also called the 50th percentile or the 2nd quartile. Once you've sorted a vector, you can easily compute any of the other percentiles or quantiles just by splitting the list into two parts somewhere else along its length. To get the 25th percentile (also known as the 1st quartile), you can split the list at one quarter of its length.

The only problem with these informal definitions in terms of length is that they don't exactly make sense if your list has an even number of entries. When there's no single number that's exactly in the middle of your data set, you need to do some trickery to produce the median. The code we wrote in the previous example handles the even-length vector case by taking the average of the two entries that would have been the median if the list had contained an odd number of entries.

To make that point clear, here is a simple example in which the median has to be invented by averaging entries and another case in which the median is exactly equal to the middle entry of the vector:

```
my.vector <- c(0, 100)
my.vector
# [1]    0 100
mean(my.vector)
#[1] 50
median(my.vector)
#[1] 50
my.vector <- c(0, 0, 100)
mean(my.vector)
#[1] 33.33333
median(my.vector)
#[1] 0
```

Returning to our original heights and weights data set, let's compute the mean and median of the heights data. This will also give us an opportunity to test our code:

```
my.mean(heights)
#[1] 66.36756
my.median(heights)
#[1] 66.31807
mean(heights) - my.mean(heights)
#[1] 0
median(heights) - my.median(heights)
#[1] 0
```

The mean and median in this example are very close to each other. In a little bit, we'll explain why we should expect that to be the case given the shape of the data we're working with.

As we've just described two of the three most prominent numbers from an intro stats course, you may be wondering why we haven't mentioned the mode. We'll talk about modes in a bit, but there's a reason we've ignored it so far: the mode, unlike the mean or median, doesn't always have a simple definition for the kinds of vectors we've been working with. Because it's not easy to automate, R doesn't have a built-in function that will produce the mode of a vector of numbers.

It's complicated to define the mode of an arbitrary vector because you need the numbers in the vector to repeat if you're going to define the mode numerically. When the numbers in a vector could be arbitrary floating-point values, it's unlikely that any single numeric value would ever be repeated in the vector. For that reason, modes are only really defined visually for many kinds of data sets.

All that said, if you're still not sure about the math and are wondering what the mode should be in theory, it's supposed to be the number that occurs most often in your data set.

Quantiles

As we said just a moment ago, the median is the number that occurs at the 50% point in your data. To get a better sense of the range of your data, you might want to know what value is the lowest point in your data. That's the minimum value of your data set, which is computed using min in R:

```
min(heights)
#[1] 54.26313
```

And to get the highest/maximum point in your data set, you should use max in R:

```
max(heights)
#[1] 78.99874
```

Together, the min and max define the range of your data:

```
c(min(heights), max(heights))
#[1] 54.26313 78.99874
range(heights)
#[1] 54.26313 78.99874
```

Another way of thinking of these numbers is to think of the min as the number that 0% of your data is below and the max as the number that 100% of your data is below. Thinking that way leads to a natural extension: how can you find the number that N% of your data is below? The answer to that question is to use the quantile function in R. The Nth quantile is exactly the number that N% of your data is below.

By default, quantile will tell you the 0%, 25%, 50%, 75%, and 100% points in your data:

```
quantile(heights)
#       0%      25%      50%      75%     100%
#54.26313 63.50562 66.31807 69.17426 78.99874
```

To get other locations, you can pass in the cut offs you want as another argument to quantile called probs:

```
quantile(heights, probs = seq(0, 1, by = 0.20))
#      0%      20%      40%      60%      80%     100%
#54.26313 62.85901 65.19422 67.43537 69.81162 78.99874
```

Here we've used the seq function to produce a sequence of values between 0 and 1 that grows in 0.20 increments:

```
seq(0, 1, by = 0.20)
#[1] 0.0 0.2 0.4 0.6 0.8 1.0
```

Quantiles aren't emphasized as much in traditional statistics texts as means and medians, but they can be just as useful. If you run a customer service branch and keep records of how long it takes to respond to a customer's concerns, you might benefit a lot more from worrying about what happens to the first 99% of your customers than worrying about what happens to the median customer. And the mean customer might be even less informative if your data has a strange shape.

Standard Deviations and Variances

The mean and median of a list of numbers are both measures of something central: the median is literally in the center of list, whereas the mean is effectively in the center only after you've weighted all the items in the list by their values.

But central tendencies are only one thing you might want to know about your data. Equally important is to ask how far apart you expect the typical values to be, which we'll call the spread of your data. You can imagine defining the range of your data in a lot of ways. As we already said, you could use the definition that the range function implements: the range is defined by the min and max values. This definition misses two things we might want from a reasonable definition of spread:

- The spread should include only most of the data, not all of it.
- The spread shouldn't be completely determined by the two most extreme values in your data set, which are often outlier values that are not representative of your data set as a whole.

The min and max will match the outliers perfectly, which makes them fairly brittle definitions of spread. Another way to think about what's wrong with the min and max definition of range is to consider what happens if you change the rest of your data while leaving those two extreme values unchanged. In practice, you can move the rest of the data as much as you'd like inside those limits and still get the same min and max. In other words, the definition of range based on min and max effectively depends on only two of your data points, regardless of whether you have two data points or two million data points. Because you shouldn't trust any summary of your data that's insensitive to the vast majority of the points in the data, we'll move on to a better definition of the spread of a data set.

Now, there are a lot of ways you could try to meet the requirements we described earlier for a good numeric summary of data. For example, you could see what range contains 50% of your data and is centered around the median. In R, this is quite easy to do:

```
c(quantile(heights, probs = 0.25), quantile(heights, probs = 0.75))
```

Or you might want to be more inclusive and find a range that contains 95% of the data:

```
c(quantile(heights, probs = 0.025), quantile(heights, probs = 0.975))
```

These are actually really good measures of the spread of your data. When you work with more advanced statistical methods, these sorts of ranges will come up again and again. But historically, statisticians have used a somewhat different measure of spread: specifically, they've used a definition called the variance. Roughly, the idea is to measure how far, on average, a given number in your data set is from the mean value. Rather than give a formal mathematical definition, let's define the variance computationally by writing our own variance function:

```
my.var <- function(x) {
  m <- mean(x)
  return(sum((x - m) ^ 2) / length(x))
}
```

As always, let's check that our implementation works by comparing it with R's var:

```
my.var(heights) - var(heights)
```

We're doing only a so-so job of matching R's implementation of var. In theory, there could be a few reasons for this, most of which are examples of how things can go wrong when you assume floating-point arithmetic is perfectly accurate. But there's actually another reason that our code isn't working the same way that the built-in function does in R: the formal definition of variance doesn't divide out by the length of a vector, but rather by the length of the vector *minus one*. This is done because the variance that you can estimate from empirical data turns out, for fairly subtle reasons, to be biased downward from its true value. To fix this for a data set with n points, you normally multiply your estimate of the variance by a scaling factor of n / (n - 1), which leads to an improved version of my.var:

```
my.var <- function(x) {
  m <- mean(x)
  return(sum((x - m) ^ 2) / (length(x) - 1))
}

my.var(heights) - var(heights)
```

With this second version of my.var, we match R's estimate of the variance perfectly. The floating-point concerns we raised earlier could easily come up if we had used longer vectors, but they didn't seem to matter with a data set of this size.

The variance is a very natural measure of the spread of our data, but unfortunately it's much larger than almost any of the values in our data set. One obvious way to see this mismatch in scale is to look at the values that are one unit of variance away from the mean:

```
c(mean(heights) - var(heights), mean(heights) + var(heights))
#[1] 51.56409 81.17103
```

This range is actually larger than the range of the entire original data set:

```
c(mean(heights) - var(heights), mean(heights) + var(heights))
#[1] 51.56409 81.17103
range(heights)
#[1] 54.26313 78.99874
```

The reason we're so far out of bounds from our original data is that we defined variance by measuring the squared distance of each number in our list from the mean value, but we never undid that squaring step. To put everything back on the original scale, we need to replace the variance with the standard deviation, which is just the square root of the variance:

```
my.sd <- function(x) {
  return(sqrt(my.var(x)))
}
```

Before we do anything else, it's always good to check that your implementation makes sense relative to R's, which is called **sd**:

```
my.sd(heights) - sd(heights)
```

Because we're now computing values on the right scale, it'll be informative to recreate our estimate of the range of our data by looking at values that are one unit of standard deviation away from the mean:

```
c(mean(heights) - sd(heights), mean(heights) + sd(heights))
# [1] 62.52003 70.21509
range(heights)
#[1] 54.26313 78.99874
```

Now that we're using units of standard deviations instead of units of variances, we're solidly inside the range of our data. Still, it would be nice to get a sense of how tightly inside the data we are. One way to do this is to compare the standard-deviation-based range against a range defined using quantiles:

```
c(mean(heights) - sd(heights), mean(heights) + sd(heights))
# [1] 62.52003 70.21509

c(quantile(heights, probs = 0.25), quantile(heights, probs = 0.75))
#    25%      75%
#63.50562 69.17426
```

By using the **quantile** function, we can see that roughly 50% of our data is less than one standard deviation away from the mean. This is quite typical, especially for data with the shape that our heights data has. But to finally make that idea about the shape of our data precise, we need to start visualizing our data and define some formal terms for describing the shape of data.

Exploratory Data Visualization

Computing numerical summaries of your data is clearly valuable. It's the stuff of classical statistics, after all. But for many people, numbers don't convey the information they want to see very efficiently. Visualizing your data is often a more effective way to discover patterns in it. In this chapter, we'll cover the two simplest forms of exploratory data visualization: single-column visualizations, which highlight the shape of your data, and two-column visualizations, which highlight the relationship between pairs of columns. Beyond showing you the tools for visualizing your data, we'll also describe some of the canonical shapes you can expect to see when you start looking at data. These idealized shapes, also called distributions, are standard patterns that statisticians have studied over the years. When you find one of these shapes in your data, you can often make broad inferences about your data: how it originated, what sort of abstract properties it will have, and so on. Even when you think the shape you see is only a vague approximation to your data, the standard distributional shapes can provide you with building blocks that you can use to construct more complex shapes that match your data more closely.

All that said, let's get started by just visualizing the heights and weights data that we've been working with so far. It's actually a fairly complex data set that illustrates many of the ideas we'll come up against again and again throughout this book. The most typical single-column visualization technique that people use is the histogram. In a histogram, you divide your data set into bins and then count the number of entries in your data that fall into each of the bins. For instance, in Figure 2-5, we create a histogram with one-inch bins to visualize our height data. We can do that in R as follows:

```
library('ggplot2')

data.file <- file.path('data', '01_heights_weights_genders.csv')

heights.weights <- read.csv(data.file, header = TRUE, sep = ',')

ggplot(heights.weights, aes(x = Height)) + geom_histogram(binwidth = 1)
```

Immediately, something should jump out at you: there's a bell curve shape in your data. Most of the entries are in the middle of your data, near the mean and median height. But there's a danger that this shape is an illusion caused by the type of histogram we're using. One way to check this is to try using several other binwidths. This is something you should always keep in mind when working with histograms: the binwidths you use *impose* external structure on your data at the same time that they reveal *internal* structure in your data. The patterns you find, even when they're real, can go away very easily if you use the wrong settings for building a histogram. In Figure 2-6, we recreate the histogram using five-inch bins with the following R code:

```
ggplot(heights.weights, aes(x = Height)) + geom_histogram(binwidth = 5)
```

When we use too broad a binwidth, a lot of the structure in our data goes away. There's still a peak, but the symmetry we saw before seems to mostly disappear. This is called

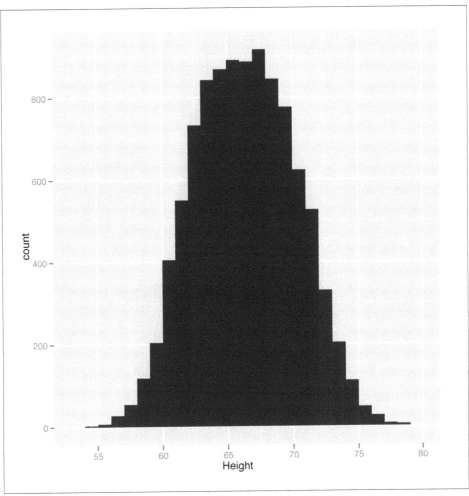

Figure 2-5. Histogram of 10,000 people's heights in inches with bindwidth = 1"

oversmoothing. And the opposite problem, called undersmoothing, is just as danger-ous. In Figure 2-7, we again adjust the binwidth, this time to a much smaller 0.001 inches:

```
ggplot(heights.weights, aes(x = Height)) + geom_histogram(binwidth = 0.001)
```

Here we've undersmoothed the data because we've used incredibly small bins. Because we have so much data, you can still learn something from this histogram, but a data set with 100 points would be basically worthless if you had used this sort of bindwidth.

Because setting bindwidths can be tedious and because even the best histogram is too jagged for our taste, we prefer an alternative to histograms called kernel density esti-mates (KDE) or density plots. Although density plots suffer from most of the same problems of oversmoothing and undersmoothing that plague histograms, we generally

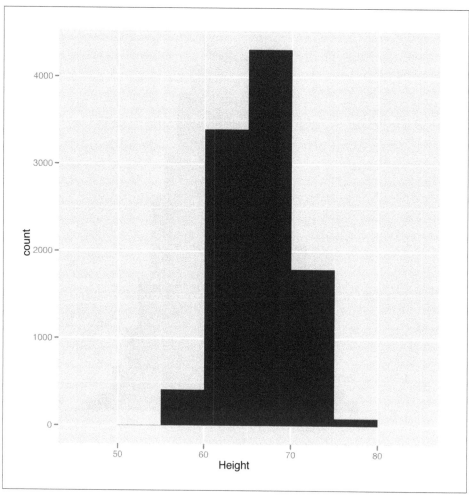

Figure 2-6. Histogram of 10,000 people's heights in inches with bindwidth = 5"

find them aesthetically superior—especially because density plots for large data sets look a lot more like the theoretical shapes we expect to find in our data. Additionally, density plots have some theoretical superiority over histograms: in theory, using a density plot should require fewer data points to reveal the underlying shape of your data than a histogram. And, thankfully, density plots are just as easy to generate in R as histograms. In Figure 2-8, we create our first density plot of the height data:

```
ggplot(heights.weights, aes(x = Height)) + geom_density()
```

The smoothness of the density plot helps us discover the sorts of patterns that we personally find harder to see in histograms. Here the density plot suggests that the data is suspiciously flat at the peak value. Because the standard bell curve shape we might expect to see isn't flat, this leads us to wonder whether there might be more structure

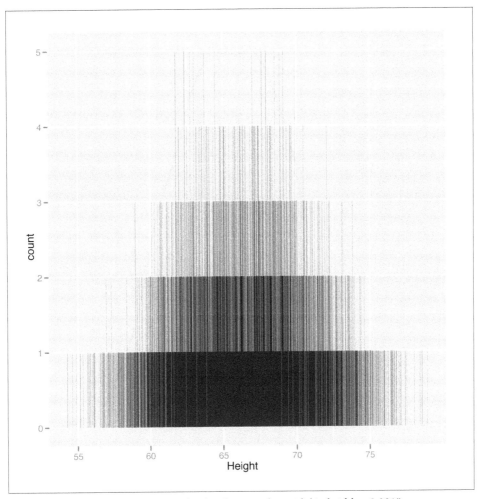

Figure 2-7. Histogram of 10,000 people's heights in inches with bindwidth = 0.001"

hidden in this data set. One thing you might try doing when you think there's some structure you're missing is to split up your plot by any qualitative variables you have available. Here we use the gender of each point to split up our data into two parts. Next, in Figure 2-9 we create a density plot in which there are two densities that get superimposed, but are colored in differently to indicate the gender they represent:

```
ggplot(heights.weights, aes(x = Height, fill = Gender)) + geom_density()
```

In this plot, we suddenly see a hidden pattern that was totally missing before: we're not looking at one bell curve, but at two different bell curves that partially overlap. This isn't surprising because men and women have different mean heights. We might expect to see the same bell curve structure in the weights for both genders. In Figure 2-10, we make a new density plot for the weights column of our data set:

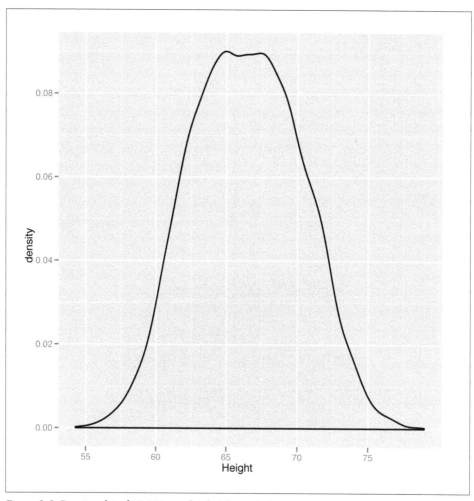

Figure 2-8. Density plot of 10,000 people's heights in inches

```
ggplot(heights.weights, aes(x = Weight, fill = Gender)) + geom_density()
```

Again, we see the same mixture of bell curves in the structure. In future chapters, we'll cover this sort of mixture of bell curves in some detail, but it's worth giving a name to the structure we're looking at right now: it's a mixture model in which two standard distributions have been mixed to produce a nonstandard distribution.

Of course, we need to describe our standard distributions more clearly to give sense to that sentence, so let's start with our first idealized data distribution: the normal distribution, which is also called the Gaussian distribution or the bell curve. We can easily see an example of the normal distribution by simply splitting up the plot into two pieces, called facets. We do this in Figure 2-11 with the density plots we've shown you so far

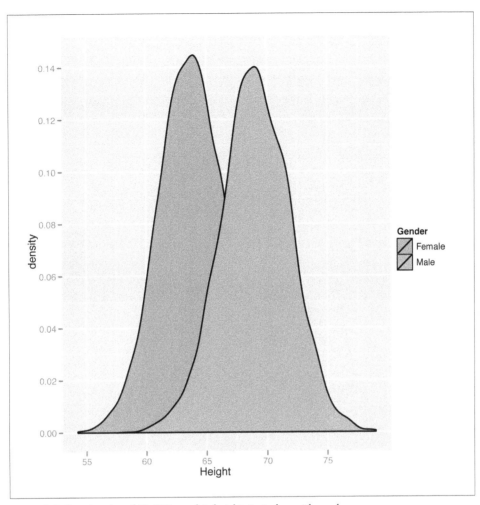

Figure 2-9. Density plot of 10,000 people's heights in inches with genders

so that you can see the two bell curves in isolation from one another. In R, we can build this sort of faceted plot as follows:

```
ggplot(heights.weights, aes(x = Weight, fill = Gender)) + geom_density() +
                    facet_grid(Gender ~ .)
```

Once we've done this, we clearly see one bell curve centered at 64" for women and another bell curve centered at 69" for men. This specific bell curve is the normal distribution, a shape that comes up so often that it's easy to think that it's the "normal" way for data to look. This isn't quite true: lots of things we care about, from people's annual incomes to the daily changes in stock prices, aren't very well described using the normal distribution. But the normal distribution is very important in the

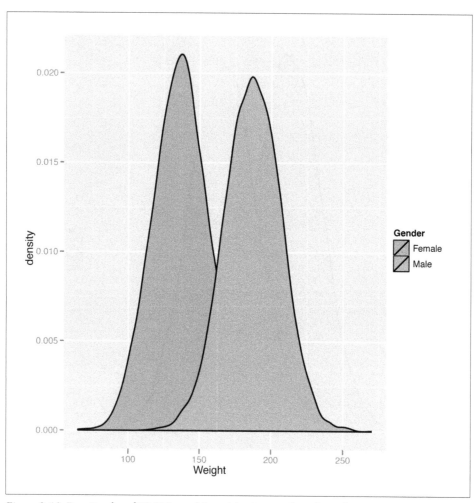

Figure 2-10. Density plot of 10,000 people's weights in pounds with genders

mathematical theory of statistics, so it's much better understood than most other distributions.

On a more abstract level, a normal distribution is just a type of bell curve. It might be any of the bell curves shown in Figures 2-12 through 2-14.

In these graphs, two parameters vary: the mean of the distribution, which determines the center of the bell curve, and the variance of the distribution, which determines the width of the bell curve. You should play around with visualizing various versions of the bell curve by playing with the parameters in the following code until you feel comfortable with how the bell curve looks. To do that, play with the values of m and s in the code shown here:

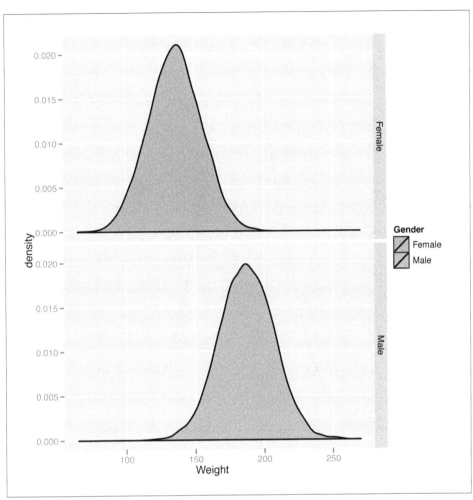

Figure 2-11. Density plot of 10,000 people's weights in pounds, facetted by gender

```
m <- 0
s <- 1
ggplot(data.frame(X = rnorm(100000, m, s)), aes(x = X)) + geom_density()
```

All of the curves you can generate with this code have the same basic shape; changing m and s only moves the center around and contracts or expands the width. As you can see from Figures 2-12 through 2-14, the exact shape of the curves will vary, but their overall shape is consistent. Unfortunately, seeing this general bell shape isn't sufficient to tell you that your data is normal, because there are other bell-shaped distributions, one of which we'll describe in just a moment. For now, let's do a quick jargon lesson, as the normal distribution lets us define several qualitative ideas about the shape of data.

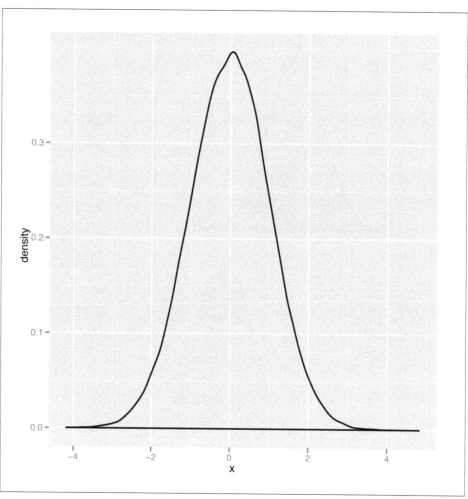

Figure 2-12. Normal distribution with mean 0 and variance 1

First, let's return to the topic of modes that we put off until now. As we said earlier, the mode of a continuous list of numbers isn't well defined, because no numbers repeat. But the mode has a clear visual interpretation: when you make a density plot, the mode of the data is the peak of the bell. For an example, look at Figure 2-15.

Estimating modes visually is much easier to do with a density plot than with a histogram, which is one of the reasons we prefer density plots over histograms. And modes make sense almost immediately when you look at density plots, whereas they often make very little sense if you try to work with the numbers directly.

Now that we've defined a mode, we should point out one of the defining traits of the normal distribution is that it has a single mode, which is also the mean and the median

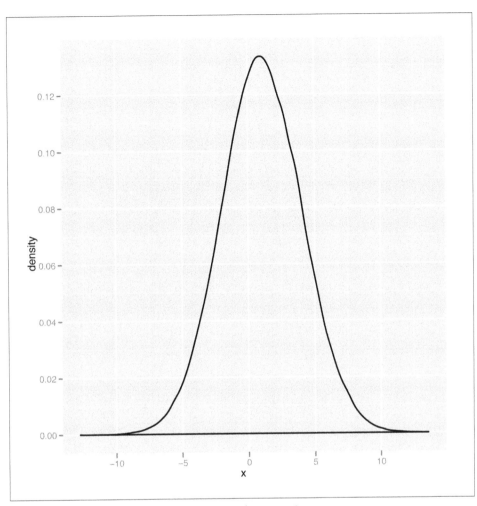

Figure 2-13. Normal distribution with mean 1 and variance 3

of the data it describes. In contrast, a graph like the one shown in Figure 2-16 has two modes, and the graph in Figure 2-17 has three modes.

When we talk about the number of modes that we see in our data, we'll use the following terms: a distribution with one mode is *unimodal*, a distribution with two modes is *bimodal*, and a distribution with two or more modes is *multimodal*.

Another important qualitative distinction can be made between data that's *symmetric* and data that's *skewed*. Figures 2-18 and 2-19 show images of symmetric and skewed data to make these terms clear.

A symmetric distribution has the same shape whether you move to the left of the mode or to the right of the mode. The normal distribution has this property, which tells us

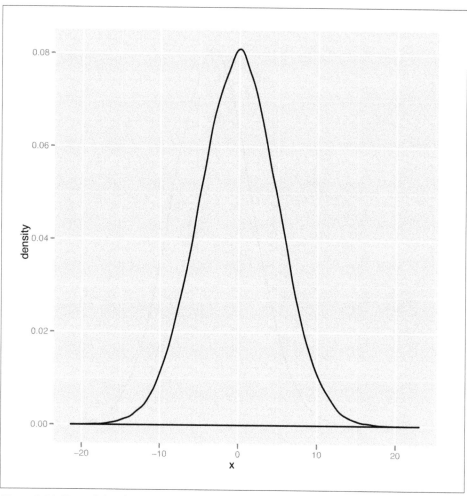

Figure 2-14. Normal distribution with mean 0 and variance 5

that we're as likely to see data that's below the mode as we are to see data that's above the mode. In contrast, the second graph, which is called the gamma distribution, is skewed to the right, which means you're much more likely to see extreme values to the right of the mode than you are to see extreme values to the left of the mode.

The last qualitative distinction we'll make is between data that's *thin-tailed* and data that's *heavy-tailed*. We'll show the standard graph that's meant to illustrate this distinction in a second, but this distinction is probably easier to make in word. A thin-tailed distribution usually produces values that are not far from the mean; let's say that it does so 99% of the time. The normal distribution, for example, produces values that are no more than three standard deviations away from the mean about 99% of the time. In contrast, another bell-shaped distribution called the Cauchy distribution produces

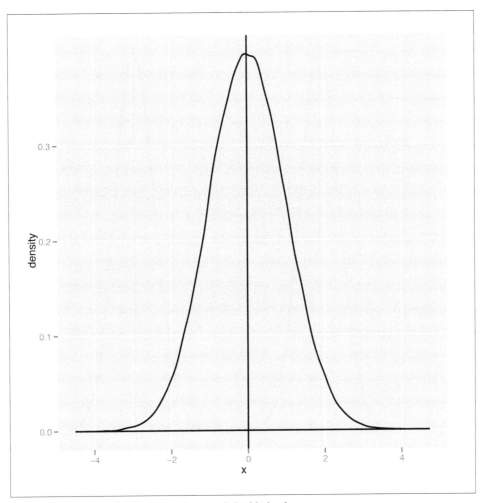

Figure 2-15. Normal distribution with its mode highlighted

only 90% of its values inside those three standard deviation bounds. And, as you get further away from the mean value, the two types of distributions become even more different: a normal distribution almost never produces values that are six standard deviations away from the mean, whereas a Cauchy will do it almost 5% of the time.

The canonical images that are usually used to explain this distinction between the thin-tailed normal and the heavy-tailed Cauchy are shown in Figures 2-20 and 2-21.

But we think you'll gain a more intuitive understanding by just generating lots of data from both of those distributions and seeing the results for yourself. R makes this quite easy, so you should try the following:

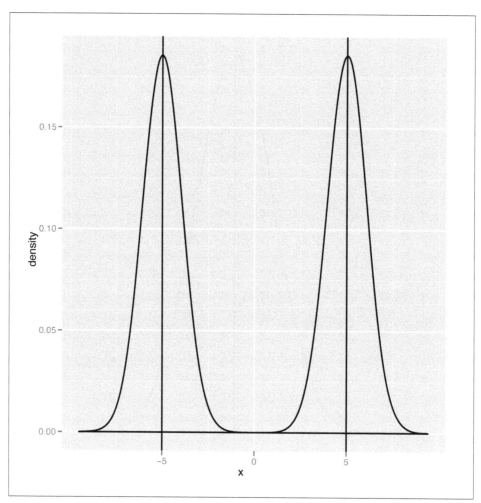

Figure 2-16. Mixture of two normal distributions with both modes highlighted

```
set.seed(1)
normal.values <- rnorm(250, 0, 1)
cauchy.values <- rcauchy(250, 0, 1)

range(normal.values)
range(cauchy.values)
```

Plotting these will also make the point clearer:

```
ggplot(data.frame(X = normal.values), aes(x = X)) + geom_density()
ggplot(data.frame(X = cauchy.values), aes(x = X)) + geom_density()
```

To end this section on the normal distribution and its cousin the Cauchy distribution, let's summarize the qualitative properties of the normal once more: it's unimodal, it's

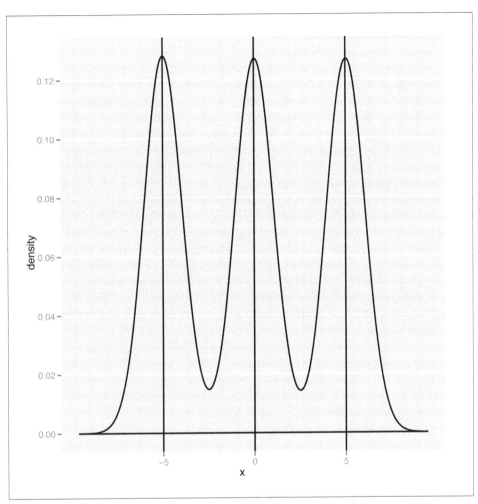

Figure 2-17. Mixture of three normal distributions with three modes highlighted

symmetric, and it has a bell shape with thin tails. The Cauchy is unimodal and symmetric, and it has a bell shape with heavy tails.

After the normal distribution, there are two more canonical images we want to show you before we bring this section on density plots to a close: a mildly skewed distribution called the *gamma* and a very skewed distribution called the *exponential*. We'll use both later on because they occur in real data, but it's worth describing them now to illustrate skewness visually.

Let's start with the gamma distribution. It's quite flexible, so we'd encourage you to play with it on your own for a bit. Here's a starting point:

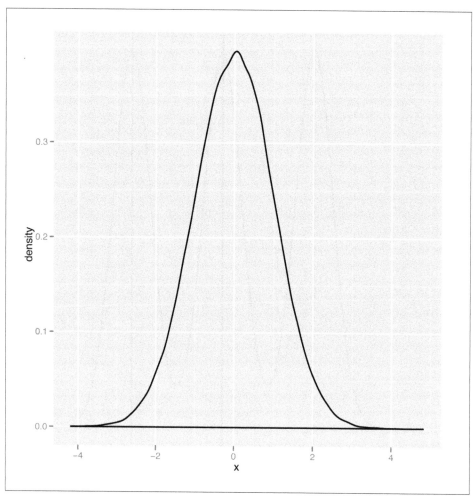

Figure 2-18. Symmetric distribution

```
gamma.values <- rgamma(100000, 1, 0.001)
ggplot(data.frame(X = gamma.values), aes(x = X)) + geom_density()
```

The resulting plot of the gamma data is shown in Figure 2-22.

As you can see, the gamma distribution is skewed to the right, which means that the median and the mean can sometimes be quite different. In Figure 2-23, we've plotted some scores we spidered from people playing the iPhone game *Canabalt*.

This real data set looks remarkably like data that could have been produced by a theoretical gamma distribution. We also bet that you'll see this sort of shape in the density plots for scores in lot of other games as well, so it seems like a particularly useful theoretical tool to have in your belt if you want to analyze game data.

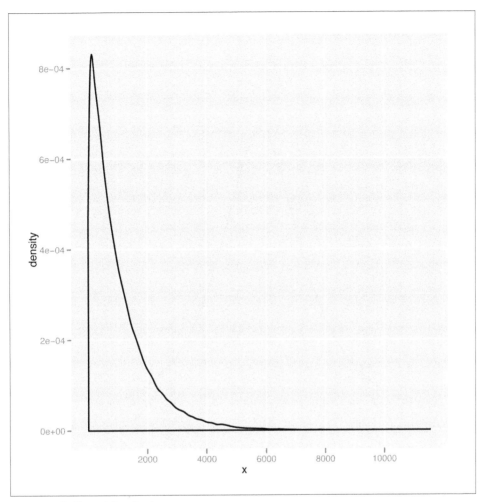

Figure 2-19. Skewed distribution

One other thing to keep in mind is that the gamma distribution produces only positive values. When we describe how to use stochastic optimization tools near the end of this book, having an all-positive distribution will come in very handy.

The last distribution we'll describe is the exponential distribution, which is a nice example of a powerfully skewed distribution. An example data set drawn from the exponential distribution is shown in Figure 2-24.

Because the mode of the exponential distribution occurs at zero, it's almost like you had cut off the positive half of a bell to produce the exponential curve. This distribution comes up quite a lot when the most frequent value in your data set is zero and only

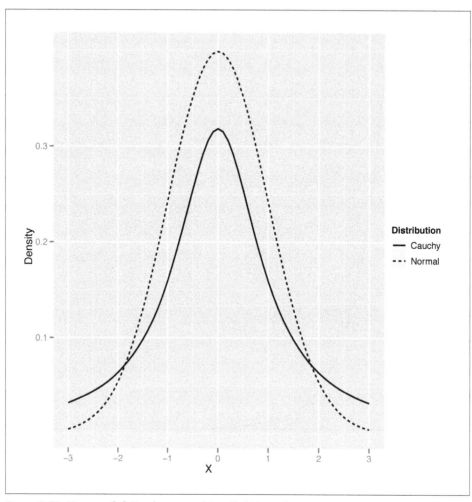

Figure 2-20. Heavy-tailed Cauchy versus thin-tailed Normal

positive values can ever occur. For example, corporate call centers often find that the length of time between the calls they receive looks like an exponential distribution.

As you build up a greater familiarity with data and learn more about the theoretical distributions that statisticians have studied, these distributions will become more familiar to you—especially because the same few distributions come up over and over again. For right now, what you really take away from this section are the simple qualitative terms that you can use to describe your data to others: unimodal versus multimodal, symmetric versus skewed, and thin-tailed versus heavy-tailed.

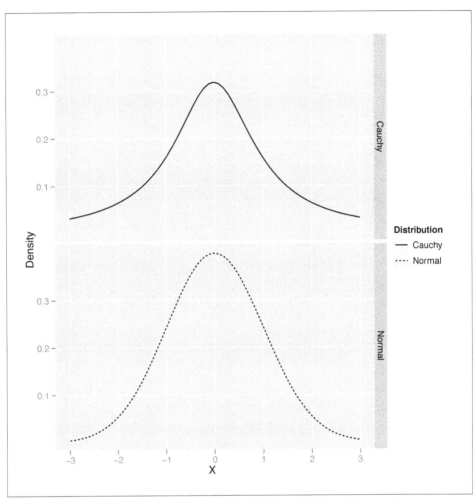

Figure 2-21. Facetted plot of heavy-tailed Cauchy and thin-tailed Normal

Visualizing the Relationships Between Columns

So far we've only covered strategies for thinking carefully about individual columns in your data set. This is clearly worth doing: often just seeing a familiar shape in your data tells you a lot about your data. Seeing a normal distribution tells us that you can use the mean and median interchangeably, and it also tells you that you can trust that most of the time you won't see data more than three standard deviations away from the mean. That's a lot to learn from just a single visualization.

But all of the material we just reviewed is what you'd expect to learn in a traditional statistics class; it doesn't have the feel of the machine learning applications that you're presumably itching to start getting involved with. To do real machine learning, we need

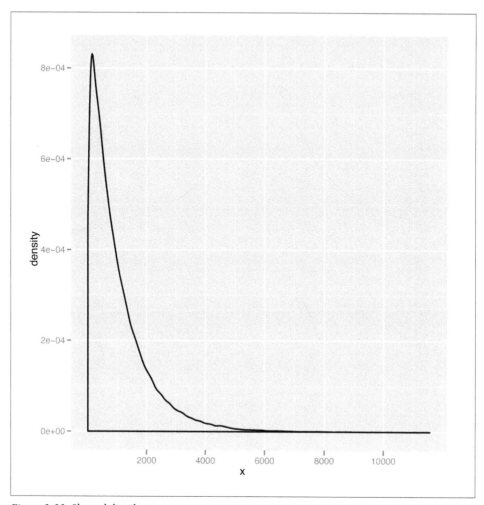

Figure 2-22. Skewed distribution

to find relationships between multiple columns in our data and use those relationships to make sense of our data and to predict things about the future. Some examples we'll touch on over the course of this book include the following prediction problems:

- Predicting someone's weight from her height
- Predicting whether an email is spam or not using the text of the email
- Predicting whether a user would want to buy a product you've never suggested to him before

As we mentioned earlier, these sorts of problems break down into two types: regression problems, in which you need to predict some number, such as weight, given a bunch of other numbers, such as height; and classification problems, in which you need to

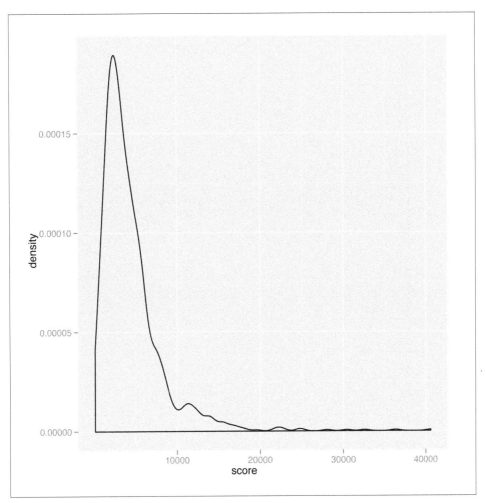

Figure 2-23. Canabalt scores

assign a label, such as spam, given a bunch of numbers, for example, word counts for spammy words such as "viagra" and "cialis." Introducing the tools we can use to perform regression and classification will take up most of the rest of this book, but there are two motivating types of data visualizations we'd like you to carry around in your head as we move forward.

The first is the stereotypical regression picture. In the regression picture, we make a scatterplot of our data and see that there's a hidden shape that relates two columns in the data set. Returning to our beloved heights and weights data, let's make a scatterplot of weights against heights.

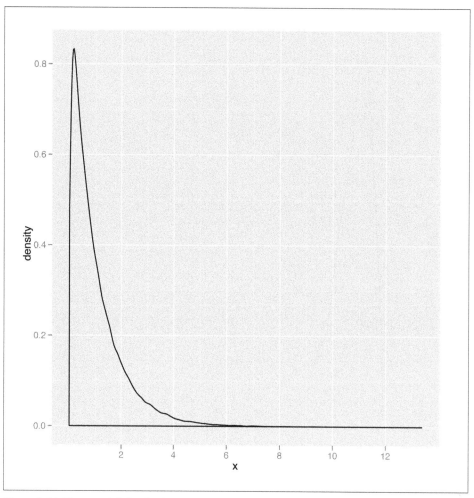

Figure 2-24. Exponential distribution

If you're not familiar with them, you should know that a scatterplot is a two-dimensional image in which one dimension corresponds to a variable X and another corresponds to a variable Y. To make our scatterplots, we'll continue using ggplot.

```
ggplot(heights.weights, aes(x = Height, y = Weight)) + geom_point()
```

The scatterplot that ggplot generates is shown in Figure 2-25.

Looking at this image, it seems pretty clear that there's a pattern relating heights with weights: people who are taller also weigh more. This is intuitively obvious, but describing general strategies for finding these sorts of patterns will take up the rest of this book.

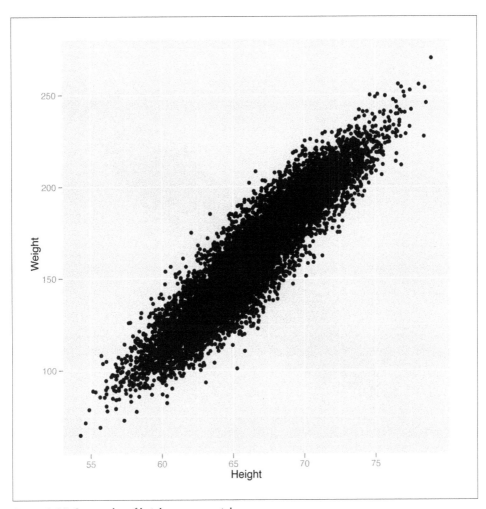

Figure 2-25. Scatterplot of heights versus weights

To start examining the pattern more carefully, we can use a smoothing tool in ggplot2 to get a visual depiction of the linear pattern we're seeing:

```
ggplot(heights.weights, aes(x = Height, y = Weight)) + geom_point() + geom_smooth()
```

The new scatterplot with a smooth pattern superimposed is shown in Figure 2-26.

geom_smooth will generate predictions for people's weights given their heights as an input. In this case, the predictions are simply a line, which is shown in blue. Around the line there is a shaded region, which describes other plausible predictions that could have been made for someone's weight based on the data you've seen. As you get more data, these guesses become more accurate and the shaded region shrinks. Because we already used all of the data, the best way to see this effect is to go in the opposite

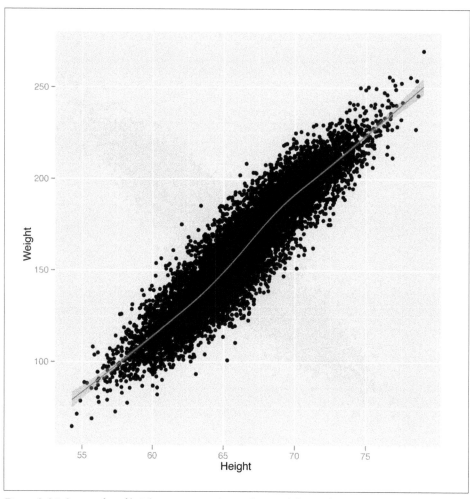

Figure 2-26. Scatterplot of heights versus weights with smooth linear fit

direction: remove some of our data, and see how the pattern gets weaker and weaker. The results are shown in Figures 2-27 through 2-29.

```
ggplot(heights.weights[1:20,], aes(x = Height, y = Weight)) + geom_point() +
                    geom_smooth()

ggplot(heights.weights[1:200,], aes(x = Height, y = Weight)) + geom_point() +
                    geom_smooth()

ggplot(heights.weights[1:2000,], aes(x = Height, y = Weight)) + geom_point() +
                    geom_smooth()
```

Recall that predicting the values in one column using another column is called regression when the values you're trying to predict are numbers. In contrast, when you're

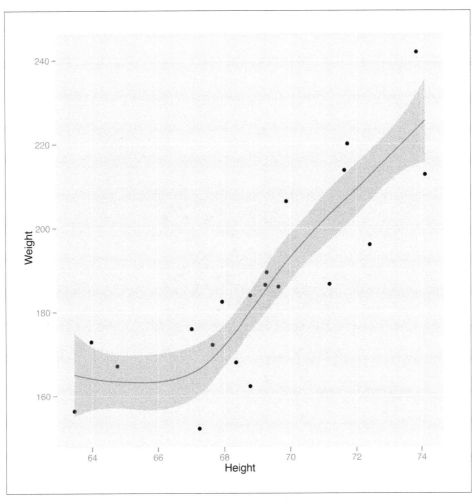

Figure 2-27. Scatterplot of heights versus weights with 20 observations

trying to predict labels, we call that classification. For classification, Figure 2-30 is the image you should keep in mind.

In this image, we've shown the heights and weights of every person in our data set, but we've also visualized their gender as the color of each point. That makes it clear that we see two distinct groups of people in our data. To generate this image in `ggplot2`, we run the following code:

```
ggplot(heights.weights, aes(x = Height, y = Weight, color = Gender)) + geom_point()
```

This image is the standard classification picture. In the classification picture, we make a scatterplot of our data but use a third column to color in the points with different labels. For our height and weight data, we added a third column, which is the gender

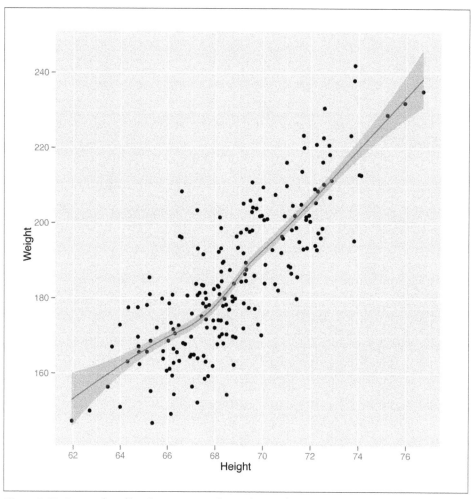

Figure 2-28. Scatterplot of heights versus weights with 200 observations

of each person in our data set. Looking at this picture, it probably seems like we could guess a person's gender using only her height and weight. Making guesses about categorical variables such as gender from other data is exactly what classification is meant to do, and we'll describe algorithms for it in some detail in the next chapter. For now, we'll just show you in Figure 2-31 what the results would look like after running a standard classification algorithm.

The line we've drawn has a very fancy-sounding name: the "separating hyperplane." It's a "separating" hyperplane because it splits the data into two groups: on one side, you guess that someone is female given her height and weight, and on the other side, you guess that he's male. This is a pretty good way to make guesses; for this data set, you'd be right about 92% of the time. In our mind, that's not bad performance when

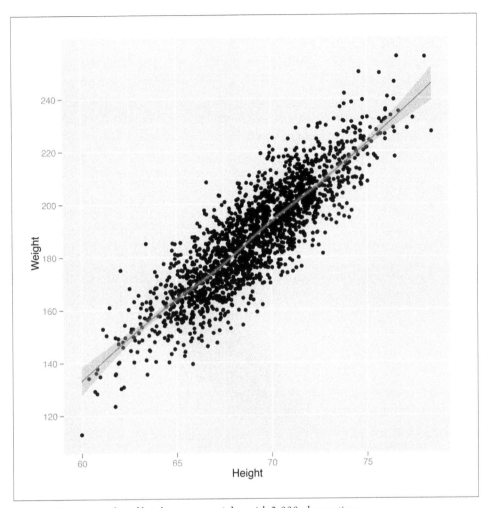

Figure 2-29. Scatterplot of heights versus weights with 2,000 observations

you're using only the simplest classification model that's out there with only heights and weights as inputs to your prediction algorithm. In our real classification tasks, we'll often have tens, hundreds, or even thousands of inputs to use for predicting classes. This data set just happens to be particularly easy to work with, which is why we started with it.

That's the end of this chapter. As a teaser to get you excited for the next chapter, we'll show you the R code that generated the predictions you just saw. As you can see, you need almost no code at all to get pretty impressive results.

```
heights.weights <- transform(heights.weights, Male = ifelse(Gender == 'Male', 1, 0))

logit.model <- glm(Male ~ Height + Weight, data = heights.weights,
```

```
                family = binomial(link = 'logit'))

ggplot(heights.weights, aes(x = Weight, y = Height, color = Gender)) +
  geom_point() +
  stat_abline(intercept = - coef(logit.model)[1] / coef(logit.model)[2],
        slope = - coef(logit.model)[3] / coef(logit.model)[2],
        geom = 'abline',
        color = 'black')
```

In the next chapter, we'll show more thoroughly how you build your own classifiers using off-the-shelf machine learning tools.

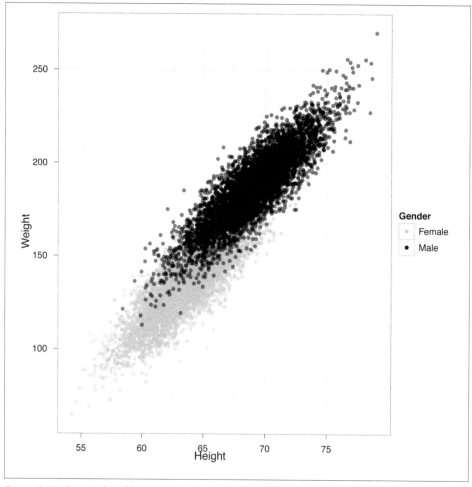

Figure 2-30. Scatterplot of heights versus weights with 2,000 observations colored by gender

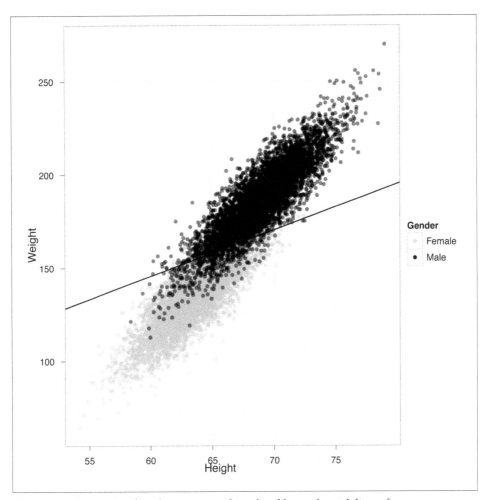

Figure 2-31. Scatterplot of heights versus weights colored by gender with linear fit

## CHAPTER 3

Classification: Spam Filtering

This or That: Binary Classification

At the very end of Chapter 2, we quickly presented an example of classification. We used heights and weights to predict whether a person was a man or a woman. With our example graph, we were able to draw a line that split the data into two groups: one group where we would predict "male" and another group where we would predict "female." This line was called a separating hyperplane, but from now on we'll use the term "decision boundary," because we'll be working with data that can't be classified properly using only straight lines. For example, imagine that your data looked like the data set shown in Example 3-1.

This plot might depict people who are at risk for a certain ailment and those who are not. Above and below the black horizontal lines we might predict that a person is at risk, but inside we would predict good health. These black lines are thus our decision boundary. Suppose that the blue dots represent healthy people and the red dots represent people who suffer from a disease. If that were the case, the two black lines would work quite well as a decision boundary for classifying people as either healthy or sick.

Producing general-purpose tools that let us handle problems where the decision boundary isn't a single straight line has been one of the great achievements of machine learning. One approach in particular that we'll focus on later is called the *kernel trick*, which has the remarkable property of allowing us to work with much more sophisticated decision boundaries at almost no additional computational cost.

But before we begin to understand how these decision boundaries are determined in practice, let's review some of the big ideas in classification.

We're going to assume that we have a set of labeled examples of the categories we want to learn how to identify. These examples consist of a label, which we'll also call a class or type, and a series of measured variables that describe each example. We'll call these measurements features or predictors. The height and weight columns we worked with earlier are examples of features that we could use to guess the "male" and "female" labels we were working with before.

Examples of classifications can be found anywhere you look for them:

- Given the results of a mammogram, does a patient have breast cancer?
- Do blood pressure measurements suggest that a patient has hypertension?
- Does a political candidate's platform suggest that she is a Republican candidate or a Democratic candidate?
- Does a picture uploaded to a social network contain a face in it?
- Was *The Tempest* written by William Shakespeare or Francis Bacon?

In this chapter, we're going to focus on problems with text classification that are closely related to the tools you could use to answer the last question in our list. In our exercise, however, we're going to build a system for deciding whether an email is spam or ham.

Our raw data comes from the SpamAssassin public corpus, available for free download at *http://spamassassin.apache.org/publiccorpus/*. Portions of this corpus are included in the *code/data/* folder for this chapter and will be used throughout this chapter. At the unprocessed stage, the features are simply the contents of the raw email as plain text.

This raw text provides us with our first problem. We need to transform our raw text data into a set of features that describe qualitative concepts in a quantitative way. In our case, that will be a 0/1 coding strategy: spam or ham. For example, we may want to determine the following: "Does containing HTML tags make an email more likely to be spam?" To answer this, we will need a strategy for turning the text in our email into numbers. Fortunately, the general-purpose text-mining packages available in R will do much of this work for us.

For that reason, much of this chapter will focus on building up your intuition for the types of features that people have used in the past when working with text data. *Feature generation* is a major topic in current machine learning research and is still very far from being automated in a general-purpose way. At present, it's best to think of the features being used as part of a vocabulary of machine learning that you become more familiar with as you perform more machine learning tasks.

 Just as learning the words of a new language builds up an intuition for what could realistically be a word, learning about the features people have used in the past builds up an intuition for what features could reasonably be helpful in the future.

When working with text, historically the most important type of feature that's been used is word count. If we think that the text of HTML tags are strong indicators of whether an email is spam, then we might pick terms like "html" and "table" and count how often they occur in one type of document versus the other. To show how this approach would work with the SpamAssassin public corpus, we've gone ahead and counted the number of times the terms "html" and "table" occurred. Table 3-1 shows the results.

Table 3-1. Frequency of "spammy" words

Term	Spam	Ham
html	377	9
table	1,182	43

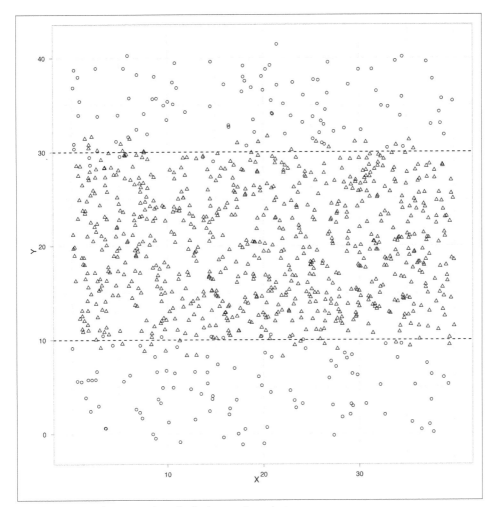

Figure 3-1. Classification with multiple decision boundaries

For every email in our data set, we've also plotted the class memberships in Figure 3-1. This plot isn't very informative, because too many of the data points in our data set overlap. This sort of problem comes up quite often when you work with data that contains only a few unique values for one or more of your variables. As this is a recurring problem, there is a standard graphical solution: we simply add random noise to the values before we plot. This noise will "separate out" the points to reduce the amount of over-plotting. This addition of noise is called *jittering*, and is very easy to produce in `ggplot2` (see Figure 3-2).

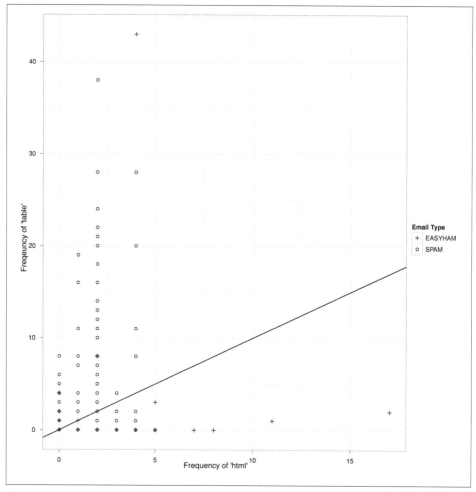

Figure 3-2. Frequency of the terms "html" and "table" by email type

This last plot suggests that we could do a so-so job of deciding whether an email is spam simply by counting the number of times the terms "html" and "table" occur.

 The commands used to create the plots in Figures 3-1 and 3-2 begin at line 129 of the *email_classify.R* file in the *code/* folder for this chapter.

In practice, we can do a much better job by using many more than just these two very obvious terms. In fact, for our final analysis we'll use several thousand terms. Even though we'll only use word-count data, we'll still get a relatively accurate classification. In the real world, you'd want to use other features beyond word counts, such as falsified headers, IP or email black lists, etc., but here we only want to introduce the basics of text classification.

Before we can proceed, we should review some basic concepts of conditional probability and discuss how they relate to classifying a message based on its text.

Moving Gently into Conditional Probability

At its core, text classification is a 20th-century application of the 18th-century concept of *conditional probability*. A conditional probability is the likelihood of observing one thing given some other thing that we already know about. For example, we might want to know the probability that a college student is female given that we already know the student's major is computer science. This is something we can look up in survey results. According to a National Science Foundation survey in 2005, only 22% of undergraduate computer science majors were female [SR08]. But 51% of undergraduate science majors overall were female, so conditioning on being a computer science major lowers the chances of being a woman from 51% to 22%.

The text classification algorithm we're going to use in this chapter, called the Naive Bayes classifier, looks for differences of this sort by searching through text for words that are either (a) noticeably more likely to occur in spam messages, or (b) noticeably more likely to occur in ham messages. When a word is noticeably more likely to occur in one context rather than the other, its occurrence can be diagnostic of whether a new message is spam or ham. The logic is simple: if you see a single word that's more likely to occur in spam than ham, that's evidence that the email as a whole is spam. If you see many words that are more likely to occur in spam than ham and very few words that are more likely to occur in ham than spam, that should be strong evidence that the email as a whole is spam.

Ultimately, our text classifier formalizes this intuition by computing (a) the probability of seeing the exact contents of an email conditioned on the email being assumed to be spam, and (b) the probability of seeing the same email's contents conditioned on the email being assumed to be ham. If it's much more likely that we would see the email in question if it were spam, we'll declare it to be spam.

How much more likely a message needs to be to merit being labeled spam depends upon an additional piece of information: the base rate of seeing spam messages. This base rate information is usually called the *prior*. You can think of the prior in the following way: if most of the birds you see in the park are ducks and you hear a bird quacking one morning, it's a pretty safe bet to assume that it's a duck. But if you have never seen a duck in the park even once, it's much riskier to assume that anything that quacks must be a duck. When working with email, the prior comes into play because the majority of email sent is spam, which means that even weak evidence that an email is spam can be sufficient to justify labeling it as spam.

In the following section we will elaborate on this logic in some detail as we write a spam classifier. To compute the probability of an email, we will assume that the occurrence counts for every word can be estimated in isolation from all of the other words. Formally, this amounts to an assumption often referred to as statistical independence. When we make this assumption without being certain that it's correct, we say that our model is naive. Because we will also make use of base rate information about emails being spam, the model will be also called a Bayes model—in homage to the 18th-century mathematician who first described conditional probabilities. Taken together, these two traits make our model a Naive Bayes classifier.

Writing Our First Bayesian Spam Classifier

As we mentioned earlier in this chapter, we will be using the SpamAssassin public corpus to both train and test our classifier. This data consists of labeled emails from three categories: "spam," "easy ham," and "hard ham." As you'd expect, "hard ham" is more difficult to distinguish from spam than the easy stuff. For instance, hard ham messages often include HTML tags. Recall that one way to easily identify spam is by the presence of these tags. To more accurately classify hard ham, we will have to include more information from many more text features. Extracting these features requires some text mining of the email files and constitutes our initial step in creating a classifier.

All of our raw email files include the headers and the message text. A typical "easy ham" email looks like Example 3-1. You'll note several features of this text that are of interest. First, the header contains a lot of information about where this email has come from. In fact, due to size constraints, we included only a portion of the total header in Example 3-1. And despite the fact that there is a lot of useful information contained in the headers, we will not be using any of this information in our classifier. Rather than focus on features contained in the transmission of the message, we are interested in how the contents of the messages themselves can help predict an email's type. This is not to say that one should always ignore the header or any other information. In fact, all sophisticated modern spam filters utilize information contained in email message headers, such as whether portions of it appear to have been forged, whether the message is from a known spammer, or whether there are bits missing.

Because we are focusing on only the email message body, we need to extract this text from the message files. If you explore some of the message files contained in this exercise, you will notice that the email message *always* begins after the first full line break in the email file. In Example 3-1, we see that the sentence "Hello, have you seen and discussed this article and his approach?" comes directly after the first line break. To begin building our classifier, we must first create R functions that can access the files and extract the message text by taking advantage of this text convention.

Example 3-1. Typical "easy ham" email

```
Received: from usw-sf-list1-b.sourceforge.net ([10.3.1.13]
   helo=usw-sf-list1.sourceforge.net) by usw-sf-list2.sourceforge.net with
   esmtp (Exim 3.31-VA-mm2 #1 (Debian)) id 17hsof-00042r-00; Thu,
   22 Aug 2002 07:20:05 -0700
Received: from vivi.uptime.at ([62.116.87.11] helo=mail.uptime.at) by
   usw-sf-list1.sourceforge.net with esmtp (Exim 3.31-VA-mm2 #1 (Debian)) id
   17hsoM-0000Ge-00 for <spamassassin-devel@lists.sourceforge.net>;
   Thu, 22 Aug 2002 07:19:47 -0700
Received: from [192.168.0.4] (chello062178142216.4.14.vie.surfer.at
   [62.178.142.216]) (authenticated bits=0) by mail.uptime.at (8.12.5/8.12.5)
   with ESMTP id g7MEI7Vp022036 for
   <spamassassin-devel@lists.sourceforge.net>; Thu, 22 Aug 2002 16:18:07
   +0200
From: David H=?ISO-8859-1?B?9g==?=hn <dh@uptime.at>
To: <spamassassin-devel@example.sourceforge.net>
Message-Id: <B98ABFA4.1F87%dh@uptime.at>
MIME-Version: 1.0
X-Trusted: YES
X-From-Laptop: YES
Content-Type: text/plain; charset="US-ASCII"
Content-Transfer-Encoding: 7bit
X-Mailscanner: Nothing found, baby
Subject: [SAdev] Interesting approach to Spam handling..
Sender: spamassassin-devel-admin@example.sourceforge.net
Errors-To: spamassassin-devel-admin@example.sourceforge.net
X-Beenthere: spamassassin-devel@example.sourceforge.net
X-Mailman-Version: 2.0.9-sf.net
Precedence: bulk
List-Help: <mailto:spamassassin-devel-request@example.sourceforge.net?subject=help>
List-Post: <mailto:spamassassin-devel@example.sourceforge.net>
List-Subscribe: <https://example.sourceforge.net/lists/listinfo/spamassassin-devel>,
   <mailto:spamassassin-devel-request@lists.sourceforge.net?subject=subscribe>
List-Id: SpamAssassin Developers <spamassassin-devel.example.sourceforge.net>
List-Unsubscribe: <https://example.sourceforge.net/lists/listinfo/spamassassin-devel>,
   <mailto:spamassassin-devel-request@lists.sourceforge.net?subject=unsubscribe>
List-Archive: <http://www.geocrawler.com/redir-sf.php3?list=spamassassin-devel>
X-Original-Date: Thu, 22 Aug 2002 16:19:48 +0200
Date: Thu, 22 Aug 2002 16:19:48 +0200

Hello, have you seen and discussed this article and his approach?

Thank you

http://www.paulgraham.com/spam.html
-- "Hell, there are no rules here-- we're trying to accomplish something."
-- Thomas Alva Edison



-------------------------------------------------------
This sf.net email is sponsored by: OSDN - Tired of that same old
cell phone?  Get a new here for FREE!
https://www.inphonic.com/r.asp?r=sourceforge1&refcode1=vs3390

Spamassassin-devel mailing list
Spamassassin-devel@lists.sourceforge.net
https://lists.sourceforge.net/lists/listinfo/spamassassin-devel
```

The "null line" separating the header from the body of an email is part of the protocol definition. For reference, see RFC822: *http://tools.ietf.org/html/frc822*.

As is always the case, the first thing to do is to load in the libraries we will use for this exercise. For text classification, we will be using the tm package, which stands for *text mining*. Once we have built our classifier and tested it, we will use the ggplot2 package to visually analyze the results. Another important initial step is to set the path variables for all of the email files. As mentioned, we have three types of messages: easy ham, hard ham, and spam. In the data file directory for this exercise, you will notice that there are two separate sets of file folders for each type of message. We will use the first set of files to train the classifier and the second set to test it.

```
library(tm)
library(ggplot2)

spam.path <- "data/spam/"
spam2.path <- "data/spam_2/"
easyham.path <- "data/easy_ham/"
easyham2.path <- "data/easy_ham_2/"
hardham.path <- "data/hard_ham/"
hardham2.path <- "data/hard_ham_2/"
```

With the requisite packages loaded and the path variables set, we can begin building up our knowledge about the type of terms used in spam and ham by creating text corpuses from both sets of files. To do this, we will write a function that opens each file, finds the first line break, and returns the text below that break as a character vector with a single text element.

```
get.msg <- function(path) {
    con <- file(path, open="rt", encoding="latin1")
    text <- readLines(con)
    # The message always begins after the first full line break
    msg <- text[seq(which(text=="")[1]+1,length(text),1)]
    close(con)
    return(paste(msg, collapse="\n"))
}
```

The R language performs file I/O in a very similar way to many other programming languages. The function shown here takes a file path as a string and opens that file in rt mode, which stands for *read as text*. Also notice that the coding is latin1. This is because many of the email messages contain non-ASCII characters, and this encoding will allow us to use these files. The readLines function will return each line of text in the file connection as a separate element of a character vector. As such, once we have read in all of the lines, we want to locate the first empty element of the text and then extract all the elements afterward. Once we have the email message as a character vector, we'll close the file connection and then collapse the vector into a single character element using the paste function and \n (new line) for the collapse argument.

To train our classifier, we will need to get the email messages from all of our spam and ham emails. One approach is to create a vector containing all of the messages, such that each element of the vector is a single email. The most straightforward way to accomplish this in R is to use an `apply` function with our newly created `get.msg` function.

```
spam.docs <- dir(spam.path)
spam.docs <- spam.docs[which(spam.docs!="cmds")]
all.spam <- sapply(spam.docs, function(p) get.msg(paste(spam.path,p,sep="")))
```

For the spam email, we begin by getting a listing of all of the filenames in the *data/ spam* directory using the `dir` function. This directory—and all of the directories holding email data—also contain a *cmds* file, which is simply a long list of Unix base commands to move files in these directories. This is not something we want to include in our training data, so we ignore it by keeping only those files that do not have *cmds* as a filename. Now `spam.docs` is a character vector containing all of the filenames for the spam messages we will use to train our classifier.

To create our vector of spam messages, we use the `sapply` function, which will apply `get.msg` to all of the spam filenames and construct a vector of messages from the returned text.

 Note that we have to pass an anonymous function to `sapply` in order to concatenate the filename with the appropriate directory path using the `paste` function. This is a very common construction in R.

Once you have executed this series of commands, you can use `head(all.spam)` to inspect the results. You will note that the name of each vector element corresponds to the filename. This is one of the advantages of using `sapply`.

The next step is to create a text corpus from our vector of emails using the functions provided by the `tm` package. Once we have the text represented as a corpus, we can manipulate the terms in the messages to begin building our feature set for the spam classifier. A huge advantage of the `tm` package is that much of the heavy lifting needed to clean and normalize the text is hidden from view. What we will accomplish in a few lines of R code would take many lines of string processing if we had to perform these operations ourselves in a lower-level language.

One way of quantifying the frequency of terms in our spam email is to construct a *term document matrix* (TDM). As the name suggests, a TDM is an N×M matrix in which the terms found among all of the documents in a given corpus define the rows and all of the documents in the corpus define the columns. The [i, j] cell of this matrix corresponds to the number of times term i was found in document j.

As before, we will define a simple function, `get.tdm`, that will take a vector of email messages and return a TDM:

```
get.tdm <- function(doc.vec) {
    doc.corpus <- Corpus(VectorSource(doc.vec))
    control <- list(stopwords=TRUE, removePunctuation=TRUE, removeNumbers=TRUE,
        minDocFreq=2)
    doc.dtm <- TermDocumentMatrix(doc.corpus, control)
    return(doc.dtm)
}

spam.tdm <- get.tdm(all.spam)
```

The `tm` package allows you to construct a corpus in several ways. In our case, we will construct the corpus from a vector of emails, so we will use the `VectorSource` function. To see the various other source types that can be used, enter `?getSources` at the R console. As is often the case when working with `tm`, once we have loaded our source text, we will use the `Corpus` function in conjunction with `VectorSource` to create a corpus object. Before we can proceed to creating the TDM, however, we must tell `tm` how we want it to clean and normalize the text. To do this we use a `control`, which is a special list of options specifying how to distill the text.

For this exercise we will use four options. First, we set `stopwords=TRUE`, which tells `tm` to remove 488 common English stop words from all of the documents. To see the list, type `stopwords()` at the R console. Next, we set `removePunctuation` and `removeNumbers` to `TRUE`, which are fairly self-explanatory and are used to reduce the noise associated with these characters—especially because many of our documents contain HTML tags. Finally, we set `minDocFreq=2`, which will ensure that only terms appearing more than once in the corpus will end up in the rows of the TDM.

We now have processed the spam emails to the point where we can begin building our classifier. Specifically, we can use the TDM to build a set of training data for spam. Within the context of R, a good approach to doing this is to construct a data frame that contains all of the observed probabilities for each term, given that we know it is spam. Just as we did with our female computer science major example, we need to train our classifier to know the probability that an email is spam, given the observation of some term.

```
spam.matrix <- as.matrix(spam.tdm)
spam.counts <- rowSums(spam.matrix)
spam.df <- data.frame(cbind(names(spam.counts),
    as.numeric(spam.counts)), stringsAsFactors=FALSE)
names(spam.df) <- c("term","frequency")
spam.df$frequency <- as.numeric(spam.df$frequency)

spam.occurrence <- sapply(1:nrow(spam.matrix),
    function(i) {length(which(spam.matrix[i,] > 0))/ncol(spam.matrix)})
spam.density <- spam.df$frequency/sum(spam.df$frequency)

spam.df <- transform(spam.df, density=spam.density,
    occurrence=spam.occurrence)
```

To create this data frame, we must first convert the TDM object to a standard R matrix using the `as.matrix` command. Then, using the `rowSums` command, we can create a vector that contains the total frequency counts for each term across all documents. Because we will use the `data.frame` function to combine a character vector with a numeric vector, by default R will convert these vectors to a common representation. The frequency counts can be represented as characters, and so they will be converted, which means we must be mindful to set `stringsAsFactors=FALSE`. Next, we will do some housekeeping to set the column names and convert the frequency counts back to a numeric vector.

With the next two steps, we will generate the critical training data. First, we calculate the percentage of documents in which a given term occurs. We do this by passing every row through an anonymous function call via `sapply`, which counts the number of cells with a positive element and then divides the total by the number of columns in the TDM—i.e., by the number of documents in the spam corpus. Second, we calculate the frequency of each word within the entire corpus. (We will not use the frequency information for classification, but it will be useful to see how these numbers compare when we consider how certain words might be affecting our results.)

In the final step, we add the `spam.occurrence` and `spam.density` vectors to the data frame using the `transform` function. We have now generated the training data for spam classification!

Let's check the data and see which terms are the strongest indicators of spam given our training data. To do this, we sort `spam.df` by the `occurrence` column and inspect its head:

```
head(spam.df[with(spam.df, order(-occurrence)),])
      term frequency     density occurrence
2122  html       377 0.005665595      0.338
538   body       324 0.004869105      0.298
4313 table      1182 0.017763217      0.284
1435 email       661 0.009933576      0.262
1736  font       867 0.013029365      0.262
1942  head       254 0.003817138      0.246
```

As we have mentioned repeatedly, HTML tags appear to be the strongest text features associated with spam. Over 30% of the messages in the spam training data contain the term `html`, as well as other common HTML-related terms, such as `body`, `table`, `font`, and `head`. Note, however, that these terms are not the most frequent by raw count. You can see this for yourself by replacing `-occurrence` with `-frequency` in the preceding statement. This is very important in terms of how we define our classifier. If we used raw count data and the subsequent densities as our training data, we might be over-weighting certain kinds of spam—specifically, spam that contains HTML tables. However, we know that not all spam messages are constructed this way. As such, a better approach is to define the conditional probability of a message being spam based on how many messages contain the term.

Now that we have the spam training data, we need to balance it with the ham training data. As part of the exercise, we will build this training data using only the easy ham messages. Of course, it would be possible to incorporate the hard ham messages into the training set; in fact, that would be advisable if we were building a production system. But within the context of this exercise, it's helpful to see how well a text classifier will work if trained using only a small corpus of easily classified documents.

We will construct the ham training data in exactly the same way we did the spam, and therefore we will not reprint those commands here. The only way this step differs from generating the spam training data is that we use only the first 500 email messages in the data/easy_ham folder.

You may note that there are actually 2,500 ham emails in this directory. So why are we ignoring four-fifths of the data? When we construct our first classifier, we will assume that each message has an equal probability of being ham or spam. As such, it is good practice to ensure that our training data reflects our assumptions. We only have 500 spam messages, so we will limit or ham training set to 500 messages as well.

 To see how we limited the ham training data in this way, see line 102 in the *email_classify.R* file for this chapter.

Once the ham training data has been constructed, we can inspect it just as we did the spam for comparison:

```
head(easyham.df[with(easyham.df, order(-occurrence)),])
        term frequency     density occurrence
3553   yahoo       185 0.008712853      0.180
966     dont       141 0.006640607      0.090
2343  people       183 0.008618660      0.086
1871   linux       159 0.007488344      0.084
1876    list       103 0.004850940      0.078
3240    time        91 0.004285782      0.064
```

The first thing you will notice in the ham training data is that the terms are much more sparsely distributed among the emails. The term that occurs in the most documents, "yahoo," does so in only 18% of them. The other terms all occur in less than 10% of the documents. Compare this to the top spam terms, which all occur in over 24% of the spam emails. Already we can begin to see how this variation will allow us to separate spam from ham. If a message contains just one or two terms strongly associated with spam, it will take a lot of nonspam words for the message to be classified as ham. With both training sets defined, we are now ready to complete our classifier and test it!

Defining the Classifier and Testing It with Hard Ham

We want to define a classifier that will take an email message file and calculate the probability that it is spam or ham. Fortunately, we have already created most of the functions and generated the data needed to perform this calculation. Before we can proceed, however, there is one critical complication that we must consider.

We need to decide how to handle terms in new emails that match terms in our training set and how to handle terms that do not match terms in our training set (see Figure 3-3). To calculate the probability that an email message is spam or ham, we will need to find the terms that are common between the training data and the message in question. We can then use the probabilities associated with these terms to calculate the conditional probability that a message is of the training data's type. This is fairly straightforward, but what do we do with the terms from the email being classified that are not in our training data?

To calculate the conditional probability of a message, we combine the probabilities of each term in the training data by taking their product. For example, if the frequency of seeing `html` in a spam message is 0.30 and the frequency of seeing `table` in a spam message is 0.10, then we'll say that the probability of seeing both in a spam message is $0.30 \times 0.10 = 0.03$. But for those terms in the email that are not in our training data, we have no information about their frequency in either spam or ham messages. One possible solution would be to assume that because we have not seen a term yet, its probability of occurring in a certain class is zero. This, however, is very misguided. First, it is foolish to assume that we will never see a term in the entire universe of spam and ham simply because we have not yet seen it. Moreover, because we calculate conditional probabilities using products, if we assigned a zero probability to terms not in our training data, elementary arithmetic tells us that we would calculate zero as the probability of most messages, because we would be multiplying all the other probabilities by zero every time we encountered an unknown term. This would cause catastrophic results for our classifier because many, or even all, messages would be incorrectly assigned a zero probability of being either spam or ham.

Researchers have come up with many clever ways of trying to get around this problem, such as drawing a random probability from some distribution or using natural language processing (NLP) techniques to estimate the "spamminess" of a term given its context. For our purposes, we will use a very simple rule: assign a very small probability to terms that are not in the training set. This is, in fact, a common way of dealing with missing terms in simple text classifiers, and for our purposes it will serve just fine. In this exercise, by default we will set this probability to 0.0001%, or one-ten-thousandth of a percent, which is sufficiently small for this data set. Finally, because we are assuming that all emails are equally likely to be ham or spam, we set our default prior belief that an email is of some type to 50%. In order to return to this problem later, however, we construct the `classify.email` function such that the prior can be varied.

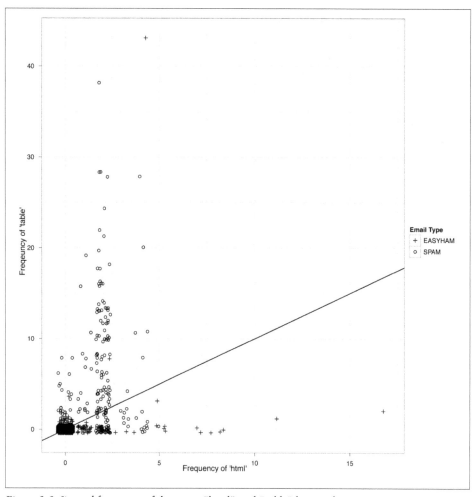

Figure 3-3. Jittered frequency of the terms "html" and "table" by email type

 Be wary of always using 0.0001% for terms not in a training set. We are using it in this example, but in others it may be too large or too small, in which case the system you build will not work at all!

```
classify.email <- function(path, training.df, prior=0.5, c=1e-6) {
    msg <- get.msg(path)
    msg.tdm <- get.tdm(msg)
    msg.freq <- rowSums(as.matrix(msg.tdm))
    # Find intersections of words
    msg.match <- intersect(names(msg.freq), training.df$term)
    if(length(msg.match) < 1) {
        return(prior*c^(length(msg.freq)))
    }
    else {
        match.probs <- training.df$occurrence[match(msg.match, training.df$term)]
        return(prior * prod(match.probs) * c^(length(msg.freq)-length(msg.match)))
    }
}
```

You will notice that the first three steps of the `classify.email` function proceed just as our training phase did. We must extract the message text with `get.msg`, turn it into a TDM with `get.tdm`, and finally calculate the frequency of terms with `rowSums`. Next, we need to find how the terms in the email message intersect with the terms in our training data, as depicted in Figure 3-3. To do so, we use the `intersect` command, passing the terms found in the email message and those in the training data. What will be returned are those terms in the gray shaded area of Figure 3-3.

The final step of the classification is to determine whether any of the words in the email message are present in the training set, and if so, we use them to calculate the probability that this message is of the class in question.

Assume for now that we are attempting to determine if this email message is spam. `msg.match` will contain all of the terms from the email message in our spam training data, `spam.df`. If that intersection is empty, then the length of `msg.match` will be less than zero, and we can update our prior only by multiplying it with the product of the number of terms in the email with our tiny probability value: `c`. The result will be a tiny probability of assigning the spam label to the email.

Conversely, if this intersection is not empty, we need to find those terms from the email in our training data and look up their occurrence probabilities. We use the `match` function to do the lookup, which will return the term's element position in the `term` column of our training data. We use these element positions to return the corresponding probabilities from the `occurrence` column, and return those values to `match.probs`. We then calculate the *product* of these values and combine it with our prior belief about the email being spam with the term probabilities and the probabilities of any missing terms. The result is our Bayesian estimate for the probability that a message is spam given the matching terms in our training data.

As an initial test, we will use our training data from the spam and easy ham messages to classify hard ham emails. We know that all of these emails are ham, so ideally our classifier will assign a higher probability of being ham to all of these messages. We also know, however, that hard ham messages are "hard" to classify because they contain terms that are also associated with spam. Now let's see how our simple classifier does!

```
hardham.docs <- dir(hardham.path)
hardham.docs <- hardham.docs[which(hardham.docs != "cmds")]

hardham.spamtest <- sapply(hardham.docs,
    function(p) classify.email(paste(hardham.path, p, sep=""),
    training.df=spam.df))

hardham.hamtest <- sapply(hardham.docs,
    function(p) classify.email(paste(hardham.path, p, sep=""),
    training.df=easyham.df))

hardham.res <- ifelse(hardham.spamtest > hardham.hamtest, TRUE, FALSE)
summary(hardham.res)
```

Just as before, we need to get all of the file paths in order, and then we can test the classifier for all hard ham messages by wrapping both a spam test and ham test in `sapply` calls. The vectors `hardham.spamtest` and `hardham.hamtest` contain the conditional probability calculations for each hard ham email of being either spam or ham given the appropriate training data. We then use the `ifelse` command to compare the probabilities in each vector. If the value in `hardham.spamtest` is greater than that in `hardham.hamtest`, then the classifier has classified the message as spam; otherwise, it is ham. Finally, we use the `summary` command to inspect the results, listed in Table 3-2.

Table 3-2. Testing our classifier against "hard ham"

Email type	Number classified as ham	Number classified as spam
Hard ham	184	65

Congratulations! You've written your first classifier, and it did *fairly well* at identifying hard ham as nonspam. In this case, we have approximately a 26% false-positive rate. That is, about one-quarter of the hard ham emails are incorrectly identified as spam. You may think this is poor performance, and in production we would not want to offer an email platform with these results, but considering how simple our classifier is, it is doing quite well. Of course, a better test is to see how the classifier performs against not only hard ham, but also easy ham and spam.

Testing the Classifier Against All Email Types

The first step is to build a simple function that will do the the probability comparison we did in the previous section all at once for all emails.

```
spam.classifier <- function(path) {
    pr.spam <- classify.email(path, spam.df)
    pr.ham <- classify.email(path, easyham.df)
    return(c(pr.spam, pr.ham, ifelse(pr.spam > pr.ham, 1, 0)))
}
```

For simplicity's sake, the spam.classifier function will determine whether an email is spam based on the spam.df and easyham.df training data. If the probability that a message is spam is greater than its probability of being ham, it returns one; otherwise, it returns zero.

As a final step in this exercise, we will test the second sets of spam, easy ham, and hard ham using our simple classifier. These steps proceed exactly as they did in previous sections: wrapping the spam.classifier function in an lapply function, passing email file paths, and building a data frame. As such, we will not reproduce these function calls here, but you are encouraged to reference the *email_classifier.R* file starting at line 158 to see how this is done.

The new data frame contains the likelihoods of being either spam or ham, the classification, and the email type for each message in all three data sets. The new data set is called class.df, and we can use the head command to inspect its contents:

```
head(class.df)
        Pr.SPAM        Pr.HAM Class    Type
1 2.712076e-307 1.248948e-282 FALSE EASYHAM
2  9.463296e-84  1.492094e-58 FALSE EASYHAM
3  1.276065e-59  3.264752e-36 FALSE EASYHAM
4  0.000000e+00 3.539486e-319 FALSE EASYHAM
5  2.342400e-26  3.294720e-17 FALSE EASYHAM
6 2.968972e-314 1.858238e-260 FALSE EASYHAM
```

From the first six entries, it seems the classifier has done well, but let's calculate the false-positive and false-negative rates for the classifier across all data sets. To do this, we will construct an N × M matrix of our results, where the rows are the actual classification types and the columns are the predicted types. Because we have three types of email being classified into two types, our confusion matrix will have three rows and two columns (as shown in Table 3-3). The columns will be the percent predicted as ham or spam, and if our classifier works perfectly, the columns will read [1,1,0] and [0,0,1], respectively.

Table 3-3. Matrix for classifier results

Email type	% Classified as ham	% Classified as spam
Easy ham	0.78	0.22
Hard ham	0.73	0.27
Spam	0.15	0.85

Unfortunately, we did not write a perfect classifier, but the results are still quite good. Similar to our initial test, we get about a 25% false-positive rate, with our classifier doing slightly better on easy ham than the hard stuff. On the other hand, the false-negative rate is much lower at only 15%. To get a better sense of how our classifier fared, we can plot the results using a scatterplot, with the predicted probabilities of being ham on the x-axis and spam on the y-axis.

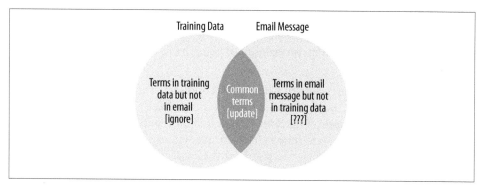

Figure 3-4. Processing strategy for terms in new emails

Figure 3-5 shows this scatterplot in log-log scale. A log transformation is done because many of the predicted probabilities are very tiny, while others are not. With this high degree of variance, it is difficult to compare the results directly. Taking logs is a simple way of altering the visual scale to more easily compare values.

We have also added a simple decision boundary to the plots where y = x, or a perfect linear relationship. This is done because our classifier compares the two predicted probabilities and determines the email's type based on whether the probability of being spam is greater than that of ham. All dots above the black diagonal line, therefore, should be spam, and all those below should be ham. As you can see, this is not the case —but there is considerable clustering of message types.

Figure 3-5 also gives some intuition about how the classifier is underperforming with respect to false-positives. There appear to be two general ways it is failing. First, there are many hard ham messages that have a positive probability of being spam but a near-zero probability of being ham. These are the points pressed up against the y-axis. Second, there are both easy and hard ham messages that have a much higher relative probability of being ham. Both of these observations may indicate a weak training data set for ham emails, as there are clearly many more terms that should be associated with ham that currently are not.

Improving the Results

In this chapter we have introduced the idea of text classification. To do this, we constructed a very simple Bayesian classifier using a minimal number of assumptions and features. At its core, this type of classification is an application of classic conditional probability theory in a contemporary context. Despite the fact that we trained our classifier with only a fraction of the total available data, this simple method performed reasonably well.

That said, the false-positive and false-negative rates found in the test data are far too high for any production spam filter. As we mentioned throughout this chapter, there

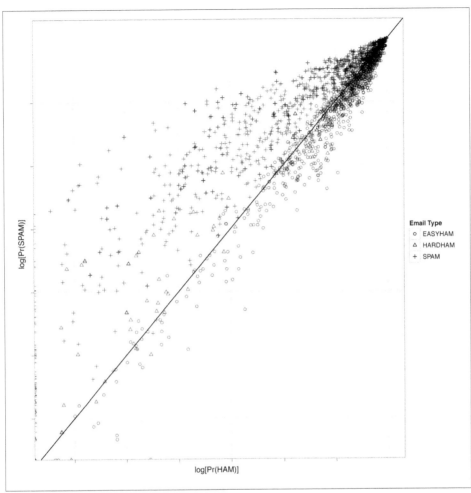

Figure 3-5. Scatterplot of predicted probabilities for email classification in log-log scale

are many simple tweaks we could apply to improve the results of the current model. For example, our approach assumes *a priori* that each email has an equal probability of being ham or spam. In practice, however, we know that this relationship is actually much closer to 80%–20% ham-to-spam. One way we might improve results, then, would be to simply alter our prior beliefs to reflect this fact and recalculate the predicted probabilities.

```
spam.classifier<-function(path) {
    pr.spam<-classify.email(path, spam.df, prior=0.2)
    pr.ham<-classify.email(path, easyham.df, prior=0.8)
    return(c(pr.spam, pr.ham, ifelse(pr.spam > pr.ham, 1, 0)))
}
```

You'll remember that we left the `prior` parameter as something that could vary in the `classify.email` function, so we now only need to make the simple change to `spam.classify` shown in the preceding example. We could rerun the classifier now and compare the results, and we encourage you to do so. These new assumptions, however, violate the distributions of ham and spam messages in our training data. To be more accurate, we should go back and retrain the classifier with the complete easy ham data set. Recall that we limited our original ham training data to only the first 500 messages so that our training data would reflect the Bayesian assumptions. In that vein, we must incorporate the full data set in order to reflect our new assumptions.

When we rerun the classifier with the new `easyham.df` and `classify.email` parameterization, we see a notable improvement in performance on false-positives (see Table 3-4).

Table 3-4. Matrix for improved classifier results

Email type	% Classified as ham	% Classified as spam
Easy ham	0.90	0.10
Hard ham	0.82	0.18
Spam	0.18	0.82

With these simple changes, we have reduced our false-positive rate by more than 50%! What is interesting, however, is that by improving performance in this way, our false-negative results suffer. In essence, what we are doing is moving the decision boundaries (recall Example 3-1). By doing so, we are explicitly trading off false positives for improvement in false negatives. This is an excellent example of why model specification is critical, and how each assumption and feature choice can affect all results.

In the following chapter we will expand our view of classification beyond the simple binary—this or that—example in this exercise. As we mentioned at the outset, often it is difficult or impossible to classify observations based on a single decision boundary. In the next chapter we will explore how to rank emails based on features that are associated with higher priority. What remain important as we increase the spectrum of classification tasks are the features we decide to include in our model. As you'll see next, the data may limit feature selection, which can have a serious impact on our model design.

## CHAPTER 4

Ranking: Priority Inbox

How Do You Sort Something When You Don't Know the Order?

In Chapter 3 we discussed in detail the concept of *binary classification*—that is, placing items into one of two types or classes. In many cases, we will be satisfied with an approach that can make such a distinction. But what if the items in one class are not created equally and we want to rank the items within a class? In short, what if we want to say that one email is the most spammy and another is the second most spammy, or we want to distinguish among them in some other meaningful way? Suppose we not only wanted to filter spam from our email, but we also wanted to place "more important" messages at the top of the queue. This is a very common problem in machine learning, and it will be the focus of this chapter.

Generating rules for ranking a list of items is an increasingly common task in machine learning, yet you may not have thought of it in these terms. More likely, you have heard of something like a *recommendation system*, which implicitly produces a ranking of products. Even if you have not heard of a recommendation system, it's almost certain that you have used or interacted with a recommendation system at some point. Some of the most successful ecommerce websites have benefited from leveraging data on their users to generate recommendations for other products their users might be interested in.

For example, if you have ever shopped at Amazon.com, then you have interacted with a recommendation system. The problem Amazon faces is simple: what items in their inventory are you most likely to buy? The implication of that statement is that the items in Amazon's inventory have an ordering specific to each user. Likewise, Netflix.com has a massive library of DVDs available to its customers to rent. In order for those customers to get the most out of the site, Netflix employs a sophisticated recommendation system to present people with rental suggestions.

For both companies, these recommendations are based on two kinds of data. First, there is the data pertaining to the inventory itself. For Amazon, if the product is a television, this data might contain the type (e.g., plasma, LCD, LED), manufacturer, price, and so on. For Netflix, this data might be the genre of a film, its cast, director, running time, etc. Second, there is the data related to the browsing and purchasing behavior of the customers. This sort of data can help Amazon understand what accessories most people look for when shopping for a new plasma TV and can help Netflix understand which romantic comedies George A. Romero fans most often rent. For both types of data, the features are well identified. That is, we know the labels for categorical data such as *product type* or *movie genre*; likewise, user-generated data is well structured in the form of purchase/rental records and explicit ratings.

Because we usually have *explicit examples* of the outputs of interest when doing ranking, this is a type of machine learning problem that is often called *supervised learning*. This is in contrast to *unsupervised learning*, where there are no pre-existing examples of the outputs when we start working with the data. To better understand the difference, think of supervised learning as a process of learning through instruction. For example, if you want to teach someone how to bake a cherry pie, you might hand him a recipe and then let him taste the pie that results. After seeing how the result tastes, he might decide to adjust the ingredients a bit. Having a record of the ingredients he has used (i.e., the inputs) and the taste of the result (i.e., the output) means that he can analyze the contributions of each ingredient and try to find the perfect cherry pie recipe.

Alternatively, if you only knew that dishes with refried beans tend to also come with tortillas, whereas dishes with baked cherries tend to come with dough, you might be able to group other ingredients into classes that would ultimately resemble the sorts of things you'd use to make Mexican food versus the sorts of things you'd use to make American desserts. Indeed, a common form of unsupervised learning is clustering, where we want to assign items to a fixed number of groups based on commonalities or differences.

If you have already read and worked through the exercise in Chapter 3, then you have already solved a supervised learning problem. For spam classification, we knew the terms associated with spam and ham messages, and we trained our classifier using that recipe. That was a very simple problem, and so we were able to obtain relatively good classification results using a feature set with only a single element: email message terms. For ranking, however, we need to assign a unique weight to each item to stratify them in a finer way.

So in the next section we will begin to address the question proposed in the title of this section: how do you sort something when you don't already know its order? As you may have guessed, to do this in the context of ordering emails by their importance, we will have to reword the question in terms of the features available to us in the email data and how those features relate to an email's priority.

Ordering Email Messages by Priority

What makes an email important? To begin to answer this, let's first step back and think about what email is. First, it is a transaction-based medium. People send and receive messages over time. As such, in order to determine the importance of an email, we need to focus on the transactions themselves. Unlike the spam classification task, where we could use static information from all emails to determine their type, to rank emails by importance we must focus on the dynamics of the in- and out-bound transactions. Specifically, we want to make a determination as to the likelihood a person will interact with a new email once it has been received. Put differently, given the set of features we have chosen to study, how likely is the reader to perform an action on this email in the immediate future?

The critical new dimension that this problem incorporates is *time*. In a transaction-based context, in order to rank things by importance, we need to have some concept of time. A natural way to use time to determine the importance of an email is to measure how long it takes a user to perform some action on an email. The shorter the average time it takes a user to perform some action on an email, given its set of features, the more *important* emails of that type may be.

The implicit assumption in this model is that more important emails will be acted on sooner than less important emails. Intuitively, this makes sense. All of us have stared at the queue in our inbox and filtered through emails that needed an immediate response versus those that could wait. The filtering that we do naturally is what we will attempt to teach our algorithm to do in the following sections. Before we can begin, however, we must determine which features in email messages are good proxy measures for priority.

Priority Features of Email

If you use Google's Gmail service for your email, you will know that the idea of a "priority inbox" was first popularized by Google in 2010. Of course, it was this problem that inspired the case study on ranking for this chapter, so it will be useful to revisit the approach that Google took in implementing their ranking algorithm as we move toward designing our own. Fortunately, several months after the priority inbox feature was released by Google, they published a paper entitled "The Learning Behind Gmail Priority Inbox," which describes their strategy for designing the supervised learning approach and how to implement it at scale [DA10]. For the purposes of this chapter, we are interested only in the former, but we highly recommend the paper as a supplement to what we discuss here. And at four pages in length, it is well worth the time commitment.

As we mentioned, measuring time is critical, and in Google's case they have the luxury of a long and detailed history of users' interactions with email. Specifically, Google's priority inbox attempts to predict the probability that a user will perform some action on an email within a fixed number of seconds from its delivery. The set of actions a user can perform in Gmail is large: reading, replying, labeling, etc. Also, *delivery* is not explicitly the time at which an email is received by the server, but the time at which it is delivered to the user—i.e., when she checks her email.

As with spam classification, this is a relatively simple problem to state: what is the probability that a user will perform some actions, within our set of possible actions, between some minimum and maximum numbers of seconds, given a set of features for that email and the knowledge that the user has recently checked his email?

Within the universe of possible email features, which did Google decide to focus on? As you might expect, they incorporated a very large number. As the authors of the paper note, unlike spam classification—which nearly all users will code the same way—everyone has a different way of ordering the priority of email. Given this variability in how users may evaluate the feature set, Google's approach needed to incorporate multiple features. To begin designing the algorithm, Google engineers explored various different types of email features, which they describe as follows:

> There are many hundred features falling into a few categories. *Social features* are based on the degree of interaction between sender and recipient, e.g. the percentage of a sender's mail that is read by the recipient. *Content features* attempt to identify headers and recent terms that are highly correlated with the recipient acting (or not) on the mail, e.g. the presence of a recent term in the subject. Recent user terms are discovered as a pre-processing step prior to learning. *Thread features* note the user's interaction with the thread so far, e.g. if a user began a thread. *Label features* examine the labels that the user applies to mail using filters. We calculate feature values during ranking and we temporarily store those values for later learning. Continuous features are automatically partitioned into binary features using a simple ID3 style algorithm on the histogram of the feature values.

As we mentioned, Google has a long history of its users' interactions with Gmail, which affords them a rich perspective into what actions users perform on emails and when. Unfortunately, such detailed email logs are not available to us in this exercise. Instead, we will again use the SpamAssassin public corpus, available for free download at *http://spamassassin.apache.org/publiccorpus/*.

Though this data set was distributed as a means of testing spam classification algorithms, it also contains a convenient timeline of a single user's email. Given this single thread, we can repurpose the data set to design and test a priority email ranking system. Also, we will focus only on the ham emails from this data set, so we know that all of the messages we will examine are those that the user would want in her inbox.

Before we can proceed, however, we must consider how our data differs from that of a full-detail email log—such as Google's—and how that affects the features we will be able to use in our algorithm. Let's begin by going through each of the four categories proposed by Google and determining how they might fit into the data we are using.

 The most critical difference between a full-detail email log and what we will be working with is that we can only see the messages received. This means that we will be effectively "flying half-blind," as we have no data on when and how a user responded to emails, or if the user was the originator of a thread. This is a *significant limitation*, and therefore the methods and algorithms used in this chapter should be considered as exercises only and not examples of how enterprise priority inbox systems should be implemented. What we hope to accomplish is to show how, even with this limitation, we can use the data we have to create proxy measures for email importance and still design a relatively good ranking system.

Given that email is a transaction-based medium, it follows that social features will be paramount in assessing the importance of an email. In our case, however, we can see only one half of that transaction. In the full-detail case, we would want to measure the volume of interactions between the user and various email senders in order to determine which senders receive more immediate actions from the user. With our data, however, we can measure only incoming volume. So we can assume that this one-way volume is a good proxy for the type of social features we are attempting to extract from the data.

Clearly this is not ideal. Recall, however, that for this exercise we will be using only the ham messages from the SpamAssassin public corpus. If one receives a large volume of ham email messages from a certain address, then it may be that the user has a strong social connection to the sender. Alternatively, it may be the case that the user is signed up to a mailing list with a high volume and would prefer that these emails not receive a high priority. This is exactly the reason why we must incorporate other features to balance these types of information when developing our ranking system.

One problem with looking only at the volume of messages from a given address is that the temporal component is protracted. Because our data set is static compared to a fully detailed email log, we must partition the data into temporal segments and measure volume over these periods to get a better understanding of the temporal dynamics.

As we will discuss in detail later, for this exercise we will simply order all of the messages chronologically, then split the set in half. The first half will be used to train the ranking algorithm, and the second half will be used to test. As such, message volume from each email address over the entire time period covered by the training data will be used to train our ranker's social feature.

Given the nature of our data, this may be a good start, but we will need to achieve a deeper understanding if we hope to rank messages more accurately. One way to partition the data to gain a more granular view of these dynamics is to identify conversation threads and then measure the intra-thread activity. (To identify threads, we can borrow techniques used by other email clients and match message subjects with key thread terms, such as "RE:".) Although we do not know what actions the user is taking on a thread, the assumption here is that if it is very active, then it is likely to be more important than less active threads. By compressing the temporal partitions into these small pieces, we can get a much more accurate proxy for the thread features we need to model email priority.

Next, there are many content features we could extract from the emails to add to our feature set. In this case, we will continue to keep things relatively simple by extending the text-mining techniques we used in Chapter 3 to this context. Specifically, if there are common terms in the subjects and bodies of emails received by a user, then future emails that contain these terms in the subject and body may be more important than those that do not. This is actually a common technique, and it is mentioned briefly in the description of Google's priority inbox. By adding content features based on terms for both the email subject and body, we will encounter an interesting problem of *weighting*. Typically, there are considerably fewer terms in an email's subject than the body; therefore, we should not weight the relative importance of common terms in these two features equally.

Finally, there are also many features used in enterprise distributed priority inbox implementations—like Gmail's—that are simply unavailable to us in this exercise. We have already mentioned that we are blind to much of the social feature set, and therefore must use proxies to measure these interactions. Furthermore, there are many user actions that we do not even have the ability to approximate. For example, user actions such as labeling or moving email messages are completely hidden from our view. In the Google priority inbox implementation, these actions form a large portion of the action set, but they are completely missing here. Again, although this is a weakness to the approach described here when compared to those that use full-detail email logs, because they are not available in this case, the fact that they are missing will not affect our results.

We now have a basic blueprint for the feature set we will use to create our email ranking system. We begin by ordering the messages chronologically because in this case much of what we are interested in predicting is contained in the temporal dimension. The first half of these messages are used to train our ranker. Next, we have four features we will use during training. The first is a proxy for the social feature, which measures the volume of messages from a given user in the training data. Next, we attempt to compress the temporal measurements by looking for threads and ranking active threads higher than inactive ones. Finally, we add two content features based on frequent terms in email subjects and message bodies. Figure 4-1 is an illustration of how these features are extracted from an email.

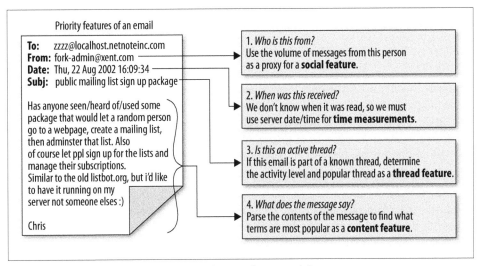

Figure 4-1. *Strategy for extracting priority features from email data*

In the next section, we will implement the priority inbox approach we just described. Using the features listed here, we will specify a weighting scheme that attempts to quickly push more important messages to the top of the stack. As before, however, our first steps will be to take the raw email data and extract the relevant pieces to fit into our feature set.

Writing a Priority Inbox

By now you will have noticed a trend: before we can get to the sexy parts of machine learning, we need to get our hands dirty hacking at the data to split, pull, and parse it until it's in a shape fit for our analysis. So far, we have had to suffer only slightly during this process. To build the spam classifier, we simply had to extract the email message body, and then we let the tm package do all of the heavy lifting. For this exercise, however, we are adding several other features to our data set and complicating the process by adding a temporal dimension as well. As such, we will have to operate on the data considerably more. But we are hackers, and getting dirty with data is what we like!

For this exercise, we will be focusing on only the ham email messages from the SpamAssassin public corpus. Unlike the spam classification exercise, here we are not concerned with the type of email, but rather with how each should be ranked in terms of priority. Therefore, we will use the largest easy ham data set and won't worry about including other types of emails. Because we may safely assume a user would not distinguish among emails in this way when determining which emails have a higher priority, there is no reason to carry this information into our ranking system.[1] Instead, we want to be able to learn as much about our features sets from a single user's emails, which is why we will use the emails in the first easy ham data set.

```
library(tm)
library(ggplot2)

data.path <- "../../03-Classification/code/data/"
easyham.path <- paste(data.path, "easy_ham/", sep="")
```

Similarly to Chapter 3, the only R packages we will be using in this exercise are tm, for extracting common terms from the emails subjects and bodies, and ggplot2, for visualizing the the results. Also, because the the SpamAssassin public corpus is a relatively large text data set, we will not duplicate it in the *data/* folder for this chapter. Instead, we will set the relative path for the data back to its location in the Chapter 3 files.

Next, we will create a series of functions that will work together to parse each email into the feature set illustrated in Example 4-1. From this diagram we know that we need to extract four elements from each email message: the sender's address, date received, subject, and message body.

Functions for Extracting the Feature Set

Recall that in Chapter 2 we introduced the idea of data as rectangles. For this exercise, therefore, the task of constructing the training data is one of "rectangularization." We need to shape the email data set to fit into a usable feature set. The features we extract from the emails will be the columns of our training data, and each row will be the unique values from a single email filling in the rectangle. Conceptualizing data this way is very useful, as we need to take the semi-structured text data in the email messages and turn them into a highly structured training data set that we can use to rank future emails.

```
parse.email <- function(path) {
    full.msg <- msg.full(path)
    date <- get.date(full.msg)
    from <- get.from(full.msg)
    subj <- get.subject(full.msg)
    msg <- get.msg(full.msg)
    return(c(date, from, subj, msg, path))
}
```

To explore this process, we will work backward and begin by examining the parse.email function. This will call a series of helper functions that extract the appropriate data from each message and then order these elements into a single vector. The vector created by the command c(date, from, subj, msg, path) constitutes the single row of data that will populate our training data. The process of turning each email message into these vectors, however, requires some classic text hacking.

---

1. Put more simply, this is the assumption that users are not acting on emails that were harder to identify as ham than those that were easy.

We include the path string as the final column because it will make ordering the data easier during the testing phase.

```
msg.full <- function(path) {
    con <- file(path, open="rt", encoding="latin1")
    msg <- readLines(con)
    close(con)
    return(msg)
}
```

If you worked through the exercise in Chapter 3, this `msg.full` function will look very familiar. Here we are simply opening a connection file path and reading the file's contents into a character vector. The `readLines` function will produce a vector whose elements are each line in the file. Unlike in Chapter 3, here we do not preprocess the data at this step, because we need to extract various elements from the messages. Instead, we will return the entire email as a character vector and write separate functions to work on this vector to extract the necessary data.

With the message vector in hand, we must begin to fight our way through the data in order to extract as much usable information as possible from the email messages—and organize them in a uniform way—to build our training data. We will begin with the relatively easy task of extracting the sender's address. To do this—and all of the data extraction in this section—we need to identify the text patterns in the email messages that identify the data we are looking for. To do so, let's take a look at a few email messages.

Example 4-1. Examples of emails "From" text pattern variations

Email #1

....

X-Sender: fortean3@pop3.easynet.co.uk (Unverified)
Message-Id: <p05100300ba138e802c7d@[194.154.104.171]>
To: Yahoogroups Forteana <zzzzteana@yahoogroups.com>
From: Joe McNally <joe@flaneur.org.uk>
X-Yahoo-Profile: wolf_solent23
MIME-Version: 1.0
Mailing-List: list zzzzteana@yahoogroups.com; contact
    forteana-owner@yahoogroups.com

....

Email #2

....

Return-Path: paul-bayes@svensson.org
Delivery-Date: Fri Sep 6 17:27:57 2002
From: paul-bayes@svensson.org (Paul Svensson)
Date: Fri, 6 Sep 2002 12:27:57 -0400 (EDT)
Subject: [Spambayes] Corpus Collection (Was: Re: Deployment)
In-Reply-To: <200209061431.g86EVM114413@pcp02138704pcs.reston01.va.comcast.net>
Message-ID: <Pine.LNX.4.44.0209061150430.6840-100000@familjen.svensson.org>

....

After exploring a few email messages, we can observe key patterns in the text that identify the sender's email address. Example 4-1 shows two excerpts from emails that highlight these patterns. First, we need to identify the line in each message that contains the email address. From the examples, we can see that this line *always* has the term "From: ", which again is specified by the email protocol mentioned in Chapter 2. So, we will use this information to search the character vector for each email to identify the correct element. As we can see from Example 4-1, however, there is variation among emails in how the email address is written. This line always contains the name of the sender and the sender's email address, but sometimes the address is encapsulated in angled brackets (Email #1) whereas in others it is not enclosed in brackets (Email #2). For that reason, we will write a `get.from` function that uses regular expressions to extract the data for this feature.

```
get.from <- function(msg.vec) {
    from <- msg.vec[grepl("From: ", msg.vec)]
    from <- strsplit(from, '[":<> ]')[[1]]
    from <- from[which(from !="" & from !=" ")]
    return(from[grepl("@", from)][1])
}
```

As we have already seen, R has many powerful functions for working with regular expressions. The `grepl` function works just like a regular `grep` function for matching regular expression patterns, but the "l" stands for *logical*. So, rather than returning vector indices, it will return a vector of the same length as `msg.vec` with Boolean values indicating where the pattern was matched in the character vector. After the first line in this function, the `from` variable is a character vector with a single element: the "From :" lines highlighted in Example 4-1.

Now that we have the correct line, we need to extract the address itself. To do this, we will use the `strsplit` function, which will split a character element into a list by a given regular expression pattern. In order to properly extract the addresses, we need to account for the variation in the text patterns observed in Example 4-1. To do so, we create a set of characters for our pattern by using the square brackets. Here, the characters we want to split the text by are colons, angle brackets, and an empty character. This pattern will always put the address as the first element in the list, so we can pull that from the list with `[[1]]`. Because of the variation in the pattern, however, it will also add empty elements to this vector. In order to return only the email address itself, we will ignore those empty elements, then look for the remaining element containing the "@" symbol and return that. We now have parsed one-fourth of the data needed to generate our training data.

```
get.msg <- function(msg.vec) {
    msg <- msg.vec[seq(which(msg.vec == "")[1] + 1, length(msg.vec), 1)]
    return(paste(msg, collapse="\n"))
}
```

Extracting the next two features, the message subject and body, is relatively simple. In Chapter 3, we needed to extract the message body in order to quantify the terms in spam and ham email messages. The get.msg function, therefore, simply replicates the pattern we used to perform the same task here. Recall that the message body always appears after the first empty line break in the email. So, we simply look for the first empty element in msg.vec and return all of the elements after that. To simplify the text mining process, we collapse these vectors into a single character vector with the paste function and return that.

```
get.subject <- function(msg.vec) {
    subj <- msg.vec[grepl("Subject: ", msg.vec)]
    if(length(subj) > 0) {
        return(strsplit(subj, "Subject: ")[[1]][2])
    }
    else {
        return("")
    }
}
```

Extracting the email's subject is akin to extracting the sender's address, but is actually a bit simpler. With the get.subject function, we will again use the grepl function to look for the "Subject: " pattern in each email to find the line in the message that contains the subject. There is a catch, however: as it turns out, not every message in the data set actually has a subject. As such, the pattern matching we are using will blow up on these edge cases. In order to guard against this, we will simply test to see whether our call to grepl has actually returned anything. To test this, we check that the length of subj is greater than zero. If it is, we split the line based on our pattern and return the second element. If not, we return an empty character. By default in R, when matching functions such as grepl do not make a match, special values such as integer(0) or character(0) will be returned. These values have a zero length, so this type of check is always a good idea when running a function over a lot of messy data.

 In the *code/data/hard_ham/* folder in the files for Chapter 3, see file *00175.** for a problematic email message. As is often the case when attempting to work a data set into your problem, you will run into edge cases like this. Getting through them will take some trial and error, as it did for us in this case. The important thing is to stay calm and dig deeper into the data to find the problem. You're not doing it right if you do not stumble on your way to parsing a data set into a workable form!

We now have three-quarters of our features extracted, but it is the final element—the date and time the message was received—that will cause us to suffer the most. This field will be difficult to work with for two reasons. First, dealing with dates is almost always a painful prospect, as different programming languages often have slightly different ways of thinking about time, and in this case, R is no different. Eventually we will want to convert the date strings into POSIX date objects in order to sort the data chronologically. But to do this, we need a common character representation of the dates, which leads directly to the second reason for our suffering: there is considerable variation within the SpamAssassin public corpus in how the receival dates and times of messages are represented. Example 4-2 illustrates a few examples of this variation.

Example 4-2. Examples of email date and time received text pattern variation

Email #1

....
Date: Thu, 22 Aug 2002 18:26:25 +0700

  Date: **Wed, 21 Aug 2002 10:54:46 -0500**
  From: Chris Garrigues lt;cwg-dated-1030377287.06fa6d@DeepEddy.Comgt;
  Message-ID: lt;1029945287.4797.TMDA@deepeddy.vircio.comgt;
....

Email #2

....
List-Unsubscribe: lt;https://example.sourceforge.net/lists/listinfo/sitescooper-talkgt;,
    lt;mailto:sitescooper-talk-request@lists.sourceforge.net?subject=unsubscribegt;
List-Archive: lt;http://www.geocrawler.com/redir-sf.php3?list=sitescooper-talkgt;
X-Original-Date: 30 Aug 2002 08:50:38 -0500
Date: 30 Aug 2002 08:50:38 -0500
....

Email #3

....
Date: Wed, 04 Dec 2002 11:36:32 GMT
Subject: [zzzzteana] Re: Bomb Ikea
Reply-To: zzzzteana@yahoogroups.com
Content-Type: text/plain; charset=US-ASCII
....

Email #4

....
Path: not-for-mail
From: Michael Hudson lt;mwh@python.netgt;
Date: 04 Dec 2002 11:49:23 +0000
Message-Id: lt;2madyyyyqa0s.fsf@starship.python.netgt;
....

As you can see, there are many things that we need to be cognizant of when extracting the date and time information from each email. The first thing to notice from the examples in Example 4-2 is that the data we want to extract is always identified by "Date: "; however, there are many traps in using this pattern that we must be mindful of. As Email #1 from Example 4-2 illustrates, sometimes there will be multiple lines that match this pattern. Likewise, Email #2 shows that some lines may be partial matches, and in either case the data on these lines can be conflicting—as it is in Email #1. Next, we can observe even in these four examples that dates and times are not stored in a uniform way across all emails. In all emails, there are extraneous GMT offsets and other types of labeling information. Finally, the format for the date and time in Email #4 is totally different from the previous two.

All of this information will be critical in getting the data into a uniform and workable form. For now, however, we need to focus only on extracting the date and time information without the extraneous offset information by defining a `get.date` function.

Once we have all of the date/time strings, we will need to deal with converting the conflicting date/time formats to a uniform POSIX object, but this will not be handled by the get.date function.

```
get.date <- function(msg.vec) {
    date.grep <- grepl("^Date: ", msg.vec)
    date.grepl <- which(date.grep == TRUE)
    date <- msg.vec[date.grep[1]]
    date <- strsplit(date, "\\+|\\-|: ")[[1]][2]
    date <- gsub("^\\s+|\\s+$", "", date)
    return(strtrim(date, 25))
}
```

As we mentioned, many emails have multiple full or partial matches to the "Date: " pattern. Notice, however, from Emails #1 and #2 in Example 4-2 that only one line from the email has "Date: " at the start of the string. In Email #1, there are several empty characters preceding this pattern, and in Email #2 the pattern is partially matched to "X-Original-Date: ". We can force the regular expression to match only strings that have "Date: " at the start of the string by using the caret operator with "^Date: ". Now grepl will return TRUE only when that pattern starts an element of the message vector.

Next, we want to return the first element in msg.vec that matches this pattern. We may be able to get away with simply returning the element in msg.vec that matches our pattern in grepl, but what if an email message contains a line that begins "Date: "? If this edge case were to occur, we know the first element that matched our pattern will come from the message's header because header information always comes before the message body. To prevent this problem, we always return the first matching element.

Now we need to process this line of text in order to return a string that can eventually be converted into a POSIX object in R. We've already noted that there is extraneous information and that the dates and times are not stored in a uniform format. To isolate the date and time information, we will split the string by characters to denote extraneous information. In this case, that will be a colon, a plus sign, or a minus character. In most cases, this will leave us with only the date and time information, plus some trailing empty characters. The use of the gsub function in the next line will substitute any leading or trailing whitespace in the character string. Finally, to deal with the kind of extraneous data we observe in Email #3 in Example 4-2, we will simply trim off any characters after a 25-character limit. A standard data/time string is 25 characters long, so we know that anything over this is extraneous.

```
easyham.docs <- dir(easyham.path)
easyham.docs <- easyham.docs[which(easyham.docs != "cmds")]
easyham.parse <- lapply(easyham.docs, function(p) parse.email(paste(easyham.path,
                                                                     p, sep="")))


ehparse.matrix <- do.call(rbind, easyham.parse)
allparse.df <- data.frame(ehparse.matrix, stringsAsFactors=FALSE)
names(allparse.df) <- c("Date", "From.EMail", "Subject", "Message", "Path")
```

Congratulations! You have successfully suffered though transforming this amorphous set of emails into a structured rectangle suitable for training our ranking algorithm. Now all we have to do is throw the switch. Similar to what we did in Chapter 3, we will create a vector with all of the "easy ham" files, remove the extra "cmds" file from the vector, and then use the lapply function to apply the parse.email function to each email file. Because we are pointing to files in the data directory for the previous chapter, we also have to be sure to concatenate the relative path to these files using the paste function and our easyham.path inside the lapply call.

Next, we need to convert the list of vectors returned by lapply into a matrix—i.e., our data rectangle. As before, we will use the do.call function with rbind to create the ehparse.matrix object. We will then convert this to a data frame of character vectors, and then set the column names to c("Date", "From.EMail", "Subject", "Message", "Path"). To check the results, use head(allparse.df) to inspect the first few rows of the data frame. To conserve space, we will not reproduce this here, but we recommend that you do.

Before we can proceed to creating a weighting scheme from this data, however, there is still some remaining housekeeping.

```
date.converter <- function(dates, pattern1, pattern2) {
    pattern1.convert <- strptime(dates, pattern1)
    pattern2.convert <- strptime(dates, pattern2)
    pattern1.convert[is.na(pattern1.convert)] <-
    pattern2.convert[is.na(pattern1.convert)]
    return(pattern1.convert)
}

pattern1 <- "%a, %d %b %Y %H:%M:%S"
pattern2 <- "%d %b %Y %H:%M:%S"

allparse.df$Date <- date.converter(allparse.df$Date, pattern1, pattern2)
```

As we mentioned, our first trial with extracting the dates was simply isolating the text. Now we need to take that text and convert it into POSIX objects that can be compared logically. This is necessary because we need to sort the emails chronologically. Recall that running through this entire exercise is the notion of *time*, and how temporal differences among observed features can be used to infer importance. The character representation of dates and times will not suffice.

As we saw in Example 4-2, there are two variations on the date format. From these examples, Email #3 has a date/time string of the format "Wed, 04 Dec 2002 11:36:32," whereas Email #4 is of the format "04 Dec 2002 11:49:23". To convert these two strings into POSIX formats, we will need to use the strptime function, but pass it two different date/time formats to make the conversion. Each element of these strings matches a specific POSIX format element, so we will need to specify conversion strings that match these variants.

R uses the standard POSIX date/time format strings to make these conversions. There are many options for these strings, and we recommend reading through the documentation in the strptime function using the ?strptime command to see all of the options. Here we will be using only a select few, but understanding them in greater depth will be very useful for working with dates and times in R.

We need to convert the strings in the Date column of allparse.df to the two different POSIX formats separately, then recombine them back into the data frame to complete the conversion. To accomplish this, we will define the date.converter function to take two different POSIX patterns and a character vector of date strings. When the pattern passed to strptime does not match the string passed to it, the default behavior is to return NA. We can use this to recombine the converted character vectors by replacing the elements with NA from the first conversion with those from the second. Because we know there are only two patterns present in the data, the result will be a single vector with all date strings converted to POSIX objects.

```
allparse.df$Subject <- tolower(allparse.df$Subject)
allparse.df$From.EMail <- tolower(allparse.df$From.EMail)

priority.df <- allparse.df[with(allparse.df, order(Date)),]

priority.train <- priority.df[1:(round(nrow(priority.df) / 2)),]
```

The final bit of cleanup is to convert the character vectors in the Subject and From email columns to all lowercase. Again, this is done to ensure that all data entries are as uniform as possible before we move into the training phase. Next, we sort the data chronologically using a combination of the with and order commands in R. (R has a particularly unintuitive way of doing sorting, but this shorthand is something you will find yourself doing very often, so it is best to get familiar with it.) The combination will return a vector of the element indices in ascending chronological order. Then, to order the data frame by these indices, we need to reference the elements of allparse.df in that order, and add the final comma before closing the square bracket so all columns are sorted this way.

Finally, we store the first half of the chronologically sorted data frame as prior ity.train. The data in this data frame will be used to train our ranker. Later, we will use the second half of priority.df to test the ranker. With the data fully formed, we are ready to begin designing our ranking scheme. Given our feature set, one way to proceed is to define weights for each observed feature in the training data.

Creating a Weighting Scheme for Ranking

Before we can proceed to implementing a weighting scheme, we need to digress briefly to discuss scales. Consider for a moment your own email activity. Do you interact with roughly the same people on a regular basis? Do you know about how many emails you receive in a day? How many emails do you receive from total strangers in a week? If you are like us, and we suspect, like most other people, your email activity crudely adheres to the 80/20 cliche. That is, about 80% of your email activity is conducted with about 20% of the total number of people in your address book. So, why is this important?

We need to be able to devise a scheme for weighting the observation of certain features in our data, but because of the potential differences in scale among these observations, we cannot compare them directly. More precisely, we cannot compare their absolute values directly. Let's take the training data that we have just finished parsing. We know that one of the features that we are adding to our ranker is an approximation of social interaction based on the volume of emails received from each address in our training data.

```
from.weight <- ddply(priority.train, .(From.EMail), summarise, Freq=length(Subject))
```

To begin to explore how this scaling affects our first feature, we will need to count the number of times each email address appears in our data. To do this, we will use the `plyr` package, which we have already loaded in as a dependency for `ggplot2`. If you worked through the example in Chapter 1, you have already seen `plyr` in action. Briefly, the family of functions in `plyr` are used to chop data into smaller squares and cubes so that we can operate over these pieces all at once. (This is very similar to the popular Map-Reduce paradigm used in many large-scale data analysis environments.) Here we will perform a very simple task: find all of the columns with matching addresses in the `From.Email` column and count them.

To do this, we use the `ddply` function, which operates on data frames, with our training data. The syntax has us define the data grouping we want first—which in this case is only the `From.EMail` dimension—and then the operation we will run over that grouping. Here we will use the `summarise` option to create a new column named `Freq` with the count information. You can use the `head(from.weight)` command to inspect the results.

 In this case, the operation asks for the `length` of the vector at column `Subject` in the chopped-up data frame, but we actually could have used any column name from the training data to get the same result because all columns matching our criteria will have the same length. Becoming more familiar with using `plyr` for manipulating data will be extremely valuable to you going forward, and we highly recommend the package author's documentation [HW11].

To get a better sense of the scale of this data, let's plot the results. Figure 4-2 shows a bar chart of the volume of emails from users who have sent more than six emails. We have performed this truncation to make it easier to read, but even with this data removed, we can already see how quickly the data scales. The top emailer, *tim.one@comcast.ent*, has sent 45 messages in our data. That's about 15 times more emails than the average person in our training data! But *tim.one@comcast.ent* is pretty unique. As you can see from Figure 4-2, there are only a few other senders near his level, and the frequency drops off very quickly after them. How could we weight an observation from an average person in our training data without skewing that value to account for outliers like our top emailers?

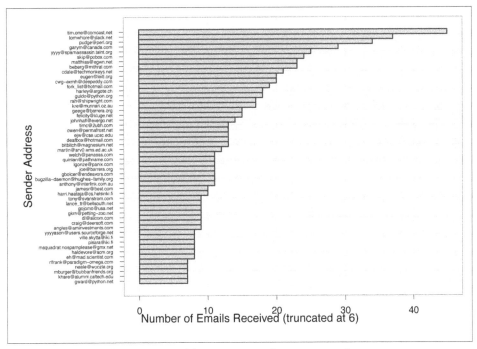

Figure 4-2. Number of emails received from various senders in training data

A log-weighting scheme

The answer comes in transforming the scales. We need to make the numerical relationship among the units in our feature set less extreme. If we compare the absolute frequency counts, then an email from *tim.one@comcast.ent* will be weighted as 15 times more important than email from an average sender. This is very problematic because we will want to establish a threshold for being either a priority message or not, based on the range of weight values produced by our ranker at the learning stage. With such extreme skewness, our threshold will be either far too low or far too high, so we need to rescale the units to account for the nature of our data.

This brings us to *logarithms* and *log-transformations*. You are probably familiar with logarithms from elementary mathematics, but if not, the concept is quite simple. A logarithm is a function that returns the exponent value that would satisfy an equation where some base number that is being raised to that exponent equals the number given to the logarithmic function.

The base value in a log-transformation is critical. As hackers, we are familiar with thinking of things in base two, or *binary*. We may very easily construct a log-transformation of base two. In this case, we would solve an equation for the exponent value where the input value is equal to two raised to that exponent. For example, if we transformed 16 by log base-two, it would equal four because two raised to the fourth power equals 16. In essence, we are "reversing" an exponential, so these types of transformations work best when the data fits such a function.

The two most common log-transformations are the so-called *natural log* and the *log base-10* transformation. In the former, the base is the special value *e*, which is an irrational constant (like *pi*) equal to approximately 2.718. The name *natural log* is often denoted ln. Rates of change by this constant are very often observed in nature, and in fact the derivation can be done geometrically as a function of the angles inside a circle. You are likely very familiar with shapes and relationships that follow a natural log, although you may not have thought of them in these terms. Figure 4-3 illustrates a natural log spiral, which can be observed in many naturally occurring phenomenon. Some examples include the interior structure of a nautilus shell and the spiraling winds of a hurricane (or tornado). Even the scattering of interstellar particles in our galaxy follows a natural logarithmic spiral. Also, many professional camera settings' apertures are set to vary by natural logs.

Given the intimate relationship between this value and many naturally occurring phenomena, it is a great function for rescaling social data—such as email activity—that is exponential. Alternatively, the log base-10 transformation, often denoted log10, replaces the e value in the natural log-transform with a 10. Given how log-transforms work, we know that the log base-10 transformation will reduce large values to much smaller ones than the natural log. For example, the log base-10 transformation of 1,000 is 3 because 10 raised to the third is 1,000, whereas the natural log is approximately 6.9. Therefore, it makes sense to use a log base-10 transformation when our data scales by a very large exponent.

The ways in which both of these options would transform our email volume data are illustrated in Figure 4-4. In this figure, we can see that the volume of emails sent by the users in the training data follows a fairly steep exponential. By transforming those values by the natural log and log base-10, we significantly flatten out that line. As we know, the log base-10 transforms the values substantially, whereas the natural log still provides some variation that will allow us to pull out meaningful weights from this training data. For this reason, we will use the natural log to define the weight for our email volume feature.

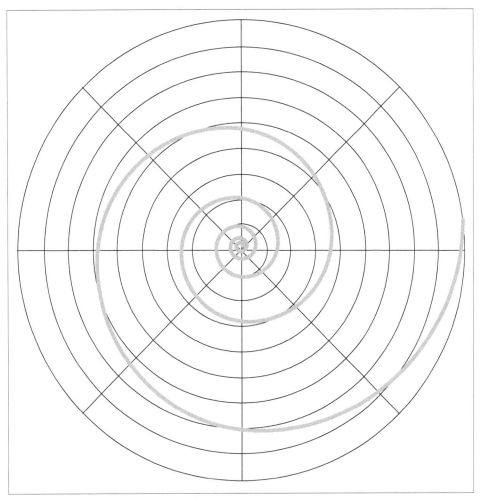

Figure 4-3. A natural-log spiral, often observed in nature

 As we have done here and as we explained in detail in Chapter 2, it is always a good idea to explore your data visually as you are working through any machine learning problem. We want to know how all of the observations in our feature set relate to one another in order to make the best predictions. Often the best way to do this is through data visualization.

```
from.weight <- transform(from.weight, Weight=log(Freq + 1))
```

Finally, recall from grade school mathematics your rules for exponents. Anything raised to zero always equals one. This is very important to keep in mind when using log-transformation in a weighting scheme because any observation equal to one will be

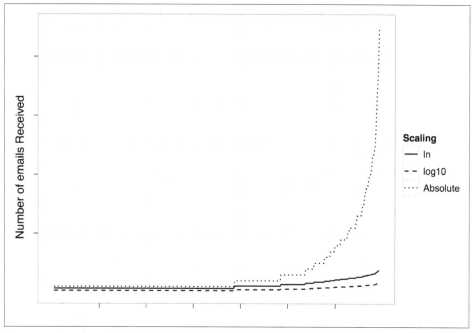

Figure 4-4. Number of emails received, with absolute counts and ln and log10 transformations

transformed to zero. This is problematic in a weighting scheme because multiplying other weights with zero will zero out the entire value. To avoid this, *we always add one to all observations before taking logs.*

 There is actually a function in R called log1p that computes log(1 + p), but for the purposes of learning and being explicit, we will do this addition "by hand."

Given the rescaling, this does not affect our results, and it keeps all weights greater than zero. In this case, we are using the default base value for the log function, which is the natural log.

 For our purposes we will never have an observation in our feature set that is equal to zero, because we are counting things. If there are no observations of something, then it simply doesn't enter our training data. In some cases, however, this will not be true, and you may have zero observations in your data. The log of zero is undefined, and if you try to compute it in R, it will return the special value -Inf. Often, having instances of -Inf in your data will cause things to blow up.

Weighting from Email Thread Activity

The second feature we want to extract from the data is email thread activity. As noted, we have no way of knowing whether the user we are building this ranking for has responded to any emails, but we can group messages by their thread and measure how active they have been since they started. Again, our assumption in building this feature is that time is important, and therefore threads that have more messages sent over a short period of time are more active and consequently more important.

The emails in our data set do not contain specific thread IDs, but a logical way to identify threads within the training data is to look for emails with a shared subject line. That is, if we find a subject that begins with "re: ", then we know that this is part of some thread. When we see a message like this, we can look around for other messages in that thread and measure the activity.

```
find.threads <- function(email.df) {
    response.threads <- strsplit(email.df$Subject, "re: ")
    is.thread <- sapply(response.threads, function(subj) ifelse(subj[1] == "", TRUE,
                        FALSE))
    threads <- response.threads[is.thread]
    senders <- email.df$From.EMail[is.thread]
    threads <- sapply(threads, function(t) paste(t[2:length(t)], collapse="re: "))
    return(cbind(senders,threads))
}

threads.matrix<-find.threads(priority.train)
```

This is precisely what the `find.threads` function attempts to do with our training data. If we split every subject in our training data by "re: ", then we can find threads by looking for split character vectors with an empty character as the first element. Once we know which observations in the training data are part of threads, we can extract the senders from those threads and the subject. The result matrix will have all of the senders and initial thread subject in our training data.

```
email.thread <- function(threads.matrix) {
    senders <- threads.matrix[, 1]
    senders.freq <- table(senders)
    senders.matrix <- cbind(names(senders.freq), senders.freq, log(senders.freq + 1))
    senders.df <- data.frame(senders.matrix, stringsAsFactors=FALSE)
    row.names(senders.df) <- 1:nrow(senders.df)
    names(senders.df) <- c("From.EMail", "Freq", "Weight")
    senders.df$Freq <- as.numeric(senders.df$Freq)
    senders.df$Weight <- as.numeric(senders.df$Weight)
    return(senders.df)
}

senders.df <- email.thread(threads.matrix)
```

Next we will create a weighting based on the senders who are most active in threads. This will be a supplement to the volume-based weighting we just did for the entire data set, but now we will focus only on those senders present in the `threads.matrix`. The function `email.thread` will take the `threads.matrix` as input and generate this secondary volume-based weighting. This will be very similar to what we did in the previous section, except this time we will use the `table` function to count the frequency of senders in the threads. This is done simply to show a different method for accomplishing the same calculation on a matrix in R, rather than a data frame using `plyr`. Most of this function simply performs housekeeping on the `senders.df` data frame, but notice that we are again using a natural-log weighting.

As the final piece to the email thread feature, we will create a weighting based on threads that we know are active. We have already identified all of the threads in our training data and created a weighting based on the terms in those threads. Now we want to take that knowledge and give additional weight to known threads that are also active. The assumption here is that if we already know the threads, we expect a user to place more importance on those threads that are more active.

```
get.threads <- function(threads.matrix, email.df) {
    threads <- unique(threads.matrix[, 2])
    thread.counts <- lapply(threads, function(t) thread.counts(t, email.df))
    thread.matrix <- do.call(rbind, thread.counts)
    return(cbind(threads, thread.matrix))
}

thread.counts <- function(thread, email.df) {
    thread.times <- email.df$Date[which(email.df$Subject == thread
    | email.df$Subject == paste("re:", thread))]
    freq <- length(thread.times)
    min.time <- min(thread.times)
    max.time <- max(thread.times)
    time.span <- as.numeric(difftime(max.time, min.time, units="secs"))
    if(freq < 2) {
        return(c(NA,NA,NA))
    }
    else {
        trans.weight <- freq / time.span
        log.trans.weight <- 10 + log(trans.weight, base=10)
        return(c(freq,time.span, log.trans.weight))
    }
}

thread.weights <- get.threads(threads.matrix, priority.train)
thread.weights <- data.frame(thread.weights, stringsAsFactors=FALSE)
names(thread.weights) <- c("Thread","Freq","Response","Weight")
thread.weights$Freq <- as.numeric(thread.weights$Freq)
thread.weights$Response <- as.numeric(thread.weights$Response)
thread.weights$Weight <- as.numeric(thread.weights$Weight)
thread.weights <- subset(thread.weights, is.na(thread.weights$Freq) == FALSE)
```

Using the `threads.matrix` we just created, we will go back into the training data to find all of the emails inside each thread. To do this, we create the `get.threads` function, which will take the `threads.matrix` and our training data as arguments. Using the `unique` command, we create a vector of all thread subjects in our data. Now we need to take this information and measure each thread's activity.

The `thread.counts` function will do this. Using the thread subject and training data as parameters, we will collect all of the date- and timestamps for all emails matching the thread in the `thread.times` vector. We can measure how many emails have been received in training data for this thread by measuring the length of `thread.times`.

Finally, to measure the activity level, we need to know how long the thread has existed in our training data. Implicitly, there is truncation on either side of this data. That is, there may be emails that were received in a thread before our training data started or after data collection was completed. There is nothing we can do about this, so we will take the minimum and maximum date/times for each thread and use these to measure the time span. The function `difftime` will calculate the amount of time elapsed between two POSIX objects in some units. In our case, we want the smallest unit possible: seconds.

Due to the truncation, it may be that we observe only a single message in a thread. This could be a thread that ended just as the training data got collected or just started when collection ended. Before we can create a weight based on the activity over the time span of a thread, we must flag those threads for which we have only one message. The if-statement at the end of `thread.counts` does this check and returns a vector of `NA` if the current thread has only one message. We will use this later to scrub these from the activity-based weighting data.

The final step is to create a weighting for those messages we can measure. We start by calculating the ratio of messages-to-seconds elapsed in the thread. So, if a message were sent every second in a given thread, the result would be one. Of course, in practice, this number is much lower: the average number of messages in each thread is about 4.5, and the average elapsed time is about 31,000 seconds (8.5 hours). Given these scales, the vast majority of our ratios are tiny fractions. As before, we still want to transform these values using logs, but because we are dealing with fractional values, this will result in negative numbers. We cannot have a negative weight value in our scheme, so we will have to perform an additional transformation that is formally called an *affine transformation*.

An affine transformation is simply a linear movement of points in space. Imagine a square drawn on piece of graph paper. If you wanted to move that square to another position on the paper, you could do so by defining a function that moved all of the points in the same direction. This is an affine transformation. To get non-negative weights in `log.trans.weight`, we will simply add 10 to all the log-transformed values. This will ensure that all of the values will be proper weights with a positive value.

As before, once we have generated the weight data with `get.threads` and `thread.counts`, we will perform some basic housekeeping on the `thread.weights` data frame to keep the naming consistent with the other weight data frames. In the final step, we use the `subset` function to remove any rows that refer to threads with only one message (i.e., *truncated* threads). We can now use `head(thread.weights)` to check the results.

```
head(thread.weights)
                                          Thread Freq Response    Weight
1            please help a newbie compile mplayer :-)    4   42309 5.975627
2                             prob. w/ install/uninstall    4   23745 6.226488
3                                    http://apt.nixia.no/   10  265303 5.576258
4                   problems with 'apt-get -f install'    3   55960 5.729244
5                            problems with apt update    2    6347 6.498461
6 about apt, kernel updates and dist-upgrade    5  240238 5.318328
```

The first two rows are good examples of how this weighting scheme values thread
activity. In both of these threads, there have been four messages.
The `prob. w/ install/uninstall` thread, however, has been in the data for about half
as many seconds. Given our assumptions, we would think that this thread is more
important and therefore should have a higher weight. In this case, we give messages
from this thread about 1.04 times more weight than those from the `please help a
newbie compile mplayer :-)` thread. This may or may not seem reasonable to you, and
therein lies part of the art in designing and applying a scheme such as this to a general
problem. It may be that in this case our user would not value things this way, whereas
others might, but because we want a general solution, we must accept the consequences
of our assumptions.

```
term.counts <- function(term.vec, control) {
    vec.corpus <- Corpus(VectorSource(term.vec))
    vec.tdm <- TermDocumentMatrix(vec.corpus, control=control)
    return(rowSums(as.matrix(vec.tdm)))
}

thread.terms <- term.counts(thread.weights$Thread,
  control=list(stopwords=stopwords()))
thread.terms <- names(thread.terms)

term.weights <- sapply(thread.terms,
  function(t) mean(thread.weights$Weight[grepl(t, thread.weights$Thread,
  fixed=TRUE)]))
term.weights <- data.frame(list(Term=names(term.weights), Weight=term.weights),
  stringsAsFactors=FALSE, row.names=1:length(term.weights))
```

The final weighting data we will produce from the threads are the frequent terms in
these threads. Similar to what we did in Chapter 3, we create a general function called
`term.counts` that takes a vector of terms and a `TermDocumentMatrix` control list to produce the TDM and extract the counts of terms in all of the threads. The assumption in
creating this weighting data is that frequent terms in active thread subjects are more
important than terms that are either less frequent or not in active threads. We are
attempting to add as much information as possible to our ranker in order to create a
more granular stratification of emails. To do so, rather than look only for already-active
threads, we want to also weight threads that "look like" previously active threads, and
term weighting is one way to do this.

```
msg.terms <- term.counts(priority.train$Message,
    control=list(stopwords=stopwords(),
    removePunctuation=TRUE, removeNumbers=TRUE))
```

```
msg.weights <- data.frame(list(Term=names(msg.terms),
    Weight=log(msg.terms, base=10)), stringsAsFactors=FALSE,
    row.names=1:length(msg.terms))

msg.weights <- subset(msg.weights, Weight > 0)
```

The final weighting data we will build is based on term frequency in all email messages in the training data. This will proceed almost identically to our method for counting terms in the spam classification exercise; however, this time we will assign log-transformed weights based on these counts. As with the term-frequency weighting for thread subjects, the implicit assumption in the `msg.weights` data frame is that a new message that looks like other messages we have seen before is more important than a message that is totally foreign to us.

We now have five weight data frames with which to perform our ranking! This includes `from.weight` (social activity feature), `senders.df` (sender activity in threads), `thread.weights` (thread message activity), `term.weights` (terms from active threads), and `msg.weights` (common terms in all emails). We are now ready to run our training data through the ranker to find a threshold for marking a message as important.

Training and Testing the Ranker

To generate a priority rank for each message in our training data, we must multiply all of the weights produced in the previous section. This means that for each message in the data, we will need to parse the email, take the extracted features, and then match them to corresponding weight data frames to get the appropriate weighting value. We will then take the product of these values to produce a single—and unique—rank value for each message. The following `rank.message` function is a single function that takes a file path to a message and produces a priority ranking for that message based on the features we have defined and their subsequent weights. The `rank.message` function relies on many functions we have already defined, as well as a new function, `get.weights`, which does the weight lookup when the feature does not map to a single weight—i.e., subject and message terms.

```
get.weights <- function(search.term, weight.df, term=TRUE) {
    if(length(search.term) > 0) {
        if(term) {
            term.match <- match(names(search.term), weight.df$Term)
        }
        else {
            term.match <- match(search.term, weight.df$Thread)
        }
        match.weights <- weight.df$Weight[which(!is.na(term.match))]
        if(length(match.weights) > 1) {
            return(1)
        }
        else {
            return(mean(match.weights))
        }
```

```
    }
    else {
        return(1)
    }
}
```

We first define `get.weights`, which takes three arguments: some search terms (a string), the weight data frame in which to do the lookup, and a single Boolean value for `term`. This final parameter will allow us to tell the application whether it is doing a lookup on a term data frame or on a thread data frame. We will treat these lookups slightly differently due to differences in column labels in the `thread.weights` data frame, so we need to make this distinction. The process here is fairly straightforward, as we use the `match` function to find the elements in the weight data frame that match `search.term` and return the weight value. What is more important to notice here is how the function is handling nonmatches.

First, we do one safety check to make sure that the search term being passed to `get.weights` is valid by checking that it has some positive length. This is the same type of check we performed while parsing the email data to check that an email actually had a subject line. If it is an invalid search term, then we simply return a 1 (which elementary mathematics tells us will not alter the product computed in the next step because of the rules for multiplication by 1). Next, the `match` function will return an `NA` value for any elements in the search vector that do not match `search.term`. Therefore, we extract the weight values for only those matched elements that are not `NA`. If there are no matches, the `term.match` vector will be all `NA`s, in which case `match.weights` will have a zero length. So, we do an additional check for this case, and if we encounter this case, we again return 1. If we have matched some weight values, we return the mean of all these weights as our result.

```
rank.message <- function(path) {
    msg <- parse.email(path)
    # Weighting based on message author

    # First is just on the total frequency
    from <- ifelse(length(which(from.weight$From.EMail == msg[2])) > 0,
        from.weight$Weight[which(from.weight$From.EMail == msg[2])], 1)

    # Second is based on senders in threads, and threads themselves
    thread.from <- ifelse(length(which(senders.df$From.EMail == msg[2])) > 0,
        senders.df$Weight[which(senders.df$From.EMail == msg[2])], 1)

    subj <- strsplit(tolower(msg[3]), "re: ")
    is.thread <- ifelse(subj[[1]][1] == "", TRUE, FALSE)
    if(is.thread) {
        activity <- get.weights(subj[[1]][2], thread.weights, term=FALSE)
    }
    else {
        activity <- 1
    }

    # Next, weight based on terms
```

```
        # Weight based on terms in threads
        thread.terms <- term.counts(msg[3], control=list(stopwords=stopwords()))
        thread.terms.weights <- get.weights(thread.terms, term.weights)

        # Weight based terms in all messages
        msg.terms <- term.counts(msg[4], control=list(stopwords=stopwords(),
            removePunctuation=TRUE, removeNumbers=TRUE))
        msg.weights <- get.weights(msg.terms, msg.weights)

        # Calculate rank by interacting all weights
        rank <- prod(from, thread.from, activity,
            thread.terms.weights, msg.weights)

        return(c(msg[1], msg[2], msg[3], rank))
}
```

The rank.message function uses rules similar to the get.weights function for assigning weight values to the features extracted from each email in the data set. First, it calls the parse.email function to extract the four features of interest. It then proceeds to use a series of if-then clauses to determine whether any of the features extracted from the current email are present in any of the weight data frames used to rank, and assigns weights appropriately. from and thread.from use the social interaction features to find weight based on the sender's email address. Note that, in both cases, if the ifelse function does not match anything in the data weight data frames, a 1 is returned. This is the same strategy implemented in the get.weights function.

For the thread- and term-based weighting, some internal text parsing is done. For threads, we first check that the email being ranked is part of a thread in the exact same way we did during the training phase. If it is, we look up a rank; otherwise, we assign a 1. For term-based weighting, we use the term.counts function to get the terms of interest from the email features and then weight accordingly. In the final step, we generate the rank by passing all of the weight values we have just looked up to the prod function. The rank.message function then returns a vector with the email's date/time, sender's address, subject, and rank.

```
    train.paths <- priority.df$Path[1:(round(nrow(priority.df) / 2))]
    test.paths <- priority.df$Path[((round(nrow(priority.df) / 2)) + 1):nrow(priority.df)]

    train.ranks <- lapply(train.paths, rank.message)
    train.ranks.matrix <- do.call(rbind, train.ranks)
    train.ranks.matrix <- cbind(train.paths, train.ranks.matrix, "TRAINING")
    train.ranks.df <- data.frame(train.ranks.matrix, stringsAsFactors=FALSE)
    names(train.ranks.df) <- c("Message", "Date", "From", "Subj", "Rank", "Type")
    train.ranks.df$Rank <- as.numeric(train.ranks.df$Rank)

    priority.threshold <- median(train.ranks.df$Rank)

    train.ranks.df$Priority <- ifelse(train.ranks.df$Rank >= priority.threshold, 1, 0)
```

We are now ready to fire up our ranker! Before we can proceed, we will split our data into two chronologically divided sets. The first will be the training data, which we call `train.paths`. We will use the ranking data generated from here to establish a threshold value for a "priority" message. Once we have this, we can run the ranker over the emails in `test.paths` to determine which ones are priority and to estimate their internal rank ordering. Next, we will apply the `rank.messages` function to the `train.paths` vector to generate a list of vectors containing the features and priority rank for each email. We then perform some basic housekeeping to convert this list to a matrix. Finally, we convert this matrix to a data frame with column names and properly formatted vectors.

 You may notice that `train.ranks <- lapply(train.paths, rank.mes sage)` causes R to throw a warning. This is not a problem, but simply a result of the way we have built the ranker. You may wrap the `lapply` call in the `suppressWarnings` function if you wish to turn off this warning.

We now perform the critical step of calculating a threshold value for priority email. As you can see, for this exercise we have decided to use the median rank value as our threshold. Of course, we could have used many other summary statistics for this threshold, as we discussed in Chapter 2. Because we are not using pre-existing examples of how emails ought to be ranked to determine this threshold, we are performing a task that is not really a standard sort of supervised learning. But we have chosen the median for two principled reasons. First, if we have designed a good ranker, then the ranks should have a smooth distribution, with most emails having low rank and many fewer emails having a high rank. We are looking for "important emails," i.e., those that are most unique or unlike the normal flow of email traffic. Those will be the emails in the right tail of the rank distribution. If this is the case, those values greater than the median will be those that are somewhat greater than the typical rank. Intuitively, this is how we want to think about recommending priority email: choosing those with rank larger than the typical email.

Second, we know that the test data will contain email messages that have data that does not match anything in our training data. New emails are flowing in constantly, but given our setup, we have no way of updating our ranker. As such, we may want to have a rule about priority that is more inclusive than exclusive. If not, we may miss messages that are only partial matches to our features. As a final step, we add a new binary column `Priority` to `train.ranks.df`, indicating whether the email will be recommended as priority by our ranker.

Figure 4-5 shows the density estimate for the ranks calculated on our training data. The vertical dashed line is the median threshold, which is about 24. As you can see, our ranks are very heavy-tailed, so we have created a ranker that performs well on the training data. We can also see that the median threshold is very inclusive, with a large portion of the downward-sloping density included as priority email. Again, this is done intentionally. A much less inclusive threshold would be to use the standard deviation of the distributions, which we can calculate with `sd(train.ranks.df$Rank)`. The standard deviation is about 90, which would almost exactly exclude any emails outside of the tail.

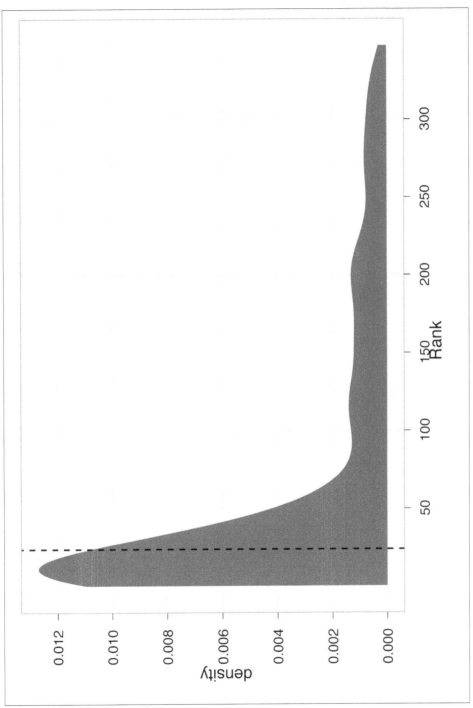

Figure 4-5. Density of the weights in training data, with a priority threshold as one standard deviation of weights

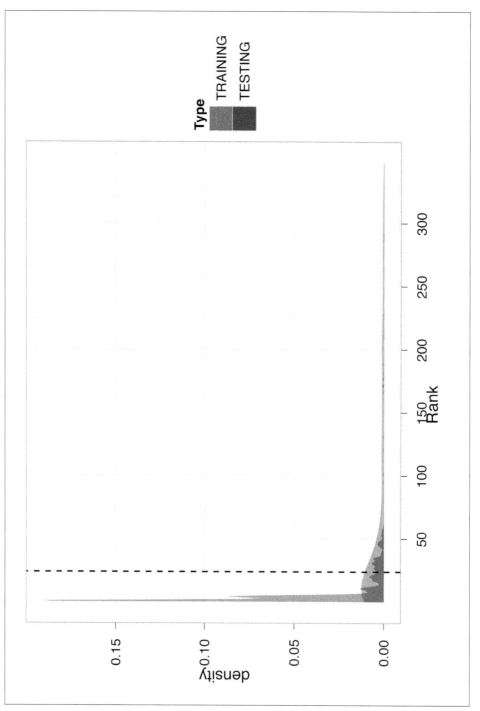

Figure 4-6. Density of weights for our test data overlaid on training data density

We will now calculate the rank values for all of the emails in our test set. This process proceeds exactly the same way as it did for our training data, so to save space we will not reproduce the code here. To see the code, refer to the *code/priority_inbox.R* file included for this chapter, starting at about line 308. Once we have calculated the ranks for the test data, we can compare the results and see how well our ranker did on new emails.

Figure 4-6 overlays the density of ranks from the test data on the densities in Figure 4-5. This illustration is very informative regarding the quality of our ranker. First, we notice that there is much more density in the test data at the very low end of the distributions. This means that there are many more emails with a low rank. Additionally, the test density estimate is much less smooth than the training data. This is evidence that the test data includes many observations not in our training data. Because these observations do not match anything in our training data, the ranker effectively ignores this information.

Although this is problematic, we avoid disaster because we used an inclusive threshold for priority email. Note that there is still a reasonable amount of density for the test data to the right of the threshold line. This means our ranker was still able to find emails to recommend as important from the test data. As a final check, let's actually see which emails our ranker pushed to the top (Table 4-1).

 There is an inherent "unknowable" quality to creating a ranker of this type. Throughout this entire exercise, we have posited assumptions about each feature we included in our design and attempted to justify these intuitively. However, we can never know the "ground truth" as to how well our ranker is doing, because we can't go back and ask the user for whom these emails were sent whether the ordering is good or makes sense. In the classification exercise, we knew the labels for each email in the training and test set, so we could measure explicitly how well the classifier was doing using the confusion matrix. In this case we can't, but we can try to infer how well the ranker is doing by looking at the results. This is what makes this exercise something distinct from standard supervised learning.

Table 4-1 shows the 40 newest emails in the test data that have been labeled as priority by our ranker. The table is meant to mimic what you might see in your email inbox if you were using this ranker to perform priority inbox sorting over your emails, with the added information of the email's rank. If you can excuse the somewhat odd or controversial subject headings, we'll explore these results to check how the ranker is grouping emails.

Table 4-1. Results of priority inbox testing

Date	From	Subject	Rank
12/1/02 21:01	geege@barrera.org	RE: Mercedes-Benz G55	31.97963566
11/25/02 19:34	deafbox@hotmail.com	Re: Men et Toil	34.7967621
10/10/02 13:14	yyyy@spamassassin.taint.org	Re: [SAdev] fully-public corpus of mail available	53.94872021
10/9/02 21:47	quinlan@pathname.com	Re: [SAdev] fully-public corpus of mail available	29.48898756
10/9/02 18:23	yyyy@spamassassin.taint.org	Re: [SAtalk] Re: fully-public corpus of mail available	44.17153847
10/9/02 13:30	haldevore@acm.org	Re: From	25.02939914
10/9/02 12:58	jamesr@best.com	RE: The Disappearing Alliance	26.54528998
10/8/02 23:42	harri.haataja@cs.helsinki.fi	Re: Zoot apt/openssh & new DVD playing doc	25.01634554
10/8/02 19:17	tomwhore@slack.net	Re: The Disappearing Alliance	56.93995821
10/8/02 17:02	johnhall@evergo.net	RE: The Disappearing Alliance	31.50297057
10/8/02 15:26	rah@shipwright.com	Re: The absurdities of life.	31.12476712
10/8/02 12:18	timc@2ubh.com	[zzzzteana] Lioness adopts fifth antelope	24.22364367
10/8/02 12:15	timc@2ubh.com	[zzzzteana] And deliver us from weevil	24.41118141
10/8/02 12:14	timc@2ubh.com	[zzzzteana] Bashing the bishop	24.18504926
10/7/02 21:39	geege@barrera.org	RE: The absurdities of life.	34.44120977
10/7/02 20:18	yyyy@spamassassin.taint.org	Re: [SAtalk] Re: AWL bug in 2.42?	46.70665631
10/7/02 16:45	jamesr@best.com	Re: erratum [Re: no matter ...] & errors	27.16350661
10/7/02 15:30	tomwhore@slack.net	Re: The absurdities of life.	47.3282386
10/7/02 14:20	cdale@techmonkeys.net	Re: The absurdities of life.	35.11063991
10/7/02 14:02	johnhall@evergo.net	RE: The absurdities of life.	28.16690172
10/6/02 17:29	geege@barrera.org	RE: Our friends the Palestinians, Our servants in government.	28.05735369
10/6/02 15:24	geege@barrera.org	RE: Our friends the Palestinians, Our servants in government.	27.32604275
10/6/02 14:02	johnhall@evergo.net	RE: Our friends the Palestinians, Our servants in government.	27.08788823
10/6/02 12:22	johnhall@evergo.net	RE: Our friends the Palestinians, Our servants in government.	26.48367996
10/6/02 10:20	owen@permafrost.net	Re: Our friends the Palestinians, Our servants in government.	26.77329071
10/6/02 10:02	fork_list@hotmail.com	Re: Our friends the Palestinians, Our servants in government.	29.60084489
10/6/02 0:34	geege@barrera.org	RE: Our friends the Palestinians, Our servants in government.	29.35353465

What's most encouraging about these results is that the ranker is grouping threads together very well. You can see several examples of this in the table, where emails from the same thread have all been marked as priority and are grouped together. Also, the ranker appears to be giving appropriately high ranks to emails from frequent senders, as is the case for outlier senders such as *tomwhore@slack.net* and *yyyy@spamassassin.taint.org*. Finally, and perhaps most encouraging, the ranker is prioritizing messages that were not present in the training data. In fact, only 12 out of the 85 threads in the test data marked as priority are continuations from the training data (about 14%). This shows that our ranker is able to apply observations from training data to new threads in the test data and make recommendations without updating. This is very good!

In this chapter we have introduced the idea of moving beyond a feature set with only one element to a more complex model with many features. We have actually accomplished a fairly difficult task, which is to design a ranking model for email when we can see only one half of the transactions. Relying on social interactions, thread activity, and common terms, we specified four features of interest and generated five weighting data frames to perform the ranking. The results, which we have just explored, were encouraging, though without *ground truth*, difficult to test explicitly.

With the last two chapters behind us, you've worked through a relatively simple example of supervised learning used to perform spam classification and a very basic form of heuristic-based ranking. You are ready to move on to the workhorse of statistical learning: regression.

## CHAPTER 5

Regression: Predicting Page Views

Introducing Regression

In the abstract, regression is a very simple concept: you want to predict one set of numbers given another set of numbers. For example, actuaries might want to predict how long a person will live given their smoking habits, while meteorologists might want to predict the next day's temperature given the previous day's temperature. In general, we'll call the numbers you're given *inputs* and the numbers you want to predict *outputs*. You'll also sometimes hear people refer to the inputs as *predictors* or *features*.

What makes regression different from classification is that the outputs are really numbers. In classification problems like those we described in Chapter 3, you might use numbers as a dummy code for a categorical distinction so that 0 represents ham and 1 represents spam. But these numbers are just symbols; we're not exploiting the "numberness" of 0 or 1 when we use dummy variables. In regression, the essential fact about the outputs is that they really are numbers: you want to predict things like temperatures, which could be 50 degrees or 71 degrees. Because you're predicting numbers, you want to be able to make strong statements about the relationship between the inputs and the outputs: you might want to say, for example, that when the number of packs of cigarettes a person smokes per day doubles, their predicted life span gets cut in half.

The problem, of course, is that wanting to make precise numerical predictions isn't the same thing as actually being able to make predictions. To make quantitative predictions, we need to come up with some rule that can leverage the information we have access to. The various regression algorithms that statisticians have developed over the last 200 years all provide different ways to make predictions by turning inputs into outputs. In this chapter, we'll cover the workhorse regression model, which is called *linear regression*.

The Baseline Model

It might seem silly to say this, but the simplest possible way to use the information we have as inputs is to ignore the inputs entirely and to predict future outcomes based only on the mean value of the output we've seen in the past. In the example of an actuary, we could completely ignore a person's health records and simply guess that they'll live as long as the average person lives.

Guessing the mean outcome for every case isn't as naive as it might seem: if we're interested in making predictions that are as close to the truth as possible without using any other information, guessing the mean output turns out to be the best guess we can possibly make.

 A little bit of work has to go into defining "best" to give this claim a definite meaning. If you're uncomfortable with us throwing around the word "best" without saying what we mean, we promise that we'll give a formal definition soon.

Before we discuss how to make the best possible guess, let's suppose that we have data from an imaginary actuarial database, a portion of which is shown in Table 5-1.

Table 5-1. Actuarial data on longevity

Smokes?	Age at death
1	75
1	72
1	66
1	74
1	69
...	...
0	66
0	80
0	84
0	63
0	79
...	...

Because this is a totally new data set, it's a good idea to follow our suggestions in Chapter 2 and explore the data a bit before doing any formal analysis. We have one numeric column and another column that's a dummy-coded factor, and so it's natural to make density plots to compare smokers with nonsmokers (see the resulting plot in Figure 5-1):

```
ages <- read.csv('data/longevity.csv')

ggplot(ages, aes(x = AgeAtDeath, fill = factor(Smokes))) +
```

```
geom_density() +
  facet_grid(Smokes ~ .)
```

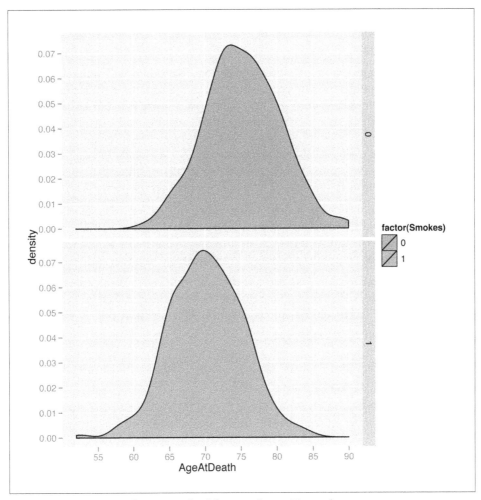

Figure 5-1. Density plot of 1,000 people's life spans, facetted by smokers

The resulting plot makes it seem reasonable to believe that smoking matters for longevity because the center of the nonsmokers' life span distribution is shifted to the right of the center of the smokers' life spans. In other words, the average life span of a nonsmoker is longer than the average life span of a smoker. But before we describe how you can use the information we have about a person's smoking habits to make predictions about her longevity, let's pretend for a minute that you didn't have any of this information. In that case, you'd need to pick a single number as your prediction for every new person, regardless of her smoking habits. So what number should you pick?

That question isn't a trivial one, because the number you should pick depends on what you think it means to make good predictions. There are a lot of reasonable ways to define the accuracy of predictions, but there is a single measure of quality that's been dominant for virtually the entire history of statistics. This measure is called squared error. If you're trying to predict a value y (the true output) and you guess h (your hypothesis about y), then the squared error of your guess is simply (y - h) ^ 2.

Beyond the value inherent in following conventions that others will understand, there are a lot of good reasons for why you might want to use squared error to measure the quality of your guesses. We won't get into them now, but we will talk a little bit more about the ways one can measure error in Chapter 7, when we talk about optimization algorithms in machine learning. For now, we'll just try to convince you of something fundamental: if we're using squared error to measure the quality of our predictions, then the best guess we can possibly make about a person's life span—without any additional information about a person's habits—is the average person's longevity.

To convince you of this claim, let's see what happens if we use other guesses instead of the mean. With the longevity data set, the mean AgeAtDeath is 72.723, which we'll round up to 73 for the time being. We can then ask: "How badly would we have predicted the ages of the people in our data set if we'd guessed that they all lived to be 73?"

To answer that question in R, we can use the following code, which combines all of the squared errors for each person in our data set by computing the mean of the squared errors, which we'll call the mean squared error (or MSE for short):

```
ages <- read.csv('data/longevity.csv')

guess <- 73

with(ages, mean((AgeAtDeath - guess) ^ 2))
#[1] 32.991
```

After running this code, we find that the mean squared error we make by guessing 73 for every person in our data set is 32.991. But that, by itself, shouldn't be enough to convince you that we'd do worse with a guess that's not 73. To convince you that 73 is the best guess, we need to consider how we'd perform if we made some of the other possible guesses. To compute those other values in R, we loop over a sequence of possible guesses ranging from 63 to 83:

```
ages <- read.csv('data/longevity.csv')

guess.accuracy <- data.frame()

for (guess in seq(63, 83, by = 1))
{
  prediction.error <- with(ages,
                           mean((AgeAtDeath - guess) ^ 2))
  guess.accuracy <- rbind(guess.accuracy,
                          data.frame(Guess = guess,
                                     Error = prediction.error))
}
```

```
ggplot(guess.accuracy, aes(x = Guess, y = Error)) +
  geom_point() +
  geom_line()
```

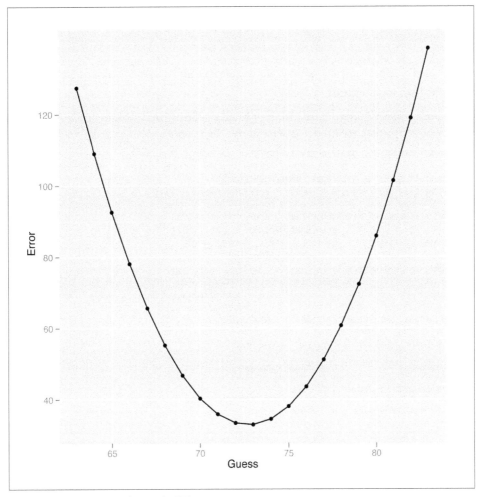

Figure 5-2. Mean squared error (MSE)

As you can see from looking at Figure 5-2, using any guess other than 73 gives us worse predictions for our data set. This is actually a general theoretical result that can be proven mathematically: to minimize squared error, you want to predict the mean value in your data set. One important implication of this is that the predictive value of having information about smoking should be measured in terms of the amount of improvement you get from using this information over just using the mean value as your guess for every person you see.

Regression Using Dummy Variables

So how can we use that information? Let's start with a simple case before we tackle the broader problem. How can we use information about whether or not people smoke to make better guesses about their longevity?

One simple idea is to estimate the mean age at death for smokers and nonsmokers separately and then to use these two separate values as our guesses for future cases, depending on whether or not a new person smokes. This time, instead of using the MSE, we'll use the root mean squared error (RMSE), which is more popular in the machine learning literature.

Here's one way to compute the RMSE in R after splitting up smokers and nonsmokers into two groups that are modeled separately (the results are listed in Table 5-2):

```
ages <- read.csv('data/longevity.csv')

constant.guess <- with(ages, mean(AgeAtDeath))
with(ages, sqrt(mean((AgeAtDeath - constant.guess) ^ 2)))

smokers.guess <- with(subset(ages, Smokes == 1),
                      mean(AgeAtDeath))
non.smokers.guess <- with(subset(ages, Smokes == 0),
                          mean(AgeAtDeath))
ages <- transform(ages,
                  NewPrediction = ifelse(Smokes == 0,
                                         non.smokers.guess,
                                         smokers.guess))
with(ages, sqrt(mean((AgeAtDeath - NewPrediction) ^ 2)))
```

Table 5-2. Prediction errors with more information

Information	Root mean squared error
Error without smoking information	5.737096
Error with smoking information	5.148622

As you can see by looking at the RMSE we get, our predictions really do get better after we include more information about the people we're studying: our prediction error when estimating people's life spans becomes 10% smaller when we include information about people's smoking habits. In general, we can do better than using just the mean value whenever we have binary distinctions that separate two types of data points— assuming that those binary distinctions are related to the output we're trying to predict. Some simple examples where binary distinctions might help are contrasting men with women or contrasting Democrats with Republicans in American political discourse.

So now we have a mechanism for incorporating dummy variables into our predictions. But how can we use richer information about the objects in our data? By richer, we mean two things: first, we want to know how we can use inputs that aren't binary distinctions, but instead continuous values such as heights or weights; second, we want to know how we can use multiple sources of information all at once to improve our estimates. In our actuarial example, suppose that we knew (a) whether or not someone was a smoker and (b) the age at which his parents died. Our intuition is that having these two separate sources of information should tell us more than either of those variables in isolation.

But making use of all of the information we have isn't an easy task. In practice, we need to make some simplifying assumptions to get things to work. The assumptions we'll describe are those that underlie linear regression, which is the only type of regression we'll describe in this chapter. Using only linear regression is less of a restriction than it might seem, as linear regression is used in at least 90% of practical regression applications and can be hacked to produce more sophisticated forms of regression with only a little bit of work.

Linear Regression in a Nutshell

The two biggest assumptions we make when using linear regression to predict outputs are the following:

Separability/additivity
> If there are multiple pieces of information that would affect our guesses, we produce our guess by adding up the effects of each piece of information as if each piece of information were being used in isolation. For example, if alcoholics live one year less than nonalcoholics and smokers live five years less than nonsmokers, then an alcoholic who's also a smoker should live 1 + 5 = 6 years less than a nonalcoholic nonsmoker. The assumption that the effects of things in isolation add up when they happen together is a very big assumption, but it's a good starting place for lots of applications of regression. Later on we'll talk about the idea of interactions, which is a technique for working around the separability assumption in linear regression when, for example, you know that the effect of excessive drinking is much worse if you also smoke.

Monotonicity/linearity
> A model is monotonic when changing one of the inputs always makes the predicted output go up or go down. For example, if you're predicting weights using heights as an input and your model is monotonic, then you're assuming that every time somebody's height increases, your prediction of their weight will go up. Monotonicity is a strong assumption because you can imagine lots of examples where the output goes up for a bit with an input and then starts to go down, but the monotonicity assumption is actually much less strong than the full assumption of the linear regression algorithm, which is called linearity. Linearity is a technical term with a very simple meaning: if you graph the input and the output on a scatterplot, you should see a line that relates the inputs to the outputs, and not something with a more complicated shape, such as a curve or a wave. For those who think less visually, linearity means that changing the input by one unit always adds N units

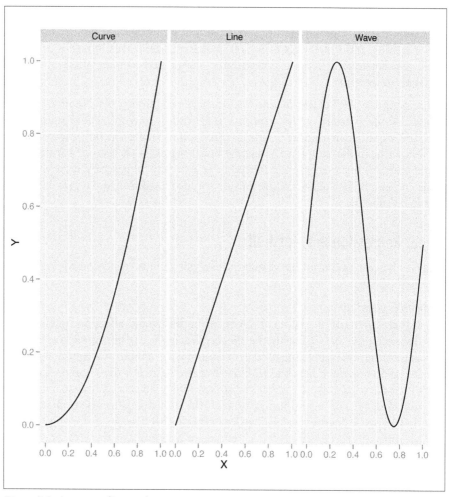

Figure 5-3. A curve, a line, and a wave

to the output or always subtracts N units from the output. Every linear model is monotonic, but curves can be monotonic without being linear. For that reason, linearity is more restrictive than monotonicity.

 Let's be perfectly clear about what we mean when we say line, curve, and wave by looking at examples of all three in Figure 5-3. Both curves and lines are monotonic, but waves are not monotonic, because they go up at times and down at other times.

Standard linear regression will work only if the data looks like a line when you plot the output against each of the inputs. It's actually possible to use linear regression to fit curves and waves, but that's a more advanced topic that we'll hold off discussing until Chapter 6.

Keeping the additivity and linearity assumptions in mind, let's start working through a simple example of linear regression. Let's go back to using our heights and weights data set one more time to show how linear regression works in this context. In Figure 5-4, we see the scatterplot that we've drawn so many times before. A small change to our plotting code will show us the line that a linear regression model will produce as a method for predicting weights using heights, as shown in Figure 5-5. We simply need to add a call to the geom_smooth function while specifying that we want to use the lm method, which implements "linear models."

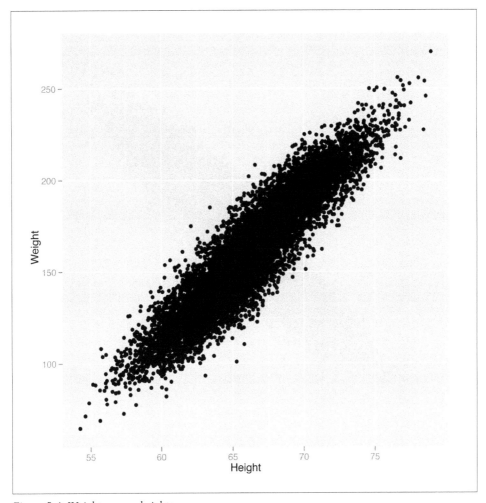

Figure 5-4. Weights versus heights

```
library('ggplot2')

heights.weights <- read.csv('data/01_heights_weights_genders.csv',
                            header = TRUE,
                            sep = ',')

ggplot(heights.weights, aes(x = Height, y = Weight)) +
  geom_point() +
  geom_smooth(method = 'lm')
```

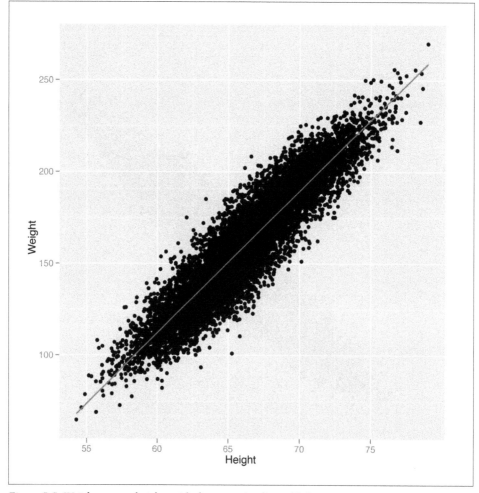

Figure 5-5. Weights versus heights with the regression line added

Looking at this plot should convince you that using a line to predict a person's weight given her height could work pretty well. For example, the line we see says that we should predict a weight of 105 pounds for someone who's 60 inches tall, and we should predict a weight of 225 pounds for someone who's 75 inches tall. So it seems reasonable to accept that using a line to make predictions is a smart thing to do. With that, the question we need to answer becomes: "How can we find the numbers that define the line we see in this plot?"

This is where R really shines as a language for doing machine learning: there's a simple function called lm in R that will do all of the work for us. To use lm, we need to specify a regression formula using the ~ operator. In our example, we're going to predict weight from height, so we write `Weight ~ Height`. If we were going to make predictions in the opposite direction, we'd write `Height ~ Weight`. If you want a way to pronounce these formulas, we personally like to say that `Height ~ Weight` means "height as a function of weight."

In addition to a specification of the regression, we need to tell R where the data we're using is stored. If the variables in your regression are global variables, you can skip this, but global variables of that sort are frowned upon by the R community.

Storing global variables in R is considered a bad practice because it is easy to lose track of what has been loaded into memory and what has not. This can cause unintentional consequences in coding, as it is easy to lose track of what it is in and out of memory. Further, it reduces the ease with which code can be shared. If global variables are not explicitly defined in code, someone who is less familiar with the data-loading process may miss something, and consequently the code may not work, because some data set or variable is missing.

It's better for you to explicitly specify the data source using the **data** parameter. Putting these together, we run a linear regression in R as follows:

```
fitted.regression <- lm(Weight ~ Height,
                        data = heights.weights)
```

Once you've run this call to lm, you can pull out the intercept of the regression line with a call to the coef function, which returns the coefficients for a linear model that relates inputs to outputs. We say "linear model" because regression can work in more than two dimensions. In two dimensions, we're fitting lines (hence the "linear" part), but in three dimensions we fit planes, and in more than three dimensions we fit hyperplanes.

If those terms don't mean anything to you, the intuition is simple: a flat surface in two dimensions is a line, whereas in three dimensions it's a plane, and in more than three dimensions, a flat surface is called a hyperplane. If that's not clear enough, we'd suggest reading *Flatland* [Abb92].

```
coef(fitted.regression)
#(Intercept)      Height
#-350.737192    7.717288
```

Understanding this output is, in some sense, what it means to understand linear regression. The simplest way to make sense of the output from coef is to write out explicitly the relationship that its output implies:

```
intercept <- coef(fitted.regression)[1]
slope <- coef(fitted.regression)[2]

# predicted.weight <- intercept + slope * observed.height
# predicted.weight == -350.737192 + 7.717288 * observed.height
```

This means that every increase of 1 inch in someone's height leads to an increase of 7.7 pounds in his weight. That strikes us as pretty reasonable. In contrast, the intercept is a bit weirder because it tells you how much a person who is 0 inches tall would weigh. According to R, she would weigh –350 pounds. If you're willing to do some algebra, you can deduce that a person has to be 45 inches tall for our prediction algorithm to say that he will weigh 0 pounds. In short, our regression model isn't so great for children or extremely short adults.

This is actually a systematic problem for linear regression in general: predictive models usually are not very good at predicting outputs for inputs that are very far removed from all of the inputs you've seen in the past.[1] Often you can do some work to improve the quality of your guesses outside of the range of data you use to train a model, but in this case there's probably no need because you're usually only going to make predictions for people who are over 4' tall and under 8' tall.

Beyond just running regressions and looking at the resulting coefficients, there's a lot more you can do in R to understand the results of a linear regression. Going through all of the different outputs that R can produce would take a whole book, so we'll just focus on a few of the most important parts after extracting the coefficients. When you're making predictions in a practical context, the coefficients are all that you need to know.

First, we want to get a sense of where our model is wrong. We do this by computing the model's predictions and comparing them against the inputs. To find the model's predictions, we use the predict function in R:

```
predict(fitted.regression)
```

Once we have our predictions in hand, we can calculate the difference between our predictions and the truth with a simple subtraction:

```
true.values <- with(heights.weights,Weight)
errors <- true.values - predict(fitted.regression)
```

The errors we calculate this way are called *residuals* because they're the part of our data that's left over after accounting for the part that a line can explain. You can get these residuals directly in R without the predict function by using the residuals function instead:

---

1. One technical way to describe this is to say that regressions are good at interpolation but not very good at extrapolation.

```
residuals(fitted.regression)
```

A common way to diagnose any obvious mistakes we're making when using linear regression is to plot the residuals against the truth:

```
plot(fitted.regression, which = 1)
```

 Here we've asked R to plot only the first regression diagnostic plot by specifying which = 1. There are other plots you can get, and we encourage you to experiment to see if you find any of the others helpful.

In this example, we can tell that our linear model works well because there's no systematic structure in the residuals. But here's a different example where a line isn't appropriate:

```
x <- 1:10
y <- x ^ 2

fitted.regression <- lm(y ~ x)
plot(fitted.regression, which = 1)
```

We can see obvious structure in the residuals for this problem. That's generally a bad thing when modeling data: a model should divide the world into signal (which **pre dict** gives you) and noise (which **residuals** gives you). If you can see signal in the residuals using your naked eye, then your model isn't powerful enough to extract all of the signal and leave behind only real noise as residuals. To solve this problem, Chapter 6 will talk about more powerful models for regression than the simple linear regression model we're working with now. But because great power brings with it great responsibility, Chapter 6 will actually focus on the unique problems that arise when we use models that are so powerful that they're actually too powerful to be used without caution.

For now, let's talk more carefully about how well we're doing with linear regression. Having the residuals is great, but there are so many of them that they can be overwhelming to work with. We'd like a single number to summarize the quality of our results.

The simplest measurement of error is to (1) take all the residuals, (2) square them to get the squared errors for our model, and (3) sum them together.

```
x <- 1:10
y <- x ^ 2

fitted.regression <- lm(y ~ x)

errors <- residuals(fitted.regression)
squared.errors <- errors ^ 2
sum(squared.errors)
#[1] 528
```

This simple sum of squared errors quantity is useful for comparing different models, but it has some quirks that most people end up disliking.

First, the sum of squared errors is larger for big data sets than for small data sets. To convince yourself of this, imagine a fixed data set and the sum of squared errors for that data set. Now add one more data point that isn't predicted perfectly. This new data point has to push the sum of squared errors up because adding a number to the previous sum of squared errors can only make the sum larger.

But there's a simple way to solve that problem: take the mean of the squared errors rather than the sum. That gives us the MSE measure we used earlier in this chapter. Although MSE won't grow consistently as we get more data the way that the raw sum of squared errors will, MSE still has a problem: if the average prediction is only off by 5, then the mean squared error will be 25. That's because we're squaring the errors before taking their mean.

```
x <- 1:10
y <- x ^ 2

fitted.regression <- lm(y ~ x)

errors <- residuals(fitted.regression)
squared.errors <- errors ^ 2
mse <- mean(squared.errors)
mse
#[1] 52.8
```

The solution to this problem of scale is trivial: we take the square root of the mean squared error to get the root mean squared error, which is the RMSE measurement we also tried out earlier in this chapter. RMSE is a very popular measure of performance for assessing machine learning algorithms, including algorithms that are far more sophisticated than linear regression. For just one example, the Netflix Prize was scored using RMSE as the definitive metric of how well the contestants' algorithms performed.

```
x <- 1:10
y <- x ^ 2

fitted.regression <- lm(y ~ x)

errors <- residuals(fitted.regression)
squared.errors <- errors ^ 2
mse <- mean(squared.errors)
rmse <- sqrt(mse)
rmse
#[1] 7.266361
```

One complaint that people have with RMSE is that it's not immediately clear what mediocre performance is. Perfect performance clearly gives you an RMSE of 0, but the pursuit of perfection is not a realistic goal in these tasks. Likewise, it isn't easy to recognize when a model is performing very poorly. For example, if everyone's heights are 5' and you predict 5,000', you'll get a huge value for RMSE. And you can do worse than that by predicting 50,000', and still worse by predicting 5,000,000'. The unbounded values that RMSE can take on make it difficult to know whether your model's performance is reasonable.

When you're running linear regressions, the solution to this problem is to use R^2 (pronounced "R squared"). The idea of R^2 is to see how much better your model does than we'd do if we were just using the mean. To make it easy to interpret, R^2 will always be between 0 and 1. If you're doing no better than the mean, it will be 0. And if you predict every data point perfectly, R^2 will be 1.

Because R^2 is always between 0 and 1, people tend to multiply it by 100 and say that it's the percent of the variance in the data you've explained with your model. This is a handy way to build up an intuition for how accurate a model is, even in a new domain where you don't have any experience about the standard values for RMSE.

To calculate R^2, you need to compute the RMSE for a model that uses only the mean output to make predictions for all of your example data. Then you need to compute the RMSE for your model. After that, it's just a simple arithmetic operation to produce R^2, which we've described in code here:

```
mean.rmse <- 1.09209343
model.rmse <- 0.954544

r2 <- 1 - (model.rmse / mean.rmse)
r2
#[1] 0.1259502
```

Predicting Web Traffic

Now that we've prepared you to work with regressions, this chapter's case study will focus on using regression to predict the amount of page views for the top 1,000 websites on the Internet as of 2011. The top five rows of this data set, which was provided to us by Neil Kodner, are shown in Table 5-3.

For our purposes, we're going to work with only a subset of the columns of this data set. We'll focus on five columns: Rank, PageViews, UniqueVisitors, HasAdvertising, and IsEnglish.

The Rank column tells us the website's position in the top 1,000 list. As you can see, Facebook is the number one site in this data set, and YouTube is the second. Rank is an interesting sort of measurement because it's an ordinal value in which numbers are used not for their true values, but simply for their order. One way to realize that the values don't matter is to realize that there's no real answer to questions like, "What's the 1.578th website in this list?" This sort of question *would* have an answer if the numbers being used were cardinal values. Another way to emphasize this distinction is to note that we could replace the ranks 1, 2, 3, and 4 with A, B, C, and D and not lose any information.

Table 5-3. Top websites data set

Rank	Site	Category	UniqueVisitors	Reach	PageViews	HasAd-vertising	InEnglish	TLD
1	facebook.com	Social Networks	880000000	47.2	9.1e+11	Yes	Yes	com
2	youtube.com	Online Video	800000000	42.7	1.0e+11	Yes	Yes	com
3	yahoo.com	Web Portals	660000000	35.3	7.7e+10	Yes	Yes	com
4	live.com	Search Engines	550000000	29.3	3.6e+10	Yes	Yes	com
5	wikipedia.org	Dictionaries & Encyclopedias	490000000	26.2	7.0e+09	No	Yes	org

The next column, `PageViews`, is the output we want to predict in this case study, and it tells us how many times the website was seen that year. This is a good way of measuring the popularity of sites such as Facebook with repeated visitors who tend to return many times.

> After you've finished reading this chapter, a good exercise to work on would be comparing `PageViews` with `UniqueVisitors` to find a way to tell which sorts of sites have lots of repeat visits and which sorts of sites have very few repeat visits.

The `UniqueVisitors` column tells us how many different people came to the website during the month when these measurements were taken. If you think that `PageViews` are easily inflated by having people refresh pages needlessly, the `UniqueVisitors` is a good way to measure how many *different people* see a site.

The `HasAdvertising` column tells us whether or not a website has ads on it. You might think that ads would be annoying and that people would, all else being equal, tend to avoid sites that have ads. We can explicitly test for this using regression. In fact, one of the great values of regression is that it lets us try to answer questions in which we have to talk about "all else being equal." We say "try" because the quality of a regression is only as good as the inputs we have. If there's an important variable that's missing from our inputs, the results of a regression can be very far from the truth. For that reason, you should always assume that the results of a regression are tentative: "If the inputs we had were sufficient to answer this question, then the answer would be...."

The `IsEnglish` column tells us whether a website is primarily in English. Looking through the list, it's clear that most of the top sites are primarily either English-language sites or Chinese-language sites. We've included this column because it's interesting to ask whether being in English is a positive thing or not. We're also including this column because it's an example in which the direction of causality isn't at all clear from a regression; does being written in English make a site more popular, or do more popular sites decide to convert to English because it's the lingua franca of the Internet? A regression model can tell you that two things are related, but it can't tell you whether one thing causes the other thing or whether things actually work the other way around.

Now that we've described the inputs we have and decided that PageViews is going to be our output, let's start to get a sense of how these things relate to one another. We'll start by making a scatterplot that relates PageViews with UniqueVisitors. We always suggest drawing scatterplots for numerical variables before you try to relate them by using regression because a scatterplot can make it clear when the linearity assumption of regression isn't satisfied.

```
top.1000.sites <- read.csv('data/top_1000_sites.tsv',
                           sep = '\t',
                           stringsAsFactors = FALSE)

ggplot(top.1000.sites, aes(x = PageViews, y = UniqueVisitors)) +
  geom_point()
```

The scatterplot we get from this call to ggplot (shown in Figure 5-6) looks terrible: almost all the values are bunched together on the x-axis, and only a very small number jump out from the pack. This is a common problem when working with data that's not normally distributed, because using a scale that's large enough to show the full range of values tends to place the majority of data points so close to each other that they can't be separated visually. To confirm that the shape of the data is the problem with this plot, we can look at the distribution of PageViews by itself:

```
ggplot(top.1000.sites, aes(x = PageViews)) +
  geom_density()
```

This density plot (shown in Figure 5-7) looks as completely impenetrable as the earlier scatterplot. When you see nonsensical density plots, it's a good idea to try taking the log of the values you're trying to analyze and make a density plot of those log-transformed values. We can do that with a simple call to R's log function:

```
ggplot(top.1000.sites, aes(x = log(PageViews))) +
  geom_density()
```

This density plot (shown in Figure 5-8) looks much more reasonable. For that reason, we'll start using the log-transformed PageViews and UniqueVisitors from now on. Recreating our earlier scatterplot on a log scale is easy:

```
ggplot(top.1000.sites, aes(x = log(PageViews), y = log(UniqueVisitors))) +
  geom_point()
```

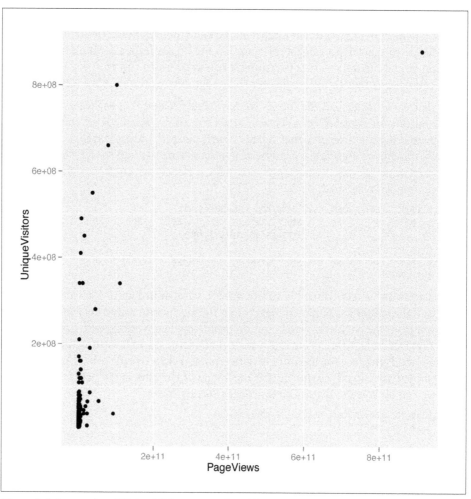

Figure 5-6. Scatterplot of UniqueVisitors versus PageViews

 The ggplot2 package also contains a convenience function to change the scale of an axis to the log. You can use the scale_x_log or scale_y_log in this case. Also, recall from our discussion in Chapter 4 that in some cases you will want to use the logp function in R to avoid the errors related to taking the log of zero. In this case, however, that is not a problem.

The resulting scatterplot shown in Figure 5-9 looks like there's a potential line to be drawn using regression. Before we use lm to fit a regression line, let's use geom_smooth with the method = 'lm' argument to see what the regression line will look like:

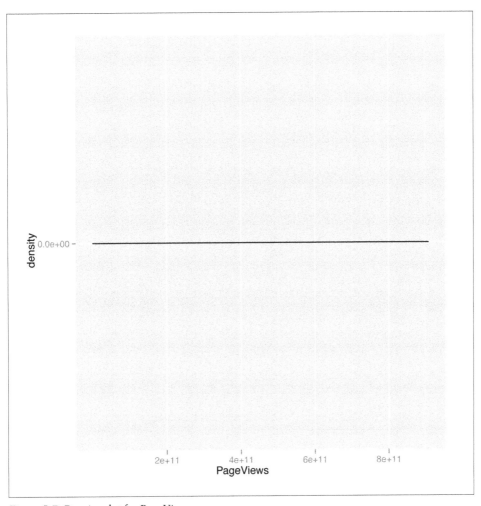

Figure 5-7. Density plot for PageViews

```
ggplot(top.1000.sites, aes(x = log(PageViews), y = log(UniqueVisitors))) +
  geom_point() +
  geom_smooth(method = 'lm', se = FALSE)
```

The resulting line, shown in Figure 5-10, looks promising, so let's find the values that define its slope and intercept by calling lm:

```
lm.fit <- lm(log(PageViews) ~ log(UniqueVisitors),
             data = top.1000.sites)
```

Now that we've fit the line, we'd like to get a quick summary of it. We could look at the coefficients using coef, or we could look at the RMSE by using residuals. But we'll introduce another function that produces a much more complex summary that we can walk through step by step. That function is conveniently called summary:

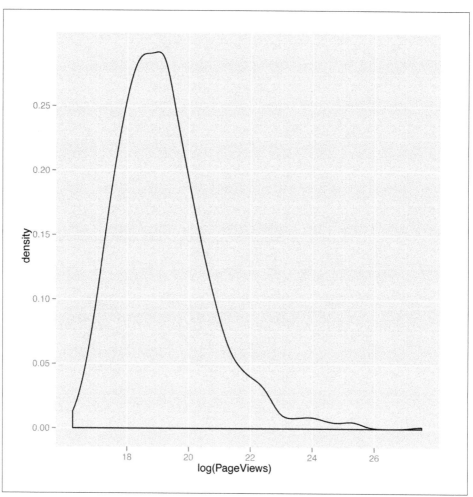

Figure 5-8. Log-scale density plot for PageViews

```
summary(lm.fit)

#Call:
#lm(formula = log(PageViews) ~ log(UniqueVisitors), data = top.1000.sites)
#
#Residuals:
#    Min     1Q  Median     3Q    Max
#-2.1825 -0.7986 -0.0741  0.6467  5.1549
#
#Coefficients:
#                    Estimate Std. Error t value Pr(>|t|)
#(Intercept)         -2.83441    0.75201  -3.769 0.000173 ***
#log(UniqueVisitors)  1.33628    0.04568  29.251 < 2e-16 ***
#---
```

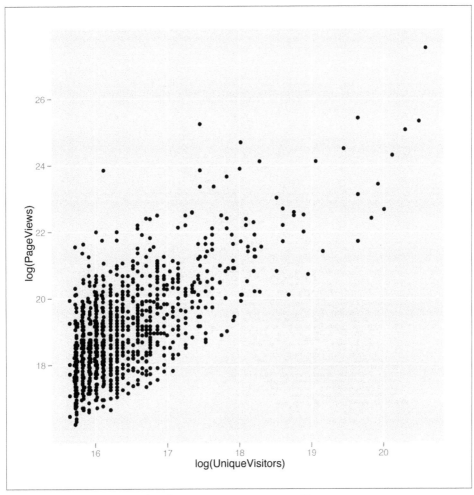

Figure 5-9. Log-scale scatterplot of UniqueVisitors versus PageViews

```
#Signif. codes:  0 '***' 0.001 '**' 0.01 '*' 0.05 '.' 0.1 ' ' 1
#
#Residual standard error: 1.084 on 998 degrees of freedom
#Multiple R-squared: 0.4616,    Adjusted R-squared: 0.4611
#F-statistic: 855.6 on 1 and 998 DF,  p-value: < 2.2e-16
```

The first thing that summary tells us is the call we made to lm. This isn't very useful when you're working at the console, but it can be helpful when you're working in larger scripts that make multiple calls to lm. When this is the case, this information helps you keep all of the models organized so you have a clear understanding of what data and variables went into each model.

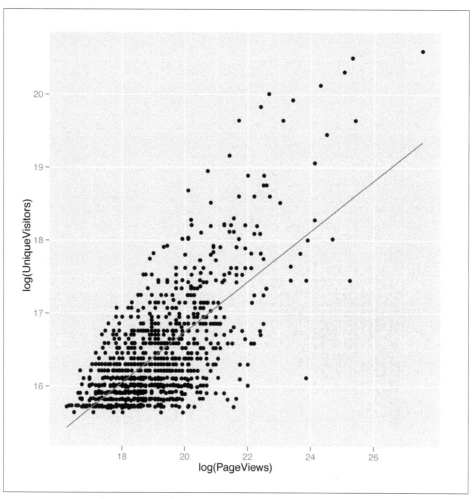

Figure 5-10. Log-scale scatterplot of UniqueVisitors versus PageViews with a regression line

The next thing that summary tells us are the quantiles of the residuals that you would compute if you called quantile(residuals(lm.fit)). Personally, we don't find this very helpful, although others may prefer looking for symmetry in the minimum and maximum residual, rather than looking at a scatterplot of the data. However, we almost always find graphical plots more informative than numerical summaries.

Next, summary tells us the coefficients of the regression in much more detail than coef would. The output from coef ends up in this table as the "Estimate" column. After that, there are columns for the "Std. Error," the "t value," and the p-value of each coefficient. These values are used to assess the uncertainty we have in the estimates we've computed; in other words, they're meant to be measurements of our confidence that the values we've computed from a specific data set are accurate descriptions of the real world that generated the data. The "Std. Error", for instance, can be used to produce a 95% confidence interval for the coefficient. The interpretation of this interval can be confusing, and it is occasionally presented in a misleading way. The interval indicates the bounds for which we can say, "95% of the time, the algorithm we use to construct intervals will include the true coefficient inside of the intervals it produces." If that's unclear to you, that's normal: the analysis of uncertainty is profoundly important, but far more difficult than the other material we're covering in this book. If you really want to understand this material, we'd recommend buying a proper statistics textbook such as *All of Statistics* [Wa03] or *Data Analysis Using Regression and Multilevel/Hierarchical Models* [GH06], and working through them in detail. Thankfully, the sort of qualitative distinctions that require attention to standard errors usually aren't necessary if you're just trying to hack together models to predict something.

The "t-value" and the p-value (written as "Pr(>|t|)" in the output from `summary`) are both measures of how confident we are that the true coefficient isn't zero. This is used to say that we are confident that there is a real relationship between the output and the input we're currently examining. For example, here we can use the "t value" column to assess how sure we are that `PageViews` really are related to `UniqueVisitors`. In our minds, these two numbers can be useful if you understand how to work with them, but they are sufficiently complicated that their usage has helped to encourage people to assume they'll never fully understand statistics. If you care whether you're confident that two variables are related, you should check whether the estimate is at least two standard errors away from zero. For example, the coefficient for `log(UniqueVisitors)` is 1.33628 and the standard error is 0.04568. That means that the coefficient is `1.33628 / 0.04568 == 29.25306` standard errors away from zero. If you're more than three standard errors away from zero, you can feel reasonably confident that your two variables are related.

 t-values and p-values are useful for deciding whether a relationship between two columns in your data is real or just an accident of chance. Deciding that a relationship exists is valuable, but understanding the relationship is another matter entirely. Regressions can't help you do that. People try to force them to, but in the end, if you want to understand the reasons why two things are related, you need more information than a simple regression can ever provide.

The traditional cutoff for being confident that an input is related to your output is to find a coefficient that's at least two standard errors away from zero.

The next piece of information that `summary` spits out are the significance codes for the coefficients. These are asterisks shown along the side that are meant to indicate how large the "t value" is or how small the p-value is. Specifically, the asterisks tell you whether you're passed a series of arbitrary cutoffs at which the p-value is less than 0.1, less than 0.05, less than 0.01, or less than 0.001. Please don't worry about these values; they're disturbingly popular in academia, but are really holdovers from a time when statistical analysis was done by hand rather than on a computer. There is literally no interesting content in these numbers that's not found in asking how many standard errors your estimate is away from 0. Indeed, you might have noticed in our earlier calculation that the "t value" for log(UniqueVisitors) was exactly the number of standard errors away from 0 that the coefficient for log(UniqueVisitors) was. That relationship between t-values and the number of standard errors away from 0 you are is generally true, so we suggest that you don't work with p-values at all.

The final pieces of information we get are related to the predictive power of the linear model we've fit to our data. The first piece, the "Residual standard error," is simply the RMSE of the model that we could compute using sqrt(mean(residuals(lm.fit) ^ 2)). The "degrees of freedom" refers to the notion that we've effectively used up two data points in our analysis by fitting two coefficients: the intercept and the coefficient for log(UniqueVisitors). This number, 998, is relevant because it's not very impressive to have a low RMSE if you've used 500 coefficients in your model to fit 1,000 data points. Using lots of coefficients when you have very little data is a form of overfitting that we'll talk about more in Chapter 6.

After that, we see the "Multiple R-squared". This is the standard "R-squared" we described earlier, which tells us what percentage of the variance in our data was explained by our model. Here we're explaining 46% of the variance using our model, which is pretty good. The "Adjusted R-squared" is a second measure that penalizes the "Multiple R-squared" for the number of coefficients you've used. In practice, we personally tend to ignore this value because we think it's slightly ad hoc, but there are many people who are very fond of it.

Finally, the last piece of information you'll see is the "F-statistic." This is a measure of the improvement of your model over using just the mean to make predictions. It's an alternative to "R-squared" that allows one to calculate a "p-value." Because we think that a "p-value" is usually deceptive, we encourage you to not put too much faith in the F-statistic. "p-values" have their uses if you completely understand the mechanism used to calculate them, but otherwise they can provide a false sense of security that will make you forget that the gold standard of model performance is predictive power on data that wasn't used to fit your model, rather than the performance of your model on the data that it was fit to. We'll talk about methods for assessing your model's ability to predict new data in Chapter 6.

Those pieces of output from summary get us quite far, but we'd like to include some other sorts of information beyond just relating PageViews to UniqueVisitors. We'll also include HasAdvertising and IsEnglish to see what happens when we give our model more inputs to work with:

```
lm.fit <- lm(log(PageViews) ~ HasAdvertising + log(UniqueVisitors) + InEnglish,
             data = top.1000.sites)
summary(lm.fit)

#Call:
#lm(formula = log(PageViews) ~ HasAdvertising + log(UniqueVisitors) +
```

```
#    InEnglish, data = top.1000.sites)
#
#Residuals:
#    Min     1Q  Median     3Q     Max
#-2.4283 -0.7685 -0.0632  0.6298  5.4133
#
#Coefficients:
#                     Estimate Std. Error t value Pr(>|t|)
#(Intercept)          -1.94502    1.14777  -1.695  0.09046 .
#HasAdvertisingYes     0.30595    0.09170   3.336  0.00088 ***
#log(UniqueVisitors)   1.26507    0.07053  17.936  < 2e-16 ***
#InEnglishNo           0.83468    0.20860   4.001 6.77e-05 ***
#InEnglishYes         -0.16913    0.20424  -0.828  0.40780
#---
#Signif. codes:  0 '***' 0.001 '**' 0.01 '*' 0.05 '.' 0.1 ' ' 1
#
#Residual standard error: 1.067 on 995 degrees of freedom
#Multiple R-squared: 0.4798,    Adjusted R-squared: 0.4777
#F-statistic: 229.4 on 4 and 995 DF,  p-value: < 2.2e-16
```

Again, we see that summary echoes our call to lm and prints out the residuals. What's new in this summary are the coefficients for all of the variables we've included in our more complicated regression model. Again, we see the intercept printed out as (Inter cept). The next entry is quite different from anything we saw before because our model now includes a factor. When you use a factor in a regression, the model has to decide to include one level as part of the intercept and the other level as something to model explicitly. Here you can see that HasAdvertising was modeled so that sites for which HasAdvertising == 'Yes' are separated from the intercept, whereas sites for which HasAdvertising == 'No' are folded into the intercept. Another way to describe this is to say that the intercept is the prediction for a website that has no advertising and has zero log(UniqueVisitors), which actually occurs when you have one UniqueVisitor.

We can see the same logic play out for InEnglish, except that this factor has many NA values, so there are really three levels of this dummy variable: NA, 'No', and 'Yes'. In this case, R treats the NA value as the default to fold into the regression intercept and fits separate coefficients for the 'No' and 'Yes' levels.

Now that we've considered how we can use these factors as inputs to our regression model, let's compare each of the three inputs we've used in isolation to see which has the most predictive power when used on its own. To do that, we can extract the R-squared for each summary in isolation:

```
lm.fit <- lm(log(PageViews) ~ HasAdvertising,
             data = top.1000.sites)
summary(lm.fit)$r.squared
#[1] 0.01073766

lm.fit <- lm(log(PageViews) ~ log(UniqueVisitors),
             data = top.1000.sites)
summary(lm.fit)$r.squared
#[1] 0.4615985
```

```
lm.fit <- lm(log(PageViews) ~ InEnglish,
             data = top.1000.sites)
summary(lm.fit)$r.squared
#[1] 0.03122206
```

As you can see, `HasAdvertising` explains only 1% of the variance, `UniqueVisitors` explains 46%, and `InEnglish` explains 3%. In practice, it's worth including all of the inputs in a predictive model when they're cheap to acquire, but if `HasAdvertising` were difficult to acquire programmatically, we'd advocate dropping it in a model with other inputs that have so much more predictive power.

Defining Correlation

Now that we've introduced linear regression, let's take a quick digression to discuss in more detail the word "correlation." In the strictest sense, two variables are correlated if the relationship between them can be described using a straight line. In other words, correlation is just a measure of how well linear regression could be used to model the relationship between two variables. 0 correlation indicates that there's no interesting line that relates the two variables. A correlation of 1 indicates that there's a perfectly positive straight line (going up) that relates the two variables. And a correlation of −1 indicates that there's a perfectly negative straight line (going down) that relates the two variables.

To make all of that precise, let's work through a short example. First, we'll generate some data that isn't strictly linear and then plot it:

```
x <- 1:10
y <- x ^ 2

ggplot(data.frame(X = x, Y = y), aes(x = X, y = Y)) +
    geom_point() +
    geom_smooth(method = 'lm', se = FALSE)
```

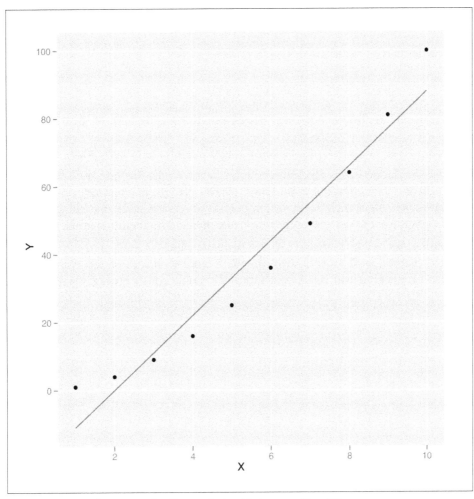

Figure 5-11. Line shows imperfect linear relationship between X and Y

This sample data is shown in Figure 5-11. As you can see, the line drawn using geom_smooth doesn't pass through all of the points, so the relationship between x and y can't be perfectly linear. But how close is it? To answer that, we compute the correlation in R using the cor function:

```
cor(x, y)
#[1] 0.9745586
```

Here we can see that x and y can be related pretty well using a straight line. The cor function gives us an estimate of how strong this relationship is. In this case it's **0.97**, which is almost 1.

How could we compute the correlation for ourselves rather than using cor? We can do that using lm, but first we need to scale both x and y. Scaling involves subtracting the mean of both variables and then dividing out by the standard deviation. You can perform scaling in R using the `scale` function:

```
coef(lm(scale(y) ~ scale(x)))
# (Intercept)       scale(x)
#-1.386469e-16  9.745586e-01
```

As you can see, in this case the correlation between x and y is exactly equal to the coefficient relating the two in linear regression after scaling both of them. This is a general fact about how correlations work, so you can always use linear regression to help you envision exactly what it means for two variables to be correlated.

Because correlation is just a measure of how linear the relationship between two variables is, it tells us nothing about causality. This leads to the maxim that "correlation is not causation." Nevertheless, it's very important to know whether two things are correlated if you want to use one of them to make predictions about the other.

That concludes our introduction to linear regression and the concept of correlation. In the next chapter, we'll show how to run much more sophisticated regression models that can handle nonlinear patterns in data and simultaneously prevent overfitting.

## CHAPTER 6

Regularization: Text Regression

Nonlinear Relationships Between Columns: Beyond Straight Lines

While we told you the truth in Chapter 5 when we said that linear regression assumes that the relationship between two variables is a straight line, it turns out you can also use linear regression to capture relationships that aren't well-described by a straight line. To show you what we mean, imagine that you have the data shown in panel A of Figure 6-1.

It's obvious from looking at this scatterplot that the relationship between X and Y isn't well-described by a straight line. Indeed, plotting the regression line shows us exactly what will go wrong if we try to use a line to capture the pattern in this data; panel B of Figure 6-1 shows the result.

We can see that we make systematic errors in our predictions if we use a straight line: at small and large values of x, we overpredict y, and we underpredict y for medium values of x. This is easiest to see in a residuals plot, as shown in panel C of Figure 6-1. In this plot, you can see all of the structure of the original data set, as none of the structure is captured by the default linear regression model.

Using `ggplot2`'s `geom_smooth` function without any `method` argument, we can fit a more complex statistical model called a Generalized Additive Model (or GAM for short) that provides a smooth, nonlinear representation of the structure in our data:

```
set.seed(1)

x <- seq(-10, 10, by = 0.01)
y <- 1 - x ^ 2 + rnorm(length(x), 0, 5)
ggplot(data.frame(X = x, Y = y), aes(x = X, y = Y)) +
  geom_point() +
  geom_smooth(se = FALSE)
```

The result, shown in panel D of Figure 6-1, lets us immediately see that we want to fit a curved line instead of a straight line to this data set.

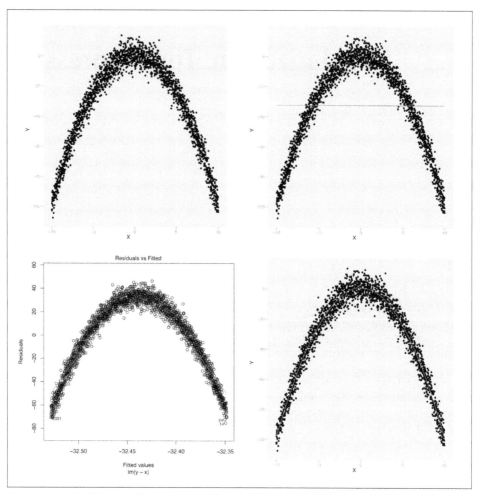

Figure 6-1. Modeling nonlinear data: (A) visualizing nonlinear relationships; (B) nonlinear relationships and linear regression; (C) structured residuals; (D) results from a generalized additive model

So how can we fit some sort of curved line to our data? This is where the subtleties of linear regression come up: linear regression can only fit lines in the input, but you can create new inputs that are nonlinear functions of your original inputs. For example, you can use the following code in R to produce a new input based on the raw input x that is the square of the raw input:

```
x.squared <- x ^ 2
```

You can then plot y against the new input, `x.squared`, to see a very different shape emerge from your data:

```
ggplot(data.frame(XSquared = x.squared, Y = y), aes(x = XSquared, y = Y)) +
  geom_point() +
  geom_smooth(method = 'lm', se = FALSE)
```

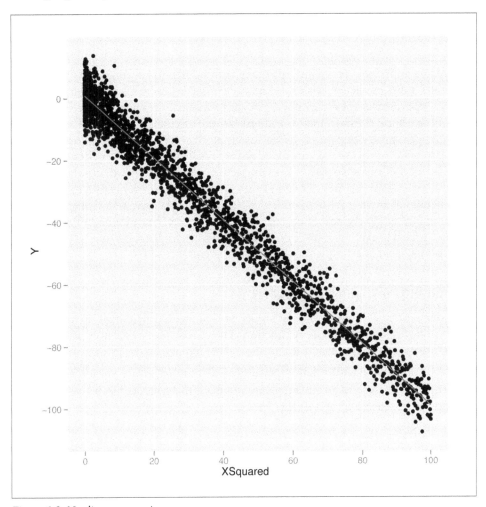

Figure 6-2. Nonlinear regression

As shown in Figure 6-2, plotting y against this new `x.squared` input gives us a fit that looks exactly like a straight line. Essentially, we've transformed our original nonlinear problem into a new problem in which the relationship between the two inputs really satisfies the linearity assumption of linear regression. This idea of replacing a complicated nonlinear problem with a simpler linear one using a transformation of the inputs comes up again and again in machine learning. Indeed, this intuition is the essence of the kernel trick that we'll discuss in Chapter 12. To see how much this simple squaring transformation improves our prediction quality, we can compare the R^2 values for linear regressions using x and x.squared:

```
summary(lm(y ~ x))$r.squared
#[1] 2.973e-06

summary(lm(y ~ x.squared))$r.squared
#[1] 0.9707
```

We've gone from accounting for 0% of the variance to accounting for 97%. That's a pretty huge jump for such a simple change in our model. In general, we might wonder how much more predictive power we can get from using more expressive models with more complicated shapes than lines. For mathematical reasons that are beyond the scope of this book, it turns out that you can capture essentially any type of relationship that might exist between two variables using more complex curved shapes. One approach to building up more complicated shapes is called polynomial regression, which we'll describe in the next part of this chapter. But the flexibility that polynomial regression provides is not a purely good thing, because it encourages us to mimic the noise in our data with our fitted model, rather than just the true underlying pattern we want to uncover. So the rest of this chapter will focus on the additional forms of discipline we need to exercise if we're going to use more complex tools such as polynomial regression instead of a simple tool like linear regression.

Introducing Polynomial Regression

With our earlier caveats in mind, let's start working with polynomial regression in R, which is implemented in the poly function. The easiest way to see how poly works is to build up from a simple example and show what happens as we give our model more expressive power to mimic the structure in our data.

We'll use a sine wave to create a data set in which the relationship between x and y could never be described by a simple line.

```
set.seed(1)

x <- seq(0, 1, by = 0.01)
y <- sin(2 * pi * x) + rnorm(length(x), 0, 0.1)

df <- data.frame(X = x, Y = y)

ggplot(df, aes(x = X, y = Y)) +
  geom_point()
```

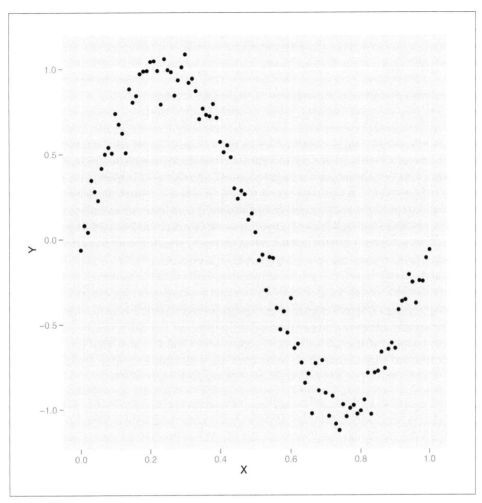

Figure 6-3. Nonlinear data

Just looking at this data, which is shown in Figure 6-3, it's clear that using a simple linear regression model won't work. But let's run a simple linear model and see how it performs.

```
summary(lm(Y ~ X, data = df))

#Call:
#lm(formula = Y ~ X, data = df)
#
#Residuals:
#     Min      1Q   Median      3Q      Max
#-1.00376 -0.41253 -0.00409  0.40664  0.85874
#
#Coefficients:
```

```
#              Estimate Std. Error t value Pr(>|t|)
#(Intercept)  0.94111    0.09057   10.39   <2e-16 ***
#X           -1.86189    0.15648  -11.90   <2e-16 ***
#---
#Signif. codes:  0 '***' 0.001 '**' 0.01 '*' 0.05 '.' 0.1 ' ' 1
#
#Residual standard error: 0.4585 on 99 degrees of freedom
#Multiple R-squared: 0.5885,  Adjusted R-squared: 0.5843
#F-statistic: 141.6 on 1 and 99 DF,  p-value: < 2.2e-16
```

Surprisingly, we're able to explain 60% of the variance in this data set using a linear model—despite the fact that we know the naive linear regression model is a bad model of wave data. We also know that a good model should be able to explain more than 90% of the variance in this data set, but we'd still like to figure out what the linear model did to produce such a good fit to the data. To answer our question, it's best to plot the results of fitting a linear regression using our preferred variant of geom_smooth in which we force geom_smooth to use a linear model by setting the option method = 'lm':

```
ggplot(data.frame(X = x, Y = y), aes(x = X, y = Y)) +
  geom_point() +
  geom_smooth(method = 'lm', se = FALSE)
```

Looking at Figure 6-4, we can see that the linear model finds a way to capture half of the sine wave's structure using a downward-sloping line. But this is not a great strategy, because you're systematically neglecting the parts of the data that aren't described by that downward-sloping line. If the sine wave were extended through another period, the R^2 for this model would suddenly drop closer and closer to 0%.

We can conclude that the default linear regression model overfits the quirks of our specific data set and fails to find its true underlying wave structure. But what if we give the linear regression algorithm more inputs to work with? Will it find a structure that's actually a wave?

One way to do this is to follow the logic we exploited at the start of this chapter and add new features to our data set. This time we'll add both the second power of x and the third power of x to give ourselves more wiggle room. As you see here, this change improves our predictive power considerably:

```
df <- transform(df, X2 = X ^ 2)
df <- transform(df, X3 = X ^ 3)

summary(lm(Y ~ X + X2 + X3, data = df))

#Call:
#lm(formula = Y ~ X + X2 + X3, data = df)
#
#Residuals:
#     Min      1Q   Median      3Q      Max
#-0.32331 -0.08538  0.00652  0.08320  0.20239
#
#Coefficients:
#              Estimate Std. Error t value Pr(>|t|)
#(Intercept)  -0.16341    0.04425  -3.693 0.000367 ***
```

```
#X            11.67844    0.38513  30.323  < 2e-16 ***
#X2          -33.94179    0.89748 -37.819  < 2e-16 ***
#X3           22.59349    0.58979  38.308  < 2e-16 ***
#---
#Signif. codes:  0 '***' 0.001 '**' 0.01 '*' 0.05 '.' 0.1 ' ' 1
#
#Residual standard error: 0.1153 on 97 degrees of freedom
#Multiple R-squared: 0.9745,  Adjusted R-squared: 0.9737
#F-statistic:  1235 on 3 and 97 DF,  p-value: < 2.2e-16
```

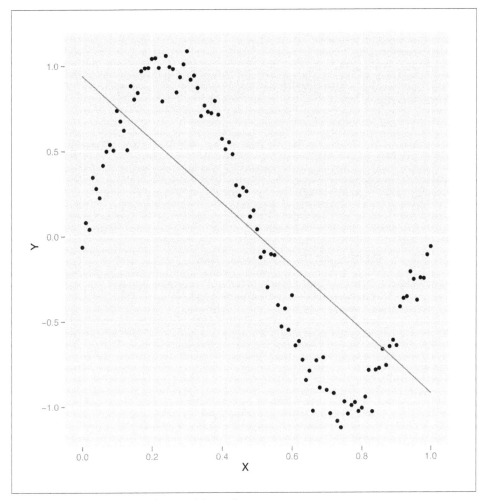

Figure 6-4. Nonlinear data with smooth linear fit

By adding two more inputs, we went from an R^2 of 60% to an R^2 of 97%. That's a huge increase. And, in principle, there's no reason why we can't follow this logic out as long as we want and keep adding more powers of X to our data set. But as we add more powers, we'll eventually start to have more inputs than data points. That's usually worrisome, because it means that we could, in principle, fit our data perfectly. But a more subtle problem with this strategy will present itself before then: the new columns we add to our data are so similar in value to the original columns that lm will simply stop working. In the output from summary shown next, you'll see this problem referred to as a "singularity."

```
df <- transform(df, X4 = X ^ 4)
df <- transform(df, X5 = X ^ 5)
df <- transform(df, X6 = X ^ 6)
df <- transform(df, X7 = X ^ 7)
df <- transform(df, X8 = X ^ 8)
df <- transform(df, X9 = X ^ 9)
df <- transform(df, X10 = X ^ 10)
df <- transform(df, X11 = X ^ 11)
df <- transform(df, X12 = X ^ 12)
df <- transform(df, X13 = X ^ 13)
df <- transform(df, X14 = X ^ 14)
df <- transform(df, X15 = X ^ 15)

summary(lm(Y ~ X + X2 + X3 + X4 + X5 + X6 + X7 + X8 + X9 + X10 + X11 + X12 + X13 +
           X14, data = df))

#Call:
#lm(formula = Y ~ X + X2 + X3 + X4 + X5 + X6 + X7 + X8 + X9 +
#    X10 + X11 + X12 + X13 + X14, data = df)
#
#Residuals:
#     Min        1Q    Median        3Q       Max
#-0.242662 -0.038179  0.002771  0.052484  0.210917
#
#Coefficients: (1 not defined because of singularities)
#              Estimate Std. Error t value Pr(>|t|)
#(Intercept) -6.909e-02  8.413e-02  -0.821    0.414
#X            1.494e+01  1.056e+01   1.415    0.161
#X2          -2.609e+02  4.275e+02  -0.610    0.543
#X3           3.764e+03  7.863e+03   0.479    0.633
#X4          -3.203e+04  8.020e+04  -0.399    0.691
#X5           1.717e+05  5.050e+05   0.340    0.735
#X6          -6.225e+05  2.089e+06  -0.298    0.766
#X7           1.587e+06  5.881e+06   0.270    0.788
#X8          -2.889e+06  1.146e+07  -0.252    0.801
#X9           3.752e+06  1.544e+07   0.243    0.809
#X10         -3.398e+06  1.414e+07  -0.240    0.811
#X11          2.039e+06  8.384e+06   0.243    0.808
#X12         -7.276e+05  2.906e+06  -0.250    0.803
#X13          1.166e+05  4.467e+05   0.261    0.795
#X14                NA         NA      NA       NA
#
#Residual standard error: 0.09079 on 87 degrees of freedom
#Multiple R-squared: 0.9858,  Adjusted R-squared: 0.9837
#F-statistic: 465.2 on 13 and 87 DF,  p-value: < 2.2e-16
```

The problem here is that the new columns we're adding with larger and larger powers of X are so correlated with the old columns that the linear regression algorithm breaks down and can't find coefficients for all of the columns separately. Thankfully, there is a solution to this problem that can be found in the mathematical literature: instead of naively adding simple powers of x, we add more complicated variants of x that work like successive powers of x, but aren't correlated with each other in the way that x and x^2 are. These variants on the powers of x are called orthogonal polynomials,[1] and you can easily generate them using the poly function in R. Instead of adding 14 powers of x to your data frame directly, you simply type poly(X, degree = 14) to transform x into something similar to X + X^2 + X^3 + ... + X^14, but with orthogonal columns that won't generate a singularity when running lm.

To confirm for yourself that the poly black box works properly, you can run lm with the output from poly and see that lm will, in fact, give you proper coefficients for all 14 powers of X:

```
summary(lm(Y ~ poly(X, degree = 14), data = df))

#Call:
#lm(formula = Y ~ poly(X, degree = 14), data = df)
#
#Residuals:
#      Min        1Q    Median        3Q       Max
#-0.232557 -0.042933  0.002159  0.051021  0.209959
#
#Coefficients:
#                        Estimate Std. Error t value Pr(>|t|)
#(Intercept)             0.010167   0.009038   1.125   0.2638
#poly(X, degree = 14)1  -5.455362   0.090827 -60.063  < 2e-16 ***
#poly(X, degree = 14)2  -0.039389   0.090827  -0.434   0.6656
#poly(X, degree = 14)3   4.418054   0.090827  48.642  < 2e-16 ***
#poly(X, degree = 14)4  -0.047966   0.090827  -0.528   0.5988
#poly(X, degree = 14)5  -0.706451   0.090827  -7.778 1.48e-11 ***
#poly(X, degree = 14)6  -0.204221   0.090827  -2.248   0.0271 *
#poly(X, degree = 14)7  -0.051341   0.090827  -0.565   0.5734
#poly(X, degree = 14)8  -0.031001   0.090827  -0.341   0.7337
#poly(X, degree = 14)9   0.077232   0.090827   0.850   0.3975
#poly(X, degree = 14)10  0.048088   0.090827   0.529   0.5979
#poly(X, degree = 14)11  0.129990   0.090827   1.431   0.1560
#poly(X, degree = 14)12  0.024726   0.090827   0.272   0.7861
#poly(X, degree = 14)13  0.023706   0.090827   0.261   0.7947
#poly(X, degree = 14)14  0.087906   0.090827   0.968   0.3358
#---
#Signif. codes:  0 '***' 0.001 '**' 0.01 '*' 0.05 '.' 0.1 ' ' 1
#
#Residual standard error: 0.09083 on 86 degrees of freedom
#Multiple R-squared: 0.986,  Adjusted R-squared: 0.9837
#F-statistic: 431.7 on 14 and 86 DF,  p-value: < 2.2e-16
```

In general, poly gives you a lot of expressive power. Mathematicians have shown that polynomial regression will let you capture a huge variety of complicated shapes in your data.

---

1. Orthogonal means uncorrelated.

But that isn't necessarily a good thing. One way to see that the added power provided by poly can be a source of trouble is to look at the shape of the models that poly generates as you increase the degree parameter. In the following example, we generate models using poly with degrees of 1, 3, 5, and 25. The results are shown in the panels of Figure 6-5.

```
poly.fit <- lm(Y ~ poly(X, degree = 1), data = df)
df <- transform(df, PredictedY = predict(poly.fit))

ggplot(df, aes(x = X, y = PredictedY)) +
  geom_point() +
  geom_line()

poly.fit <- lm(Y ~ poly(X, degree = 3), data = df)
df <- transform(df, PredictedY = predict(poly.fit))

ggplot(df, aes(x = X, y = PredictedY)) +
  geom_point() +
  geom_line()

poly.fit <- lm(Y ~ poly(X, degree = 5), data = df)
df <- transform(df, PredictedY = predict(poly.fit))

ggplot(df, aes(x = X, y = PredictedY)) +
  geom_point() +
  geom_line()

poly.fit <- lm(Y ~ poly(X, degree = 25), data = df)
df <- transform(df, PredictedY = predict(poly.fit))

ggplot(df, aes(x = X, y = PredictedY)) +
  geom_point() +
  geom_line()
```

We can continue this process indefinitely, but looking at the predicted values for our model makes it clear that eventually the shape we're fitting doesn't resemble a wave anymore, but starts to become distorted by kinks and spikes. The problem is that we're using a model that's more powerful than the data can support. Things work fine for smaller degrees such as 1, 3, or 5, but they start to break around degree 25. The problem we're seeing is the essence of overfitting. As our data grows in number of observations, we can let ourselves use more powerful models. But for any specific data set, there are always some models that are too powerful. How can we do something to stop this? And how we can get a better sense of what's going to go wrong if we give ourselves enough rope to hang ourselves with? The answer we'll propose is a mixture of *cross-validation* and *regularization*, two of the most important tools in the entire machine learning toolkit.

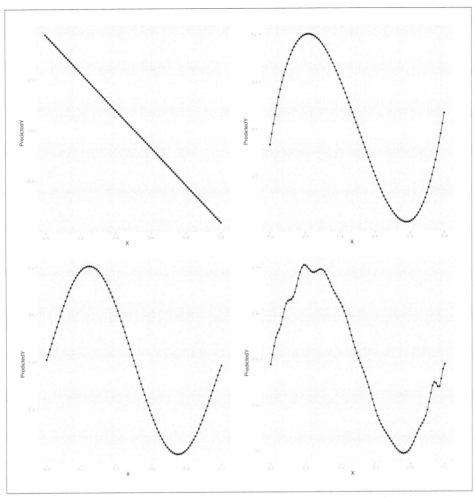

Figure 6-5. Polynomial regression: (A) degree 1; (B) degree 3; (C) degree 5; (D) degree 25

Methods for Preventing Overfitting

Before we can prevent overfitting, we need to give the term a rigorous meaning. We've talked about a model being overfit when it matches part of the noise in a data set rather than the true underlying signal. But if we don't know the truth, how can we tell that we're getting further away from it rather than closer?

The trick is to make clear what we mean by truth. For our purposes, a predictive model is close to the truth when its predictions about future data are accurate. But of course we don't have access to future data; we only have data from the past. Thankfully, we can simulate what it would be like to have access to future data by splitting up our past data into two parts.

A simple example will make our general strategy clear: imagine that we're trying to build a model to predict temperatures in the future. We have data for January through June and want to make predictions for July. We can see which of our models is best by fitting them to data from January through May and then testing these models against the data for June. If we had done this model-fitting step in May, we really would have been testing our model against future data. So we can use this data-splitting strategy to make a completely realistic simulation of the experience of testing our model against unseen data.

Cross-validation, at its core, simply refers to this ability of ours to simulate testing our model on future data by ignoring part of our historical data during the model-fitting process.

> If you went through the cases in Chapters 3 and 4, you'll remember that we did exactly this then. In each case we split our data to train and test our classification and ranking models.

Arguably, it's simply an instantiation of the scientific method that we were all taught as children: (1) formulate a hypothesis, (2) gather data, and (3) test it. There's just a bit of sleight of hand because we don't formulate a hypothesis based on existing data and then go out and gather more data. Instead, we ignore part of our data while formulating our hypotheses, so that we can magically rediscover that missing data when it comes time to test our predictions.

Before using cross-validation in a complex application, let's go through a toy example of how we might use cross-validation to select a degree for polynomial regression for the sine wave data we had before.

First, we'll recreate our sine wave data:

```
set.seed(1)

x <- seq(0, 1, by = 0.01)
y <- sin(2 * pi * x) + rnorm(length(x), 0, 0.1)
```

Then we need to split our data into two parts: a training set that we'll use to fit our model and a test set that we'll use to test the model's performance. The training set can be thought of as past data, whereas the test set is future data. For this example, we'll split the data exactly in half. For some applications, it's better to use more data for the training set (say, 80%) and less data for the test set (say, 20%) because the more data you have during model fitting, the better the fitted model will tend to be. As always, your mileage will vary, so experiment when facing any real-world problem. Let's do the split and then talk about the details:

```
n <- length(x)

indices <- sort(sample(1:n, round(0.5 * n)))
```

```
training.x <- x[indices]
training.y <- y[indices]

test.x <- x[-indices]
test.y <- y[-indices]

training.df <- data.frame(X = training.x, Y = training.y)
test.df <- data.frame(X = test.x, Y = test.y)
```

Here we've constructed a random vector of indices that defines the training set. It's always a good idea to randomly split the data when making a training set/test set split because you don't want the training set and test set to differ systematically—as might happen, for example, if you put only the smallest values for x into the training set and the largest values into the test set. The randomness comes from the use of R's sample function, which produces a random sample from a given vector. In our case we provide a vector of integers, 1 through n, and sample half of them. Once we've set the values for indices, we pull the training and test sets apart using R's vector indexing rules. Finally, we construct a data frame to store the data because it's easier to work with lm when using data frames.

Once we've split our data into a training set and test set, we want to test various degrees for our polynomial regression to see which works best. We'll use RMSE to measure our performance. To make our code a bit easier to read, we'll create a special rmse function:

```
rmse <- function(y, h)
{
  return(sqrt(mean((y - h) ^ 2)))
}
```

Then we'll loop over a set of polynomial degrees, which are the integers between 1 and 12:

```
performance <- data.frame()

for (d in 1:12)
{
  poly.fit <- lm(Y ~ poly(X, degree = d), data = training.df)

  performance <- rbind(performance,
                       data.frame(Degree = d,
                                  Data = 'Training',
                                  RMSE = rmse(training.y, predict(poly.fit))))

  performance <- rbind(performance,
                       data.frame(Degree = d,
                                  Data = 'Test',
                                  RMSE = rmse(test.y, predict(poly.fit,
                                         newdata = test.df))))
}
```

During each iteration of this loop, we're fitting a polynomial regression of degree d to the data in training.df and then assessing its performance on both training.df and test.df. We store the results in a data frame so that we can quickly analyze the results after finishing the loop.

 Here we use a slightly different data frame construction technique than we have in the past. We begin by assigning an empty data frame to the variable performance, to which we then iteratively add rows with the rbind function. As we have mentioned before, there are often many ways to accomplish the same data manipulation task in R, but rarely is a loop of this nature the most efficient. We use it here because the data is quite small and it allows the process of the algorithm to be understood most clearly, but keep this in mind when writing your own cross-validation tests.

Once the loop's finished executing, we can plot the performance of the polynomial regression models for all the degrees we've tried:

```
ggplot(performance, aes(x = Degree, y = RMSE, linetype = Data)) +
  geom_point() +
  geom_line()
```

The result, shown in Figure 6-6, makes it clear that using a degree in the middle of the range we've experimented with gives us the best performance on our test data. When the degree is as low as 1 or 2, the model doesn't capture the real pattern in the data, and we see very poor predictive performance on both the training and the test data. When a model isn't complex enough to fit even the training data, we call that underfitting.

On the opposite end of our graph near degrees 11 and 12, we see the predictions for the model start to get worse again on the test data. That's because the model is becoming too complex and noisy, and it fits quirks in the training data that aren't present in the test data. When you start to model quirks of chance in your data, that's what we call overfitting. Another way of thinking of overfitting is to notice that our performance on the training set and test set start to diverge as we go farther to the right in Figure 6-6: the training set error rate keeps going down, but the test set performance starts going up. Our model doesn't generalize to any data beyond the specific points it was trained on—and that makes it overfit.

Thankfully, our plot lets us know how to set the degree of our regression to get the best performance from our model. This intermediate point, which is neither underfit nor overfit, would be very hard to discover without using cross-validation.

Having given a quick explanation of how we can use cross-validation to deal with overfitting, we'll switch to discussing another approach to preventing overfitting, which is called regularization. Regularization is quite different from cross-validation in spirit, even though we'll end up using cross-validation to provide a demonstration that regularization is able to prevent overfitting. We'll also have to use cross-validation to calibrate our regularization algorithm, so the two ideas will ultimately become intimately connected.

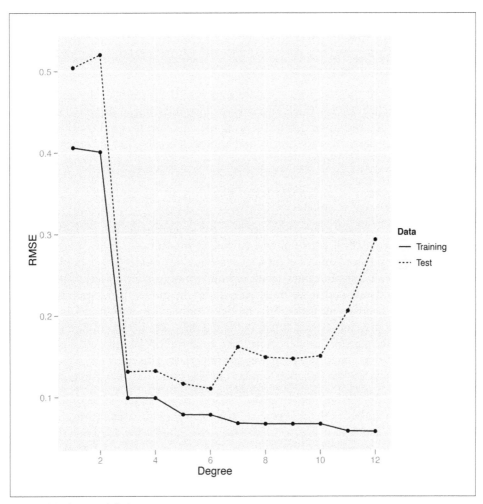

Figure 6-6. Cross-validation

Preventing Overfitting with Regularization

Throughout this chapter we've talked about models being too complex, but never gave a formal definition of complexity. One approach when working with polynomial regression would be to say that models are more complex when the degree is larger; a polynomial of degree 2 is more complex than a polynomial of degree 1, for example.

But that doesn't help us for linear regression in general. So we'll use an alternative measure of complexity: we'll say that a model is complicated when the coefficients are large. For example, we would say that the model y ~ 5 * x + 2 is more complicated than the model y ~ 3 * x + 2. By the same logic, we'll say that the model y ~ 1 * x^2 + 1 * x + 1 is more complicated than the model y ~ 1 * x + 1. To use this definition in practice, we can fit a model using lm and then measure its complexity by summing over the values returned by coef:

```
lm.fit <- lm(y ~ x)
model.complexity <- sum(coef(lm.fit) ^ 2)
```

Here we've squared the coefficients before summing them so that they don't cancel each other out when we add them all together. This squaring step is often called the *L2 norm*. An alternative approach to squaring the coefficients is to take the absolute value of the coefficients instead; this second approach is called the *L1 norm*. Here we compute the two of them in R:

```
lm.fit <- lm(y ~ x)
l2.model.complexity <- sum(coef(lm.fit) ^ 2)
l1.model.complexity <- sum(abs(coef(lm.fit)))
```

These measures of model complexity might seem strange at first, but you'll see in a moment that they really are helpful when trying to prevent overfitting. The reason is that we can use this measure of complexity to force our model to be simpler during model fitting. We'll talk about the details of how this occurs in Chapter 7, but the big idea for the time being is that we trade off making the model fit the training data as well as possible against a measure of the model's complexity. This brings us to one of the most critical decision criteria when modeling data: because we make a trade-off between fitting the data and model complexity, we'll end up selecting a simpler model that fits worse over a more complex model that fits better. This trade-off, which is what we mean by regularization, ultimately prevents overfitting by restraining our model from matching noise in the training data we use to fit it.

For now, let's talk about the tools you can use to work with regularization in R. For this chapter, we'll stick to using the glmnet package, which provides a function called glmnet that fits linear models using regularization. To see how glmnet works, let's go back one last time to our sine wave data:

```
set.seed(1)

x <- seq(0, 1, by = 0.01)
y <- sin(2 * pi * x) + rnorm(length(x), 0, 0.1)
```

To use glmnet, we first have to convert our vector copy of x to a matrix using the matrix function. After that, we call glmnet in the reverse order than the one you would use with lm and its ~-operator syntax:

```
x <- matrix(x)

library('glmnet')
glmnet(x, y)

#Call:  glmnet(x = x, y = y)
#
#       Df    %Dev    Lambda
# [1,]   0 0.00000 0.542800
# [2,]   1 0.09991 0.494600
```

```
# [3,]  1 0.18290 0.450700
# [4,]  1 0.25170 0.410600
# [5,]  1 0.30890 0.374200
...
#[51,]  1 0.58840 0.005182
#[52,]  1 0.58840 0.004721
#[53,]  1 0.58850 0.004302
#[54,]  1 0.58850 0.003920
#[55,]  1 0.58850 0.003571
```

When you call `glmnet` in this way, you get back an entire set of possible regularizations of the regression you've asked it to perform. At the top of the list is the strongest regularization that `glmnet` performed, and at the bottom of the list is the weakest regularization that was calculated. In the output we've quoted here, we show the first five rows and the last five.

Let's talk about the interpretation of each of the columns of the output for those 10 rows we've shown. Each row of the output contains three columns: (1) `Df`, (2) `%Dev`, and (3) `Lambda`. The first column, `Df`, tells you how many coefficients in the model ended up being nonzero. You should note that this does not include the intercept term, which you don't want to penalize for its size. Knowing the number of nonzero coefficients is useful because many people would like to be able to assert that only a few inputs really matter, and we can assert this more confidently if the model performs well even when assigning zero weight to many of the inputs. When the majority of the inputs to a statistical model are assigned zero coefficients, we say that the model is sparse. Developing tools for promoting sparsity in statistical models is a major topic in contemporary machine learning research.

The second column, `%Dev`, is essentially the R^2 for this model. For the top row, it's 0% because you have a zero coefficient for the one input variable and therefore can't get better performance than just using a constant intercept. For the bottom row, the `Dev` is 59%, which is the value you'd get from using `lm` directly, because `lm` doesn't do any regularization at all. In between these two extremes of regularizing the model down to only an intercept and doing no regularization at all, you'll see values for `Dev` that range from 9% to 58%.

The last column, `Lambda`, is the most important piece of information for someone learning about regularization. `Lambda` is a parameter of the regularization algorithm that controls how complex the model you fit is allowed to be. Because it controls the values you'll eventually get for the main parameters of the model, `Lambda` is often referred to as a *hyperparameter*.

We'll talk about the detailed meaning of `Lambda` in Chapter 7, but we can easily give you the main intuition. When `Lambda` is very large, you penalize your model very heavily for being complex, and this penalization pushes all of the coefficients toward zero. When `Lambda` is very small, you don't penalize your model much at all. At the farthest end of this spectrum toward weaker regularization, we can set `Lambda` to 0 and get results like those from an unregularized linear regression of the sort we'd fit using `lm`.

But it's generally somewhere inside of these two extremes that we can find a setting for Lambda that gives the best possible model. How can you find this value for Lambda? This is where we employ cross-validation as part of the process of working with regularization. Instead of playing with the degree of a polynomial regression, we can set the degree to a high value, such as 10, right at the start. And then we would fit the model with different values for Lambda on a training set and see how it performs on a held-out test set. After doing this for many values of Lambda, we would be able to see which value of Lambda gives us the best performance on the test data.

 You absolutely must assess the quality of your regularization on held-out test data. Increasing the strength of regularization can only worsen your performance on the training data, so there is literally zero information you can learn from looking at your performance on the training data.

With that approach in mind, let's go through an example now. As before, we'll set up our data and split it into a training set and a test set:

```
set.seed(1)

x <- seq(0, 1, by = 0.01)
y <- sin(2 * pi * x) + rnorm(length(x), 0, 0.1)

n <- length(x)

indices <- sort(sample(1:n, round(0.5 * n)))

training.x <- x[indices]
training.y <- y[indices]

test.x <- x[-indices]
test.y <- y[-indices]

df <- data.frame(X = x, Y = y)
training.df <- data.frame(X = training.x, Y = training.y)
test.df <- data.frame(X = test.x, Y = test.y)

rmse <- function(y, h)
{
  return(sqrt(mean((y - h) ^ 2)))
}
```

But this time we'll loop over values of Lambda instead of degrees. Thankfully, we don't have to refit the model each time, because glmnet stores the fitted model for many values of Lambda after a single fitting step.

```
library('glmnet')

glmnet.fit <- with(training.df, glmnet(poly(X, degree = 10), Y))

lambdas <- glmnet.fit$lambda
```

```
performance <- data.frame()

for (lambda in lambdas)
{
  performance <- rbind(performance,
    data.frame(Lambda = lambda,
               RMSE = rmse(test.y, with(test.df, predict(glmnet.fit, poly(X,
                           degree = 10), s = lambda)))))
}
```

Having computed the model's performance for different values of Lambda, we can construct a plot to see where in the range of lambdas we're testing we can get the best performance on new data:

```
ggplot(performance, aes(x = Lambda, y = RMSE)) +
  geom_point() +
  geom_line()
```

Looking at Figure 6-7, it seems like we get the best possible performance with Lambda near 0.05. So to fit a model to the full data, we can select that value and train our model on the entire data set. Here we do just that:

```
best.lambda <- with(performance, Lambda[which(RMSE == min(RMSE))])

glmnet.fit <- with(df, glmnet(poly(X, degree = 10), Y))
```

After fitting our final model to the whole data set, we can use coef to examine the structure of our regularized model:

```
coef(glmnet.fit, s = best.lambda)
#11 x 1 sparse Matrix of class "dgCMatrix"
#                         1
#(Intercept)  0.0101667
#1           -5.2132586
#2            0.0000000
#3            4.1759498
#4            0.0000000
#5           -0.4643476
#6            0.0000000
#7            0.0000000
#8            0.0000000
#9            0.0000000
#10           0.0000000
```

As you can see from looking at this table, we end up using only 3 nonzero coefficients, even though the model has the ability to use 10. Selecting a simpler model like this one, even when more complicated models are possible, is the major strategy behind regularization. And with regularization in our toolkit, we can employ polynomial regression with a large degree and still keep ourselves from overfitting the data.

With the basic ideas behind regularization in place, let's look at a practical application in this chapter's case study.

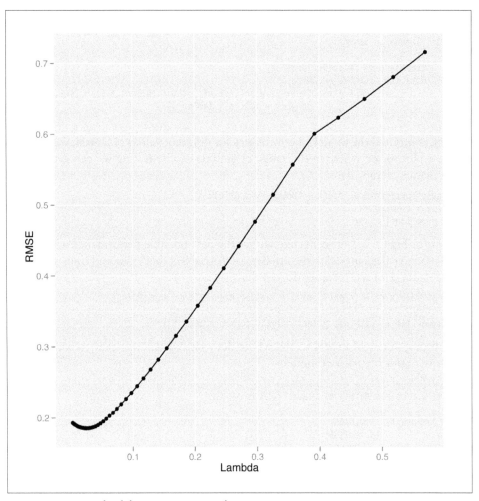

Figure 6-7. Varying lambda parameter in regularization

Text Regression

Cross-validation and regularization are both powerful tools that allow us to use complex models that can mimic very intricate patterns in our data without overfitting. One
of the most interesting cases in which we can employ regularization is when we use text
to predict some continuous output; for example, we might try to predict how volatile
a stock will be based on its IPO filings. When using text as an input for a regression
problem, we almost always have far more inputs (words) than observations (documents). If we have more observations than 1-grams (single words), we can simply consider 2-grams (pairs of words) or 3-grams (triplets of words) until we have more *n*-grams
than documents. Because our data set has more columns than rows, unregularized

linear regression will always produce an overfit model. For that reason, we have to use some form of regularization to get any meaningful results.

To give you a sense of this problem, we'll work through a simple case study in which we try to predict the relative popularity of the top-100-selling books that O'Reilly has ever published using only the descriptions of those books from their back covers as input. To transform these text descriptions into a useful set of inputs, we'll convert each book's description into a vector of word counts so that we can see how often words such as "the" and "Perl" occur in each description. The results of our analysis will be, in theory, a list of the words in a book's description that predict high sales.

 Of course, it's always possible that the prediction task simply can't be achieved. This may be the result of the model assigning high coefficients to words that are essentially arbitrary. That is, it may be that there are very few common words in the descriptions of popular O'Reilly books, but because the model does not know this it will still attempt to fit the data and assign value to some words. In this case, however, the results would provide little to no new information about what makes these words useful. This problem will not come up explicitly in this example, but it is very important to keep in mind when performing text regression.

To get started, let's load in our raw data set and transform it into a document term matrix using the tm package that we introduced in Chapter 3:

```
ranks <- read.csv('data/oreilly.csv', stringsAsFactors = FALSE)

library('tm')

documents <- data.frame(Text = ranks$Long.Desc.)
row.names(documents) <- 1:nrow(documents)

corpus <- Corpus(DataframeSource(documents))
corpus <- tm_map(corpus, tolower)
corpus <- tm_map(corpus, stripWhitespace)
corpus <- tm_map(corpus, removeWords, stopwords('english'))

dtm <- DocumentTermMatrix(corpus)
```

Here we've loaded in the ranks data set from a CSV file, created a data frame that contains the descriptions of the books in a format that tm understands, created a corpus from this data frame, standardized the case of the text, stripped whitespace, removed the most common words in English, and built our document term matrix. With that work done, we've finished all of the substantive transformations we need to make to our data. With those finished, we can manipulate our variables a little bit to make it easier to describe our regression problem to glmnet:

```
x <- as.matrix(dtm)
y <- rev(1:100)
```

Here we've converted the document term matrix into a simple numeric matrix that's easier to work with. And we've encoded the ranks in a reverse encoding so that the highest-ranked book has a y-value of 100 and the lowest-ranked book has a y-value of 1. We do this so that the coefficients that predict the popularity of a book are positive when they signal an increase in popularity; if we used the raw ranks instead, the coefficients for those same words would have to be negative. We find that less intuitive, even though there's no substantive difference between the two coding systems.

Finally, before running our regression analysis, we need to initialize our random seed and load the glmnet package:

```
set.seed(1)

library('glmnet')
```

Having done that setup work, we can loop over several possible values for Lambda to see which gives the best results on held-out data. Because we don't have a lot of data, we do this split 50 times for each value of Lambda to get a better sense of the accuracy we get from different levels of regularization. In the following code, we set a value for Lambda, split the data into a training set and test set 50 times, and then assess our model's performance on each split.

```
performance <- data.frame()

for (lambda in c(0.1, 0.25, 0.5, 1, 2, 5))
{
  for (i in 1:50)
  {
    indices <- sample(1:100, 80)
    training.x <- x[indices, ]
    training.y <- y[indices]

    test.x <- x[-indices, ]
    test.y <- y[-indices]

    glm.fit <- glmnet(training.x, training.y)
    predicted.y <- predict(glm.fit, test.x, s = lambda)
    rmse <- sqrt(mean((predicted.y - test.y) ^ 2))

    performance <- rbind(performance,
                         data.frame(Lambda = lambda,
                                    Iteration = i,
                                    RMSE = rmse))
  }
}
```

After computing the performance of the model for these different values of Lambda, we can compare them to see where the model does best:

```
ggplot(performance, aes(x = Lambda, y = RMSE)) +
  stat_summary(fun.data = 'mean_cl_boot', geom = 'errorbar') +
  stat_summary(fun.data = 'mean_cl_boot', geom = 'point')
```

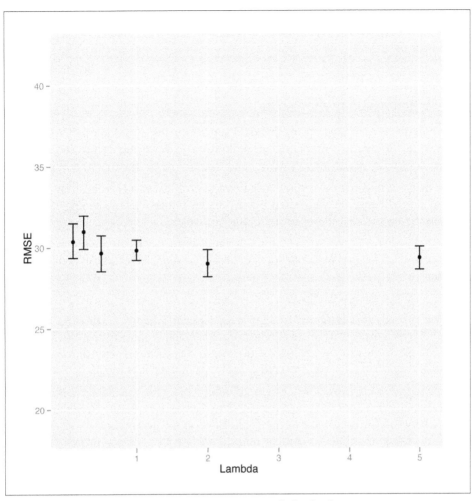

Figure 6-8. Results of varying lambda parameter on O'Reilly book sales

Unfortunately, looking at Figure 6-8 suggests that this is our first example of a failed attempt to apply a statistical method to data. It's clear that the model gets better and better with higher values of Lambda, but that occurs exactly when the model reduces to nothing more than an intercept. At that point, we're not using any text data at all. In short, there's no signal here that our text regression can find. Everything we see turns out to be noise when you test the model against held-out data.

Although that means we don't have a better idea of how to write a back cover description for a book to make sure it sells well, it's a valuable lesson for anyone working in machine learning to absorb: sometimes there's just no signal to be found in the data you're working with. The following quote summarizes the problem well:

The data may not contain the answer. The combination of some data and an aching desire for an answer does not ensure that a reasonable answer can be extracted from a given body of data.

—John Tukey

Logistic Regression to the Rescue

But we don't have to give up on this data set completely yet. Although we haven't succeeded at building a tool that predicts ranks from texts, we might try to do something simpler and see if we can predict whether a book appears in the top 50 or not.

To do that, we're going to switch our regression problem to a classification problem. Instead of predicting one of infinitely many possible ranks, we're switching to a simple categorical judgment: is this book in the top 50 or not?

Because this distinction is so much broader and simpler, we can hope that it will be easier to extract a signal from our small data set. To start, let's add class labels to our data set:

```
y <- rep(c(1, 0), each = 50)
```

Here we've used the 0/1 dummy coding we discussed in Chapter 2, where a 1 indicates that a book is in the top 50, and a 0 indicates that a book is *not* in the top 50. With that coding in place, we can use the logistic regression classification algorithm we demonstrated at the end of Chapter 2 to predict presence in the list of top 50 books.

Logistic regression is, deep down, essentially a form of regression in which one predicts the probability that an item belongs to one of two categories. Because probabilities are always between 0 and 1, we can threshold them at 0.5 to construct a classification algorithm. Other than the fact that the outputs are between 0 and 1, logistic regression behaves essentially identically to linear regression. The only difference is that you need to threshold the outputs to produce class predictions. We'll go through that thresholding step after we show you how easy it is to fit a logistic regression in R.

To start, we'll fit a logistic regression to the entire data set just so you can see how it's done:

```
regularized.fit <- glmnet(x, y, family = 'binomial')
```

The only difference between this call to `glmnet` and the call we made earlier to perform linear regression is that we set an additional parameter, `family`, which controls the type of errors you expect to see when making predictions. We didn't discuss this in Chapter 5, but linear regression assumes that the errors you see have a Gaussian distribution, whereas logistic regression assumes that the errors are binomially distributed. We won't discuss the details of the binomial distribution, but you should know that it's the statistical distribution of data you'd get from flipping a coin. For that reason, the binomial distribution produces errors that are all 0s or 1s, which, of course, is what we need for classification.

To elaborate on that, let's show you three calls you could make to `glmnet`:

```
regularized.fit <- glmnet(x, y)

regularized.fit <- glmnet(x, y, family = 'gaussian')

regularized.fit <- glmnet(x, y, family = 'binomial')
```

The first call is the one we made earlier in this chapter to perform linear regression. The second call is actually equivalent to the first call, except that we've made explicit the default value of the `family` parameter, which is set to `'gaussian'` automatically. The third call is the way we perform logistic regression. As you can see, switching an analysis from linear regression to logistic regression is just a matter of switching the error family.[2]

Having fit a logistic regression to the entire data set, let's see what the predictions from our model look like using the `predict` function:

```
predict(regularized.fit, newx = x, s = 0.001)

#1      4.884576
#2      6.281354
#3      4.892129
...
#98    -5.958003
#99    -5.677161
#100   -4.956271
```

As you can see, the output contains both positive and negative values, even though we're hoping to get predictions that are 0 or 1. There are two things we can do with these raw predictions.

The first is to threshold them at 0 and make 0/1 predictions using the `ifelse` function:

```
ifelse(predict(regularized.fit, newx = x, s = 0.001) > 0, 1, 0)

#1     1
#2     1
#3     1
...
#98    0
#99    0
#100   0
```

The second is to convert these raw predictions into probabilities, which we can more easily interpret—though we'd have to do the thresholding again at 0.5 to get the 0/1 predictions we generated previously. To convert raw logistic regression predictions into probabilities, we'll use the `inv.logit` function from the `boot` package:

---

2. There are quite a few other possible error families that can be used, but that would require a whole book to cover in depth. That said, we encourage you to explore on your own!

```
library('boot')

inv.logit(predict(regularized.fit, newx = x, s = 0.001))
#1    0.992494427
#2    0.998132627
#3    0.992550485
...
#98   0.002578403
#99   0.003411583
#100  0.006989922
```

If you want to know the details of how inv.logit works, we recommend looking at the source code for that function to figure out the mathematical transformation that it's computing. For our purposes, we just want you to understand that logistic regression expects its outputs to be transformed through the inverse logit function before you can produce probabilities as outputs. For that reason, logistic regression is often called the logit model.

Whichever way you decide to transform the raw outputs from a logistic regression, what really matters is that logistic regression provides you with a tool that does classification just as readily as we performed linear regression in Chapter 5. So let's try using logistic regression to see how well we can classify books into the top 50 or below. As you'll notice, the code to do this is essentially identical to the code we used earlier to fit our rank prediction model using linear regression:

```
set.seed(1)

performance <- data.frame()

for (i in 1:250)
{
  indices <- sample(1:100, 80)
  training.x <- x[indices, ]
  training.y <- y[indices]

  test.x <- x[-indices, ]
  test.y <- y[-indices]

  for (lambda in c(0.0001, 0.001, 0.0025, 0.005, 0.01, 0.025, 0.5, 0.1))
  {
    glm.fit <- glmnet(training.x, training.y, family = 'binomial')
    predicted.y <- ifelse(predict(glm.fit, test.x, s = lambda) > 0, 1, 0)
    error.rate <- mean(predicted.y != test.y)

    performance <- rbind(performance,
                         data.frame(Lambda = lambda,
                                    Iteration = i,
                                    ErrorRate = error.rate))
  }
}
```

The algorithmic changes in this code snippet relative to the one we used for linear regression are few: (1) the calls to glmnet, where we use the binomial error family parameter for logistic regression; (2) the thresholding step that produces 0/1 predictions from the raw logistic predictions; and (3) the use of error rates rather than RMSE as our measure of model performance. Another change you might notice is that we've chosen to perform 250 splits of the data rather than 50 so that we can get a better sense of our mean error rate for each setting of lambda. We've done this because the error rates end up being very close to 50%, and we wanted to confirm that we're truly doing better than chance when making predictions. To make this increased splitting more efficient, we've reversed the order of the splitting and lambda loops so that we don't redo the split for every single value of lambda. This saves a lot of time and serves as a reminder that writing effective machine learning code requires that you behave like a good programmer who cares about writing efficient code.

But we're more interested in our performance on this data set, so let's graph our error rate as we sweep through values of lambda:

```
ggplot(performance, aes(x = Lambda, y = ErrorRate)) +
  stat_summary(fun.data = 'mean_cl_boot', geom = 'errorbar') +
  stat_summary(fun.data = 'mean_cl_boot', geom = 'point') +
  scale_x_log10()
```

The results tell us that we've had real success replacing regression with classification. For low values of lambda, we're able to get better than chance performance when predicting whether a book will be among the top 50, which is a relief. Although this data was just not sufficient to fit a sophisticated rank prediction regression, it turns out to be large enough to fit a much simpler binary distinction that splits books into the top 50 and below.

And that's a general lesson we'll close this chapter on: sometimes simpler things are better. Regularization forces us to use simpler models so that we get higher performance on our test data. And switching from a regression model to a classification model can give you much better performance because the requirements for a binary distinction are generally much weaker than the requirements for predicting ranks directly.

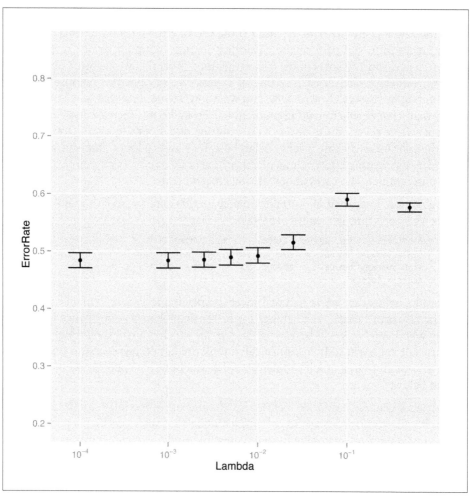

Figure 6-9. Error rates for classifying books in the top 50 versus lambda

## CHAPTER 7

Optimization: Breaking Codes

Introduction to Optimization

So far we've treated most of the algorithms in this book as partial black boxes, in that we've focused on understanding the inputs you're expected to use and the outputs you'll get. Essentially, we've treated machine learning algorithms as a library of functions for performing prediction tasks.

In this chapter, we're going to examine some of the techniques that are used to implement the most basic machine learning algorithms. As a starting point, we're going to put together a function for fitting simple linear regression models with only one predictor. That example will allow us to motivate the idea of viewing the act of fitting a model to data as an optimization problem. An optimization problem is one in which we have a machine with some knobs that we can turn to change the machine's settings and a way to measure how well the machine is performing with the current settings. We want to find the best possible settings, which will be those that maximize some simple measure of how well the machine is performing. That point will be called the *optimum*. Reaching it will be called *optimization*.

Once we have a basic understanding of how optimization works, we'll embark on our major task: building a very simple code-breaking system that treats deciphering an encrypted text as an optimization problem.

Because we're going to build our own linear regression function, let's go back to our standard example data set: people's heights and weights. As we've already done, we're going to assume that we can predict weights by computing a function of their heights. Specifically, we'll assume that a linear function works, which looks like this in R:

```
height.to.weight <- function(height, a, b)
{
  return(a + b * height)
}
```

In Chapter 5 we went through the details of computing the slope and intercept of this line using the lm function. In this example, the a parameter is the slope of the line and the b parameter is the intercept, which tells us how much a person whose height is zero should weigh.

With this function in hand, how can we decide which values of a and b are best? This is where optimization comes in: we want to first define a measure of how well our function predicts weights from heights and then change the values of a and b until we predict as well as we possibly can.

How do we do this? Well, lm already does all of this for us. It has a simple error function that it tries to optimize, and it finds the best values for a and b using a very specific algorithm that works only for ordinary linear regression.

Let's just run lm to see its preferred values for a and b:

```
heights.weights <- read.csv('data/01_heights_weights_genders.csv')

coef(lm(Weight ~ Height, data = heights.weights))
#(Intercept)      Height
#-350.737192    7.717288
```

Why are these reasonable choices for a and b? To answer that, we need to know what error function lm is using. As we said briefly in Chapter 5, lm is based on an error measure called "squared error," which works in the following way:

1. Fix values for a and b.
2. Given a value for height, make a guess at the associated weight.
3. Take the true weight, and subtract the predicted weight. Call this the error.
4. Square the error.
5. Sum the squared errors over all of your examples to get your sum of squared errors.

 For interpretation, we usually take the mean rather than the sum, and compute square roots. But for optimization, none of that is truly necessary, so we can save some small amount of computational time by just calculating the sum of squared errors.

The last two steps are closely related; if we weren't summing the errors for each data point together, squaring wouldn't be helpful. Squaring is essential precisely because summing all of the raw errors together would give us zero total error.

 Showing that this is always true isn't hard, but requires the sort of algebra we're trying to avoid in this book.

Let's go through some code that implements this approach:

```
squared.error <- function(heights.weights, a, b)
{
  predictions <- with(heights.weights, height.to.weight(Height, a, b))
  errors <- with(heights.weights, Weight - predictions)
  return(sum(errors ^ 2))
}
```

Let's evaluate `squared.error` at some specific values of a and b to get a sense of how this works (the results are in Table 7-1):

```
for (a in seq(-1, 1, by = 1))
{
  for (b in seq(-1, 1, by = 1))
  {
    print(squared.error(heights.weights, a, b))
  }
}
```

Table 7-1. Squared error over a grid

a	b	Squared error
-1	-1	536271759
-1	0	274177183
-1	1	100471706
0	-1	531705601
0	0	270938376
0	1	98560250
1	-1	527159442
1	0	267719569
1	1	96668794

As you can see, some values of a and b give much lower values for `squared.error` than others. That means we really want to find the best values for a and b now that we have a meaningful error function that tells us something about our ability to make predictions. That's the first part of our optimization problem: set up a metric that we can then try to minimize or maximize. That metric is usually called our *objective function*. The problem of optimization then becomes the problem of finding the best values for a and b to make that objective function as small or as big as possible.

One obvious approach is called grid search: compute a table like the one we just showed you for a large enough range of values of a and b, and then pick the row with the lowest value of `squared.error`. This approach will always give you the best value in the grid you've searched, so it's not an unreasonable approach. But there are some serious problems with it:

- How close should the values you use to define the grid be to each other? Should a be the values 0, 1, 2, 3? Or should a be the values 0, 0.001, 0.002, 0.003? In other words, what is the right resolution at which we should perform our search? Answering this question requires that you evaluate both grids and see which is more informative, an evaluation that is computationally costly and effectively introduces another a second optimization problem in which you're optimizing the size of the grid you use. Down that road lies infinite loop madness.
- If you want to evaluate this grid at 10 points per parameter for 2 parameters, you need to build a table with 100 entries. But if you want this evaluate this grid at 10 points per parameter for 100 parameters, you need to build a table with 10^{100} entries. This problem of exponential growth is so widespread in machine learning that it's called the Curse of Dimensionality.

Because we want to be able to use linear regression with hundreds or even thousands of inputs, grid search is out for good as an optimization algorithm. So what can we do? Thankfully for us, computer scientists and mathematicians have been thinking about the problem of optimization for a long time and have built a large set of off-the-shelf optimization algorithms that you can use. In R, you should usually make a first pass at an optimization problem using the `optim` function, which provides a black box that implements many of the most popular optimization algorithms.

To show you how `optim` works, we're going to use it to fit our linear regression model. We hope that it produces values for a and b that are similar to those produced by `lm`:

```
optim(c(0, 0),
      function (x)
      {
        squared.error(heights.weights, x[1], x[2])
      })
#$par
#[1] -350.786736    7.718158
#
#$value
#[1] 1492936
#
#$counts
#function gradient
#     111       NA
#
#$convergence
#[1] 0
#
#$message
#NULL
```

As the example shows, `optim` takes a few different arguments. First, you have to pass a numeric vector of starting points for the parameters you're trying to optimize; in this case, we say that a and b should default to the vector `c(0, 0)`. After that, you have to pass a function to `optim` that expects to receive a vector, which we've called x, that contains all of the parameters you want to optimize. Because we usually prefer writing functions with multiple named parameters, we like wrapping our error function in an anonymous function that takes only the argument x, which we then partition out to our primary error function. In this example, you can see how we've wrapped `squared.error`.

Running this call to `optim` gives us values for `a` and `b`, respectively, as the values of `par`. And these values are very close to those produced by `lm`, which suggests that `optim` is working.[1] In practice, `lm` uses an algorithm that's much more specific to linear regression than our call to `optim`, which makes the results more precise than those produced by `optim`. If you're going to work through your own problems, though, `optim` is much better to work with because it can be used with models other than linear regression.

The other outputs we get from `optim` are sometimes less interesting. The first we've shown is `value`, which tells us the value of the squared error evaluated at the parameters that `optim` claims are best. After that, the `counts` value tells us how many times `optim` evaluated the main function (here called `function`) and the gradient (here called `gradient`), which is an optional argument that can be passed if you know enough calculus to compute the gradient of the main function.

If the term "gradient" doesn't mean anything to you, don't worry. We dislike calculating gradients by hand, and so we usually let `optim` do its magic without specifying any value for the optional gradient argument. Things have worked out pretty well so far for us, though your mileage may vary.

The next value is `convergence`, which tells us whether or not `optim` found a set of parameters it's confident are the best possible. If everything went well, you'll see a 0. Check the documentation for `optim` for an interpretation of the different error codes you can get when your result isn't 0. Finally, the `message` value tells us whether anything happened that we need to know about.

In general, `optim` is based on a lot of clever ideas from calculus that help us perform optimization. Because it's quite mathematically complex, we won't get into the inner workings of `optim` at all. But the general spirit of what `optim` is doing is very simple to express graphically. Imagine that you only wanted to find the best value of `a` after you decided that `b` had to be 0. You could calculate the squared error when you vary only `a` using the following code:

```
a.error <- function(a)
{
  return(squared.error(heights.weights, a, 0))
}
```

To get a sense of where the best value of `a` is, you can graph the squared error as a function of `a` using the `curve` function in R, which will evaluate a function or expression

---

1. Or at least that it's doing the same wrong thing as `lm`.

at a set of many values of a variable x and then plot the output of that function or the value of the expression. In the following example, we've evaluated a.error at many values of x, and because of a quirk in R's evaluation of expressions, we've had to use sapply to get things to work.

```
curve(sapply(x, function (a) {a.error(a)}), from = -1000, to = 1000)
```

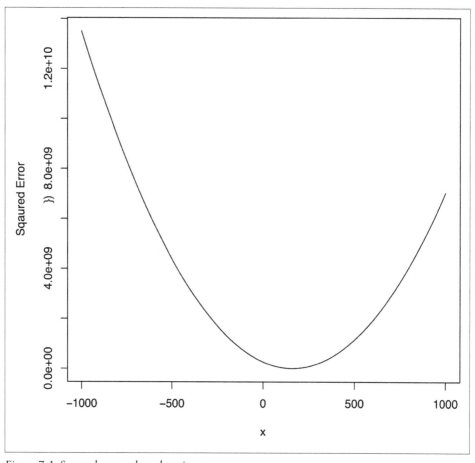

Figure 7-1. Squared error when changing a

Looking at Figure 7-1, there seems to be a single value for a that's best, and every value that moves further away from that value for a is worse. When this happens, we say that there's a *global optimum*. In cases like that, optim can use the shape of the squared error function to figure out in which direction to head after evaluating the error function at a single value of a; using this local information to learn something about the global structure of your problem lets optim hit the optimum very quickly.

To get a better sense of the full regression problem, we also need to look at how the error function responds when we change b:

```
b.error <- function(b)
{
  return(squared.error(heights.weights, 0, b))
}

curve(sapply(x, function (b) {b.error(b)}), from = -1000, to = 1000)
```

Looking at Figure 7-2, the error function looks like it also has a global optimum for b. Taken together with evidence that there's a global optimum for a, this suggests that it should be possible for optim to find a single best value for both a and b that minimizes our error function.

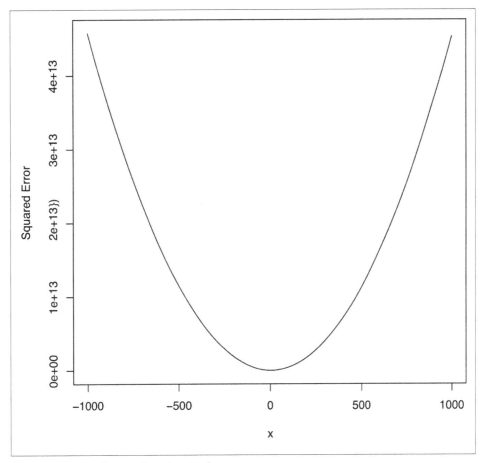

Figure 7-2. Squared error when changing b

More generally, we can say that optim works because it can search for the troughs of these graphs in all of the parameters at once by using calculus. It works faster than grid search because it can use information about the point it's currently considering to infer something about nearby points. That lets it decide which direction it should move in to improve its performance. This adaptive behavior makes it much more efficient than grid search.

Ridge Regression

Now that we know a little bit about how to use optim, we can start to use optimization algorithms to implement our own version of ridge regression. Ridge regression is a specific kind of regression that incorporates regularization, which we discussed in Chapter 6. The only difference between ordinary least squares regression and ridge regression is the error function: ridge regression considers the size of the regression coefficients to be part of the error term, which encourages the coefficients to be small. In this example, this pushes the slope and intercept toward zero.

Other than changing our error function, the only added complexity to running ridge regression is that we now have to include an extra parameter, lambda, that adjudicates between the importance of minimizing the squared error of our predictions and minimizing the values of a and b so that we don't overfit our data. The extra parameter for this regularized algorithm is called a hyperparameter and was discussed in some detail in Chapter 6. Once we've selected a value of lambda, we can write the ridge error function as follows:

```
ridge.error <- function(heights.weights, a, b, lambda)
{
  predictions <- with(heights.weights, height.to.weight(Height, a, b))
  errors <- with(heights.weights, Weight - predictions)
  return(sum(errors ^ 2) + lambda * (a ^ 2 + b ^ 2))
}
```

As we discussed in Chapter 6, we can select a value of lambda using cross-validation. For the rest of this chapter, we're simply going to assume that you've already done this and that the proper value of lambda is 1.

With the ridge error function defined in R, a new call to optim solves the ridge regression problem as easily as the original ordinary least squares problem was solved:

```
lambda <- 1

optim(c(0, 0),
      function (x)
      {
        ridge.error(heights.weights, x[1], x[2], lambda)
      })
#$par
#[1] -340.434108    7.562524
#
#$value
#[1] 1612443
#
```

```
#$counts
#function gradient
#      115       NA
#
#$convergence
#[1] 0
#
#$message
#NULL
```

Looking at the output of optim, we can see that we've produced a slightly smaller intercept and slope for our line than we had when using lm, which gave an intercept of -350 and a slope of 7.7. In this toy example that's not really helpful, but in the large-scale regressions we ran in Chapter 6, including a penalty for large coefficients was essential to getting meaningful results out of our algorithm.

In addition to looking at the fitted coefficients, we can also repeat the calls we were making to the curve function to see why optim should be able work with ridge regression in the same way that it worked for ordinary linear regression. The results are shown in Figures 7-3 and 7-4.

```
a.ridge.error <- function(a, lambda)
{
  return(ridge.error(heights.weights, a, 0, lambda))
}

curve(sapply(x, function (a) {a.ridge.error(a, lambda)}), from = -1000, to = 1000)

b.ridge.error <- function(b, lambda)
{
  return(ridge.error(heights.weights, 0, b, lambda))
}

curve(sapply(x, function (b) {b.ridge.error(b, lambda)}), from = -1000, to = 1000)
```

Hopefully this example convinces you that you can get a lot done in machine learning just by understanding how to use functions such as optim to minimize some measure of prediction error. We recommend working through a few examples on your own and then playing around with different error functions that you've invented yourself. This is particularly helpful when you try an error function like the absolute error function shown here:

```
absolute.error <- function
(heights.weights, a, b)
{
  predictions <- with(heights.weights, height.to.weight(Height, a, b))
  errors <- with(heights.weights, Weight - predictions)
  return(sum(abs(errors)))
}
```

For technical reasons related to calculus, this error term won't play nice with optim. Fully explaining why things break is a little hard without calculus, but it's actually possible to communicate the big idea visually. We just repeat the calls to curve that we've been making:

```
a.absolute.error <- function(a)
{
  return(absolute.error(heights.weights, a, 0))
}

curve(sapply(x, function (a) {a.absolute.error(a)}), from = -1000, to = 1000)
```

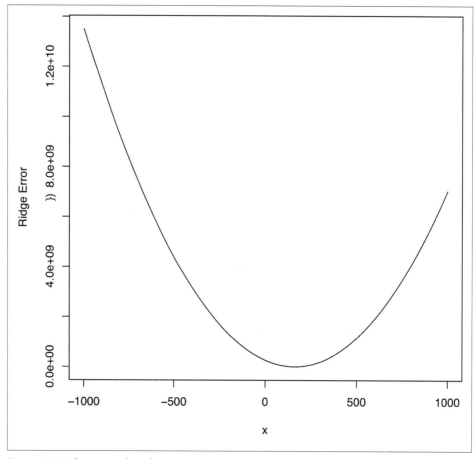

Figure 7-3. Ridge error when changing a

As you can see in Figure 7-5, the absolute error curve is much sharper than the squared error curve or the ridge error curve. Because the shape is so sharp, optim doesn't get as much information about the direction in which it should go from a single point and won't necessarily reach the global optimum, even though we can clearly see that one exists from simple visual inspection.

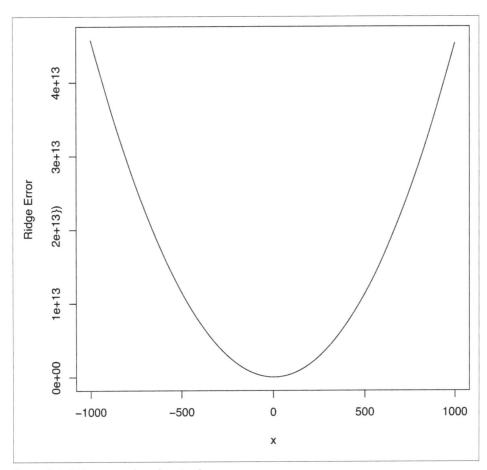

Figure 7-4. Ridge error when changing b

Because some types of error metrics break otherwise powerful algorithms, part of the art of doing machine learning well is learning when simple tools like optim will work and learning when you'll need something more powerful. There are algorithms that work for absolute error optimization, but they're beyond the scope of this book. If you're interested in learning more about this, find your local math guru and get him to talk to you about convex optimization.

Code Breaking as Optimization

Moving beyond regression models, almost every algorithm in machine learning can be viewed as an optimization problem in which we try to minimize some measure of prediction error. But sometimes our parameters aren't simple numbers, and so evaluating your error function at a single point doesn't give you enough information about nearby points to use optim. For these problems, we could use grid search, but there are other

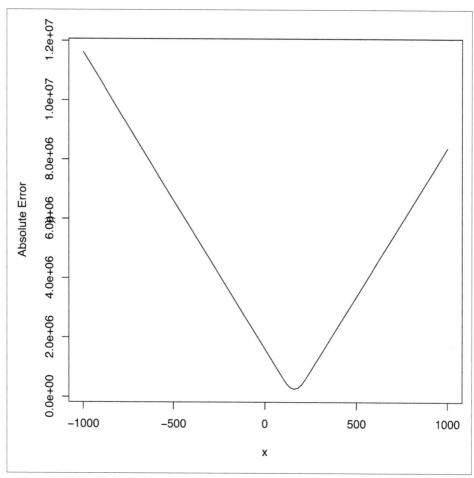

Figure 7-5. Absolute error when changing a

approaches that work better than grid search. We'll focus on one approach that's fairly intuitive and very powerful. The big idea behind this new approach, which we'll call stochastic optimization, is to move through the range of possible parameters slightly randomly, but making sure to head in directions where your error function tends to go down rather than up. This approach is related to a lot of popular optimization algorithms that you may have heard of, including simulated annealing, genetic algorithms, and Markov chain Monte Carlo (MCMC). The specific algorithm we'll use is called the Metropolis method; versions of the Metropolis method power a lot of modern machine learning algorithms.

To illustrate the Metropolis method, we'll work through this chapter's case study: breaking secret codes. The algorithm we're going to define isn't a very efficient decryption system and would never be seriously used for production systems, but it's a very clear example of how to use the Metropolis method. Importantly, it's also an example where most out-of-the-box optimization algorithms such as optim could never work.

So let's state our problem: given a string of letters that you know are encrypted using a substitution cipher, how do we decide on a decryption rule that gives us the original text? If you're not familiar with substitution ciphers, they're the simplest possible encryption system, in which you replace every letter in the unencrypted message with a fixed letter in the encrypted message. ROT13[2] is probably the most famous example, though the Caesar cipher might also be known to you. The Caesar cipher is one very simple substitution cipher in which you replace every letter with its neighbor in the alphabet: "a" becomes "b," "b" becomes "c," and "c" becomes "d." (If you're wondering about the edge case here: "z" becomes "a.")

To make sure it's clear how to work with ciphers in R, let's create the Caesar cipher for now so that we can see how to implement it in R:

```
english.letters <- c('a', 'b', 'c', 'd', 'e', 'f', 'g', 'h', 'i', 'j', 'k',
                      'l', 'm', 'n', 'o', 'p', 'q', 'r', 's', 't', 'u', 'v',
                      'w', 'x', 'y', 'z')

caesar.cipher <- list()
inverse.caesar.cipher <- list()

for (index in 1:length(english.letters))
{
  caesar.cipher[[english.letters[index]]] <- english.letters[index %% 26 + 1]
  inverse.caesar.cipher[[english.letters[index %% 26 + 1]]] <- english.letters[index]
}

print(caesar.cipher)
```

Now that we have the cipher implemented, let's build some functions so that we can translate a string using a cipher:

```
apply.cipher.to.string <- function(string, cipher)
{
  output <- ''

  for (i in 1:nchar(string))
  {
    output <- paste(output, cipher[[substr(string, i, i)]], sep = '')
  }

  return(output)
}

apply.cipher.to.text <- function(text, cipher)
{
```

2. ROT13 replaces every letter with the letter 13 positions further in the alphabet. "a" becomes "n," "b" becomes "o," and so on.

```
    output <- c()

    for (string in text)
    {
        output <- c(output, apply.cipher.to.string(string, cipher))
    }

    return(output)
}

apply.cipher.to.text(c('sample', 'text'), caesar.cipher)
```

Now we have some basic tools for working with ciphers, so let's start thinking about the problem of breaking the codes we might come across. Just as we did with linear regression, we'll solve the problem of breaking substitution ciphers in several parts:

1. Define a measure of the quality of a proposed decryption rule.
2. Define an algorithm for proposing new potential decryption rules that randomly modifies versions of our current best rule.
3. Define an algorithm for moving progressively toward better decryption rules.

To start thinking about how to measure the quality of decryption rule, let's suppose that you were given a piece of text that you knew had been encrypted using a substitution cipher. For example, if Julius Caesar had sent an encrypted message to you, it might look like this: "wfoj wjej wjdj." After inverting the Caesar cipher, this text will turn out to be the famous phrase "veni vidi vici."

Now imagine that you only had a piece of encrypted text and a guarantee that the original message was in standard English. How would you go about decoding it?

The approach we're going to take here to solving that problem is to say that a rule is good if it turns the encrypted message into normal English. Given a proposed decryption rule, you'll run the rule on our encrypted text and see whether the output is realistic English. For example, imagine that we had two proposed decryption rules, A and B, whose results are the following:

- decrypt(T, A) = xgpk xkfk xkek
- decrypt(T, B) = veni vidi vici

After seeing the outputs from the two proposed rules, you think it's pretty clear that rule B is better than rule A. How are we making this intuitive decision? We can tell that B is better than A because the text from rule B looks like real language rather than nonsense, whereas rule A's text looks completely nonsensical. To transform that human intuition into something automatic that we can program a computer to do, we'll use a lexical database that provides the probability for any word we see. Real language will then be equivalent to text built out of words that have high probability, whereas fake language will be equivalent to text with words that have low probability. The only complexity with this approach is dealing with words that don't exist at all. Because their probability is zero and we're going to estimate the probability of a piece of text as a whole by multiplying the probability of the individual words together, we'll need to replace zero with something really small, like our machine's smallest distinguishable floating-point difference, which we'll call epsilon, to use our algorithm. Once we've handled that edge case, we can use a lexical database to rank the quality of two pieces of translated text by finding the probability of each word and then multiplying these probabilities together to find an estimate of the probability of the text as a whole.

Using a lexical database to calculate the probability of the decrypted text will give us our error metric for evaluating a proposed decryption rule. Now that we have an error function, our code-breaking problem has turned entirely into a optimization problem, so we just need to find decryption rules that produce text with high probability.

Unfortunately, the problem of finding the rule with the highest text probability isn't close to being the sort of problem where `optim` would work. Decryption rules can't be graphed and don't have the smoothness that `optim` needs when it's trying to figure how to head toward better rules. So we need a totally new optimization algorithm for solving our decryption problem. That algorithm is going to be the Metropolis method that we already mentioned at the start of this section. The Metropolis algorithm turns out to work relatively well for our problem, though it's very, very slow for any reasonable length of text.[3]

The basic idea for the Metropolis method is that we'll start with an arbitrary decryption rule and then iteratively improve it many times so that it becomes a rule that could feasibly be the right one. This may seem like magic at first, but it often works in practice, as you should convince yourself by experimentation. And once we have a potential decryption rule in hand, we can use our human intuition based on semantic coherence and grammar to decide whether we've correctly decrypted the text.

To generate a good rule, we start with a completely arbitrary rule and then repeat a single operation that improves our rule a large number of times—say, 50,000 times. Because each step tends to head in the direction of better rules, repeating this operation over and over again will get us somewhere reasonable in the end, though there's no guarantee that we won't need 50,000,000 steps rather than 50,000 to get where we'd like to be. That's the reason this algorithm won't work well for a serious code-breaking system: you have no guarantee that the algorithm will give you a solution in a reasonable amount of time, and it's very hard to tell if you're even moving in the right direction while you're waiting. This case study is just a toy example that shows off how to use optimization algorithms to solve complex problems that might otherwise seem impossible to solve.

Let's be specific about how we're going to propose a new decryption rule. We'll do it by randomly disturbing the current rule in just one place. That is, we'll disturb our current rule by changing the rule's effect on a single letter of the input alphabet. If "a"

---

3. The slowness is considerably exacerbated by R's slow text-processing tools, which are much less efficient than a language like Perl's.

currently translates to "b" under our rule, we'll propose a modification that has "a" translate to "q." Because of the way substitution ciphers works, this will actually require another modification to the part of the rule that originally sent another letter—for example, "c"—to "q." To keep our cipher working, "c" now has to translate to "b." So our algorithm for proposing new rules boils down to making two swaps in our existing rule, one randomly selected and another one forced by the definition of a substitution cipher.

If we were naive, we would accept this new proposed rule only if it increased the probability of our decrypted text. That's called greedy optimization. Unfortunately, greedy optimization in this case will tend to leave us stuck at bad rules, so we'll use the following nongreedy rule to decide between our original rule A and our new rule B instead:

1. If the probability of the text decrypted with rule B is greater than the probability of the text decrypted with rule A, then we replace A with B.

2. If the probability of the text decrypted with rule B is less than the probability of the text decrypted with rule A, we'll still replace A with B sometimes, just not every time. To be specific, if the probability of the text decrypted with rule B is probability(T, B) and the probability of the text decrypted with rule A is proba bility(T, A), we'll switch over to rule B probability(T, B) / probability(T, A) percent of the time.

 If this ratio seems to have come out of left field, don't worry. For intuition's sake, what really matters isn't the specific ratio, but the fact that we accept rule B more than 0% of the time. That's what helps us to avoid the traps that greedy optimization would have us fall into.

Before we can use the Metropolis method to sort through different ciphers, we need some tools for creating the perturbed ciphers we've just described. Here they are:

```
generate.random.cipher <- function()
{
  cipher <- list()

  inputs <- english.letters
  outputs <- english.letters[sample(1:length(english.letters),
  length(english.letters))]

  for (index in 1:length(english.letters))
  {
    cipher[[inputs[index]]] <- outputs[index]
  }

  return(cipher)
}

modify.cipher <- function(cipher, input, output)
{
```

```
      new.cipher <- cipher
      new.cipher[[input]] <- output
      old.output <- cipher[[input]]
      collateral.input <- names(which(sapply(names(cipher),
                          function (key) {cipher[[key]]}) == output))
      new.cipher[[collateral.input]] <- old.output
      return(new.cipher)
    }

    propose.modified.cipher <- function(cipher)
    {
      input <- sample(names(cipher), 1)
      output <- sample(english.letters, 1)
      return(modify.cipher(cipher, input, output))
    }
```

Combining this tool for proposing new rules and the rule-swapping procedure we specified softens the greediness of our optimization approach without making us waste too much time on obviously bad rules that have much lower probability than our current rule. To do this softening algorithmically, we just compute `probability(T, B) / probability(T , A)` and compare it with a random number between 0 and 1. If the resulting random number is higher than `probability(T, B) / probability(T , A)`, we replace our current rule. If not, we stick with our current rule.

In order to compute the probabilities that we keep mentioning, we've created a lexical database that tells you how often each of the words in *usr/share/dic/words* occurs in text on Wikipedia. To load that into R, you would do the following:

```
    load('data/lexical_database.Rdata')
```

You can get a feel for the database by querying some simple words and seeing their frequencies in our sample text (see Table 7-2):

```
    lexical.database[['a']]
    lexical.database[['the']]
    lexical.database[['he']]
    lexical.database[['she']]
    lexical.database[['data']]
```

Table 7-2. Lexical database

Word	Probability
a	0.01617576
the	0.05278924
he	0.003205034
she	0.0007412179
data	0.0002168354

Now that we have our lexical database, we need some methods to calculate the probability of text. First, we'll write a function to wrap pulling the probability from the database. Writing a function makes it easier to handle fake words that need to be assigned the lowest possible probability, which is going to be your machine's floating-point epsilon. To get access to that value in R, you can use the variable .Machine $double.eps.

```
one.gram.probability <- function(one.gram, lexical.database = list())
{
  lexical.probability <- lexical.database[[one.gram]]

  if (is.null(lexical.probability) || is.na(lexical.probability))
  {
    return(.Machine$double.eps)
  }
  else
  {
    return(lexical.probability)
  }
}
```

Now that we have this method for finding the probability of isolated words, we create a method for calculating the probability of a piece of text by pulling the text apart into separate words, calculating probabilities in isolation, and putting them back together again by multiplying them together. Unfortunately, it turns out that using raw probabilities is numerically unstable because of the finite precision arithmetic that floating-point numbers provide when you do multiplication. For that reason, we actually compute the log probability of the text, which is just the sum of the log probabilities of each word in the text. That value turns out to be not to be numerically unstable.

```
log.probability.of.text <- function(text, cipher, lexical.database = list())
{
  log.probability <- 0.0

  for (string in text)
  {
    decrypted.string <- apply.cipher.to.string(string, cipher)
    log.probability <- log.probability +
      log(one.gram.probability(decrypted.string, lexical.database))
  }

  return(log.probability)
}
```

Now that we have all the administrative components we need, we can write a single step of the Metropolis method as follows:

```
metropolis.step <- function(text, cipher, lexical.database = list())
{
  proposed.cipher <- propose.modified.cipher(cipher)

  lp1 <- log.probability.of.text(text, cipher, lexical.database)
  lp2 <- log.probability.of.text(text, proposed.cipher, lexical.database)

  if (lp2 > lp1)
  {
```

```
      return(proposed.cipher)
    }
    else
    {
      a <- exp(lp2 - lp1)
      x <- runif(1)
      if (x < a)
      {
        return(proposed.cipher)
      }
      else
      {
        return(cipher)
      }
    }
  }
}
```

And now that we have the individual steps of our optimization algorithm working, let's put them together in a single example program that shows how they work. First, we'll set up some raw text as a character vector in R:

```
decrypted.text <- c('here', 'is', 'some', 'sample', 'text')
```

Then we'll encrypt this text using the Caesar cipher:

```
encrypted.text <- apply.cipher.to.text(decrypted.text, caesar.cipher)
```

From there, we'll create a random decryption cipher, run 50,000 Metropolis steps, and store the results in a data.frame called results. For each step, we'll keep a record of the log probability of the decrypted text, the current decryption of the sample text, and a dummy variable indicating whether we've correctly decrypted the input text.

 Of course, if you were really trying to break a secret code, you wouldn't be able to tell when you'd correctly decrypted the text, but it's useful to keep a record of this for demo purposes.

```
set.seed(1)
cipher <- generate.random.cipher()

results <- data.frame()

number.of.iterations <- 50000

for (iteration in 1:number.of.iterations)
{
  log.probability <- log.probability.of.text(encrypted.text, cipher, lexical.database)
  current.decrypted.text <- paste(apply.cipher.to.text(encrypted.text, cipher),
                                  collapse = ' ')
  correct.text <- as.numeric(current.decrypted.text == paste(decrypted.text,
                                                             collapse = ' '))
  results <- rbind(results,
                   data.frame(Iteration = iteration,
                              LogProbability = log.probability,
                              CurrentDecryptedText = current.decrypted.text,
```

```
                CorrectText = correct.text))
   cipher <- metropolis.step(encrypted.text, cipher, lexical.database)
}

write.table(results, file = 'data/results.csv', row.names = FALSE, sep = '\t')
```

It takes a while for this code to run, so while you're waiting, let's look at a sample of the results contained in Table 7-3.

Table 7-3. Progress of the Metropolis method

Iteration	Log probability	Current decrypted text
1	-180.218266945586	lsps bk kfvs kjvhys zsrz
5000	-67.6077693543898	gene is same sfmpwe text
10000	-67.6077693543898	gene is same spmzoe text
15000	-66.7799669880591	gene is some scmhbe text
20000	-70.8114316132189	dene as some scmire text
25000	-39.8590155606438	gene as some simple text
30000	-39.8590155606438	gene as some simple text
35000	-39.8590155606438	gene is some simple text
40000	-35.784429416419	were as some simple text
45000	-37.0128944882928	were is some sample text
50000	-35.784429416419	were as some simple text

As you can see, we're close to the correct decryption after the 45,000 step, but we're not quite there. If you drill down into the results with greater detail, you'll discover that we hit the correct text at row 45,609, but then we moved past the correct rule to a different rule. This is actually a problem with our objective function: it's not really assessing whether the translation is English, but only whether the individual words are all normal English words. If changing the rule gives you a more probable word, you'll tend to move in that direction, even if the result is grammatically broken or semantically incoherent. You could use more information about English, such as the probability of sequences of two words, to work around this. For now, we think it highlights the complexities of using optimization approaches with ad hoc objective functions: sometimes the solution you want isn't the solution that your rule will decide is best. Humans need to be kept in the loop when you're using optimization algorithms to solve your problems.

In truth, things are even more complicated than problems with our objective function not containing enough knowledge about how English works. First, the Metropolis method is always a random optimization method. Luckily we started off with a good seed value of 1, but a bad seed value could mean that it would take trillions of steps before we hit the right decryption rule. You can convince yourself of this by playing with the seed we've used and running only 1,000 iterations for each seed.

Second, the Metropolis method is always going to be willing to leave good translations. That's what makes it a nongreedy algorithm, so you can often watch it abandon the solution you want it to find if you follow the trace of its progress long enough. In Figure 7-6, we show the log probability of the decrypted text at every step along the way. You can see how erratic the method's movement is.

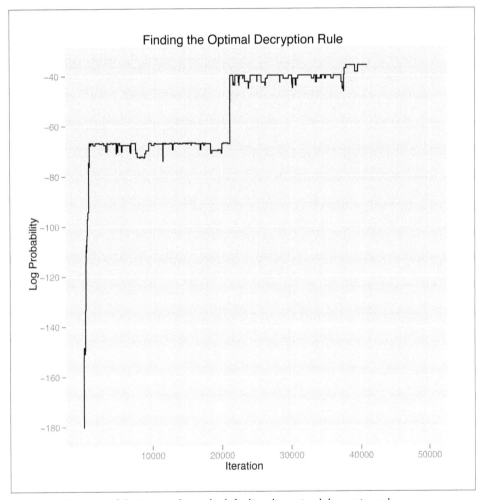

Figure 7-6. Progress of the Metropolis method: finding the optimal decryption rule

There are popular ways to deal with this random movement. One is to make the method progressively more greedy over time by accepting nongreedy proposed rules less often. That's called *simulated annealing*, and it's a very powerful approach to optimization that you can play with in our example simply by changing the way you accept new decryption rules.[4]

Another way to deal with this randomness is to embrace it and use it to produce a distribution of possible answers rather than a single right answer. In this problem that's not very helpful, but in problems where the right answer is a number, it can be very helpful to produce of variety of possible answers.

In closing, we hope that you've gained some insight into how optimization works in general and how you can use it to solve complicated problems in machine learning. We'll use some of those ideas again in later chapters, especially when talking about recommendation systems.

---

4. In fact, there's an argument to `optim` that will force `optim` to use simulated annealing instead of its standard optimization algorithm. In our example, we can't use `optim`'s implementation of simulated annealing because it works only with numerical parameters and can't handle the data structure we're using to represent ciphers.

## CHAPTER 8

PCA: Building a Market Index

Unsupervised Learning

So far, all of our work with data has been based on prediction tasks: we've tried to classify emails or web page views where we had a training set of examples for which we knew the correct answer. As we mentioned early on in this book, learning from data when we have a training sample with the correct answer is called supervised learning: we find structure in our data using a signal that tells us whether or not we're doing a good job of discovering real patterns.

But often we want to find structure without having any answers available to us about how well we're doing; we call this unsupervised learning. For example, we might want to perform dimensionality reduction, which happens when we shrink a table with a huge number of columns into a table with a small number of columns. If you have too many columns to deal with, this dimensionality reduction goes a long way toward making your data set comprehensible. Although you clearly lose information when you replace many columns with a single column, the gains in understanding are often valuable, especially when you're exploring a new data set.

One place where this type of dimensionality reduction is particularly helpful is when dealing with stock market data. For example, we might have data that looks like the real historical prices shown in Table 8-1 for 25 stocks over the period from January 2, 2002 until May 25, 2011.

Table 8-1. Historical stock prices

Date	ADC	AFL	...	UTR
2002-01-02	17.7	23.78	...	39.34
2002-01-03	16.14	23.52	...	39.49
...	...	...	...	...
2011-05-25	22.76	49.3	...	29.47

Though we've only shown 3 columns, there are actually 25, which is far too many columns to deal with in a thoughtful way. We want to create a single column that tells us how the market is doing on each day by combining information in the 25 columns that we have access to; we'll call that single column an index of the market. So how can we construct one?

The simplest approach is called principal components analysis, or PCA. The main idea of PCA is to create a new set of 25 columns that are ordered based on how much of the raw information in our data set they contain. The first new column, called the first principal component, or just the principal component for short, will often contain the vast majority of the structure in the entire data set. PCA is particularly effective when the columns in our data set are all strongly correlated. In that case, you can replace the correlated columns with a single column that matches an underlying pattern that accounts for the correlation between both columns.

So let's test whether or not PCA will work by seeing how correlated the columns in our data set are. To do that, we first need to load our raw data set into R:

```
prices <- read.csv('data/stock_prices.csv')

prices[1,]
#        Date Stock Close
#1 2011-05-25   DTE 51.12
```

Our raw data set isn't in the format we'd like to work with, so we need to do some preprocessing. The first step is to translate all of the raw datestamps in our data set to properly encoded date variables. To do that, we use the `lubridate` package from CRAN. This package provides a nice function called `ymd` that translates strings in year-month-day format into date objects:

```
library('lubridate')

prices <- transform(prices, Date = ymd(Date))
```

Once we've done this, we can use the `cast` function in the `reshape` library to create a data matrix like the table we saw earlier in this chapter. In this table, the rows will be days and the columns will be separate stocks. We do this as follows:

```
library('reshape')

date.stock.matrix <- cast(prices, Date ~ Stock, value = 'Close')
```

The `cast` function has you specify which column should be used to define the rows in the output matrix on the lefthand side of the tilde, and the columns of the result are specified after the tilde. The actual entries in the result are specified using `value`.

After exploring the result of producing this big date-stock matrix, we notice that there are some missing entries. So we go back to the `prices` data set, remove missing entries, and then rerun `cast`:

```
prices <- subset(prices, Date != ymd('2002-02-01'))
prices <- subset(prices, Stock != 'DDR')

date.stock.matrix <- cast(prices, Date ~ Stock, value = 'Close')
```

Having removed the missing entries, we use cast again to produce the matrix we want. Once that's done, we can find the correlations between all of the numeric columns in the matrix using the cor function. After doing that, we turn the correlation matrix into a single numeric vector and create a density plot of the correlations to get a sense of both a) the mean correlation, and b) the frequency with which low correlations occur:

```
cor.matrix <- cor(date.stock.matrix[,2:ncol(date.stock.matrix)])

correlations <- as.numeric(cor.matrix)

ggplot(data.frame(Correlation = correlations),
          aes(x = Correlation, fill = 1)) +
  geom_density() +
  opts(legend.position = 'none')
```

The resulting density plot is shown in Figure 8-1. As we can see, the vast majority of the correlations are positive, so PCA will probably work well on this data set.

Having convinced ourselves that we can use PCA, how do we do that in R? Again, this is a place where R shines: the entirety of PCA can be done in one line of code. We use the princomp function to run PCA:

```
pca <- princomp(date.stock.matrix[,2:ncol(date.stock.matrix)])
```

If we just type pca into R, we'll see a quick summary of the principal components:

```
Call:
princomp(x = date.stock.matrix[, 2:ncol(date.stock.matrix)])

Standard deviations:
    Comp.1      Comp.2      Comp.3      Comp.4      Comp.5      Comp.6      Comp.7
29.1001249  20.4403404  12.6726924  11.4636450   8.4963820   8.1969345   5.5438308
    Comp.8      Comp.9     Comp.10     Comp.11     Comp.12     Comp.13     Comp.14
 5.1300931   4.7786752   4.2575099   3.3050931   2.6197715   2.4986181   2.1746125
   Comp.15     Comp.16     Comp.17     Comp.18     Comp.19     Comp.20     Comp.21
 1.9469475   1.8706240   1.6984043   1.6344116   1.2327471   1.1280913   0.9877634
   Comp.22     Comp.23     Comp.24
 0.8583681   0.7390626   0.4347983

 24  variables and  2366 observations.
```

In this summary, the standard deviations tell us how much of the variance in the data set is accounted for by the different principal components. The first component, called Comp.1, accounts for 29% of the variance, while the next component accounts for 20%. By the end, the last component, Comp.24, accounts for less than 1% of the variance. This suggests that we can learn a lot about our data by just looking at the first principal component.

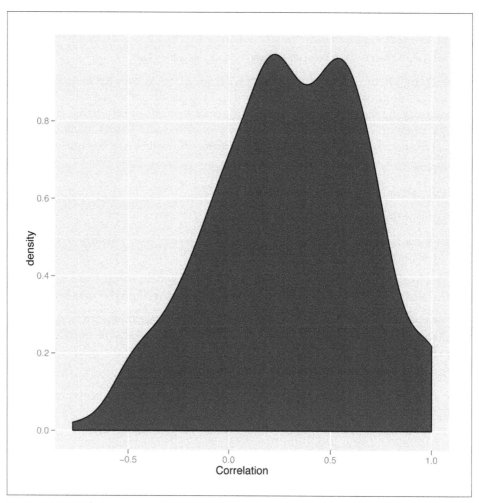

Figure 8-1. Correlations among all numeric columns in stock price data

We can examine the first principal component in more detail by looking at its loadings, which tell us how much weight it gives to each of the columns. We get those by extracting the `loadings` element of the `princomp` object stored in `pca`. Extracting `loadings` gives us a big matrix that tells us how much each of the 25 columns gets puts into each of the principal components. We're really only interested in the first principal component, so we pull out the first column of the `pca` loadings:

```
principal.component <- pca$loadings[,1]
```

Having done that, we can examine a density plot of the loadings to get a sense of how the first principal component is formed:

```
loadings <- as.numeric(principal.component)

ggplot(data.frame(Loading = loadings),
           aes(x = Loading, fill = 1)) +
  geom_density() +
  opts(legend.position = 'none')
```

This can be seen in Figure 8-2. The results are a little suspicious because there's a nice distribution of loadings, but they're overwhelmingly negative. We'll see what this leads to in a bit; it's actually a trivial nuisance that a single line of code will fix.

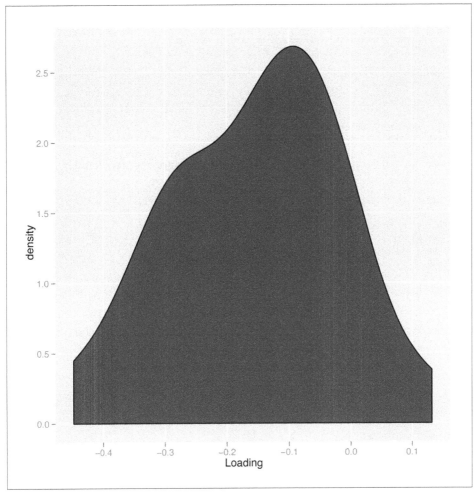

Figure 8-2. Principal component loadings

Now that we have our principal component, we might want to generate our one-column summary of our data set. We can do that using the predict function:

```
market.index <- predict(pca)[,1]
```

How can we tell whether these predictions are any good? Thankfully, this is a case where it's easy to decide whether we like our results because there are famous market indices that we can compare our results against. For this chapter, we'll use the Dow Jones Index, which we'll refer to as just the DJI.

We load the DJI into R as follows:

```
dji.prices <- read.csv('data/DJI.csv')
dji.prices <- transform(dji.prices, Date = ymd(Date))
```

Because the DJI runs for so much longer than we want, we need to do some subsetting to get only the dates we're interested in:

```
dji.prices <- subset(dji.prices, Date > ymd('2001-12-31'))
dji.prices <- subset(dji.prices, Date != ymd('2002-02-01'))
```

After doing that, we extract the parts of the DJI we're interested in, which are the daily closing prices and the dates on which they were recorded. Because they're in the opposite order of our current data set, we use the rev function to reverse them:

```
dji <- with(dji.prices, rev(Close))
dates <- with(dji.prices, rev(Date))
```

Now we can make some simple graphical plots to compare our market index generated using PCA with the DJI:

```
comparison <- data.frame(Date = dates, MarketIndex = market.index, DJI = dji)

ggplot(comparison, aes(x = MarketIndex, y = DJI)) +
  geom_point() +
  geom_smooth(method = 'lm', se = FALSE)
```

This first plot is shown in Figure 8-3. As you can see, those negative loadings that seemed suspicious before turn out to be a real source of trouble for our data set: our index is negatively correlated with the DJI.

But that's something we can easily fix. We just multiply our index by -1 to produce an index that's correlated in the right direction with the DJI:

```
comparison <- transform(comparison, MarketIndex = -1 * MarketIndex)
```

Now we can try out our comparison again:

```
ggplot(comparison, aes(x = MarketIndex, y = DJI)) +
  geom_point() +
  geom_smooth(method = 'lm', se = FALSE)
```

As you can see in Figure 8-4, we've fixed the direction of our index, and it looks like it matches the DJI really well. The only thing that's missing is to get a sense of how well our index tracks the DJI over time.

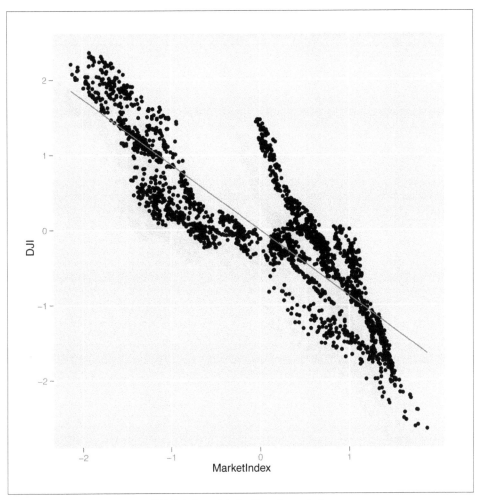

Figure 8-3. Raw comparison of PCA index with the Dow Jones Index

We can easily make that comparison. First, we use the `melt` function to get a `data.frame` that's easy to work with for visualizing both indices at once. Then we make a line plot in which the x-axis is the date and the y-axis is the price of each index.

```
alt.comparison <- melt(comparison, id.vars = 'Date')
names(alt.comparison) <- c('Date', 'Index', 'Price')

ggplot(alt.comparison, aes(x = Date, y = Price, group = Index, color = Index)) +
  geom_point() +
  geom_line()
```

Our first pass doesn't look so good, because the DJI takes on very high values, whereas our index takes on very small values. But we can fix that using `scale`, which puts both indices on a common scale:

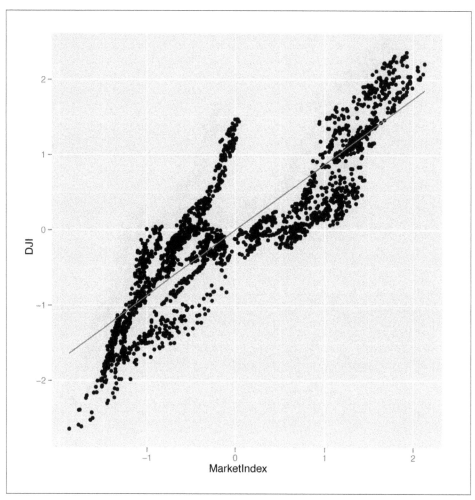

Figure 8-4. Scaled comparison of PCA index with the Dow Jones Index

```
comparison <- transform(comparisonMarketIndex = -scale(MarketIndex))
comparison <- transform(comparisonDJI = scale(DJI))

alt.comparison <- melt(comparison, id.vars = 'Date')
names(alt.comparison) <- c('Date', 'Index', 'Price')

p <- ggplot(alt.comparison, aes(x = Date, y = Price, group = Index, color = Index)) +
  geom_point() +
  geom_line()

print(p)
```

After doing that, we recreate our line plot and check the results, which are shown in Figure 8-5. This plot makes it seem like our market index, which was created entirely with PCA and didn't require any domain knowledge about the stock market, tracks the DJI incredibly well. In short, PCA really works to produce a reduced representation of stock prices that looks just like something we might create with more careful thought about how to express the general well-being of the stock market. We think that's pretty amazing.

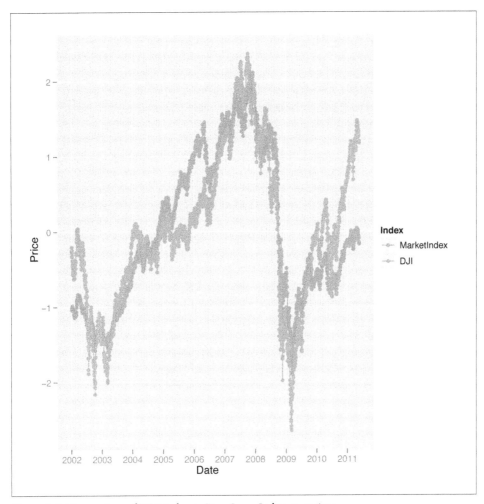

Figure 8-5. Comparison of PCA index to Dow Jones Index, over time

Hopefully this example convinces you that PCA is a powerful tool for simplifying your data and that you can actually do a lot to discover structure in your data even when you're not trying to predict something. If you're interested in this topic, we'd encourage looking into independent component analysis (ICA), which is an alternative to PCA that works well in some circumstances where PCA breaks down.

## CHAPTER 9

MDS: Visually Exploring US Senator Similarity

Clustering Based on Similarity

There are many situations where we might want to know how similar the members of a group of people are to one another. For instance, suppose that we were a brand marketing company that had just completed a research survey on a potential new brand. In the survey, we showed a group of people several features of the brand and asked them to rank the brand on each of these features using a five-point scale. We also collected a bunch of socioeconomic data from the subjects, such as age, gender, race, what zip code they live in, and their approximate annual income.

From this survey, we want to understand how the brand appeals across all of these socioeconomic variables. Most importantly, we want to know whether the brand has broad appeal. An alternative way of thinking about this problem is we want to see whether individuals who like most of the brand features have diverse socioeconomic features. A useful means of doing this would be to visualize how the survey respondents cluster. We could then use various visual cues to indicate their memberships in different socioeconomic categories. That is, we would want to see a large amount of mixing between gender, as well as among races and economic stratification.

Likewise, we could use this knowledge to see how close groups clustered based on the brand's appeal. We could also see how many people were in one cluster as compared to others, or how far away other clusters were. This might tell us what features of the brand to target at different socioeconomic categories. When phrasing these questions, we use words such as "close" and "far," which have an inherent notion of distance. To visualize the distance among clusters, therefore, we need some spatial concept of how individuals congregate.

The primary focus of this chapter is to begin to understand how to use notions of distance among a set of observations to illustrate their similarities and dissimilarities. This will require the definition of some metric for distance relevant to the type of data being analyzed. For example, in the hypothetical brand marketing situation, we could use the ordinal nature of the survey's scale to find the distances among respondents in a very straightforward way: simply calculate the absolute differences.

It is not enough, however, to only calculate these distances. In this chapter we will introduce a technique known as multidimensional scaling (MDS) for clustering observations based on a measure of distance among the observations. Applying MDS will allow us to visualize our data using only a measure of the distance between all of the points. We will first introduce the basic principles of MDS using a toy example of customer ratings for products with simulated data. Then we will move on to use real data on roll call voting in the US Senate to show how its members cluster based on these votes.

A Brief Introduction to Distance Metrics and Multidirectional Scaling

To begin, let's suppose that we have a very simple data set in which there are four customers who have rated six products. Each customer was asked to give each product a thumbs up or a thumbs down, but she could skip a product if she had no opinion about it. There are many rating systems that work this way, including Pandora's and YouTube's. Using this ratings data, we would like to measure how similar the customers are to one another.

In this simple example we will set up a 4×6 matrix in which the rows represent customers and the columns represent products. We'll fill this matrix with simulated ratings by randomly selecting a thumbs up (1), a thumbs down (–1), or a skip (0) rating for each customer/product pair. To do this, we will use the `sample` function, which will allow us to randomly select values from the vector `c(1, 0, -1)` six times with replacement. Because we will be accessing R's random number generator to simulate data, it's important that you set the seed for your generator to the same value we have used so that your outputs end up being equal to those shown in the examples. To set the seed, we'll call `set.seed()` to set the generator's seed to the number 851982.

```
set.seed(851982)
ex.matrix <- matrix(sample(c(-1,0,1), 24, replace=TRUE), nrow=4, ncol=6)
row.names(ex.matrix) <- c('A','B','C','D')
colnames(ex.matrix) <- c('P1','P2','P3','P4','P5','P6')
```

This code will create a 4×6 matrix, where each entry corresponds to the row-users rating of a column-product. We use the `row.names` and `colnames` functions just to keep things clear in this example: customers A–D and products 1–6. When we inspect the matrix, we can see exactly what our toy data set looks like. For example, customer A gave products 2 and 3 a thumbs down and did not rate any other products. On the other hand, customer B gave a thumbs down to product 1, but gave a thumbs up to products 3, 4, and 5. Now we need to use these differences to generate a distance metric among all the customers.

```
ex.matrix
  P1 P2 P3 P4 P5 P6
A  0 -1  0 -1  0  0
B -1  0  1  1  1  0
C  0  0  0  1 -1  1
D  1  0  1 -1  0  0
```

The first step in taking this data and generating a distance metric is to summarize the customer ratings for each product as they relate to all other customers, that is, rather than only to the products in the current form. Another way to think about this is that we need to convert the N-by-M matrix into an N-by-N matrix, wherein the elements of the new matrix provide summaries of the relation among users based on product rating. One way to do this is to multiply our matrix by its transpose. The effect of this multiplication is to compute the correlation between every pair of columns in the original matrix.

Matrix transposition and multiplication is something you would learn in the first few weeks of an undergraduate discrete mathematics or linear algebra class. Depending on the instructor's temperament, you may have painstakingly made these transformations by hand. Thankfully, R is perfectly happy to perform these transformations for you.

Here we provide a brief introduction to matrix operations and their use in constructing a distance metric for ratings data. If you are already familiar with matrix operations, you may skip this section.

Matrix transposition inverts a matrix so that the rows become the columns and the columns become the rows. Visually, transposition turns a matrix 90 degrees clockwise and then flips it vertically. For example, in the previous code block we can see our customer-by-review matrix, ex.matrix, but in the following code block we use the t function to transpose it. We now have a review-by-customer matrix:

```
t(ex.matrix)
    A  B  C  D
P1  0 -1  0  1
P2 -1  0  0  0
P3  0  1  0  1
P4 -1  1  1 -1
P5  0  1 -1  0
P6  0  0  1  0
```

Matrix multiplication is slightly more complicated, but involves only basic arithmetic. To multiply two matrices, we loop over the rows of the first matrix and the columns of the second matrix. For each row-column pair, we multiply each pair of entries and sum them together. We will go over a brief example in a second, but there are a few important things to keep in mind when performing matrix multiplication. First, because we are multiplying the row elements of the first matrix by the column elements of the second, these dimensions must conform across the two matrices. In our case, we could not simply multiply ex.matrix by a 2×2 matrix; as we'll see, the arithmetic would not work out. As such, the result of a matrix multiplication will always have the same number of rows as the first matrix and the same number of columns as the second matrix.

An immediate consequence of this is that order matters in matrix multiplication. In our case, we want a matrix that summarizes differences among customers, so we multiply our customer-by-review matrix by its transpose to get a customer-by-customer matrix as the product. If we did the inverse, i.e., multiply the review-by-customer matrix by itself, we would have the differences among the reviews. This might be interesting in another situation, but it is not useful right now.

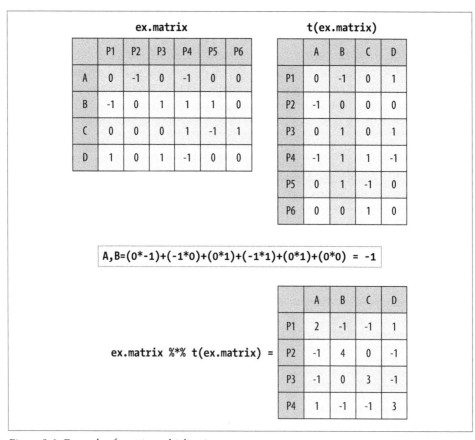

Figure 9-1. Example of matrix multiplication

In Figure 9-1 we walk through how matrix multiplication works. In the top left is ex.matrix, and in the top right is its transpose. These are the two matrices we are going to multiply, and we will multiply them in that order. As an example of the multiplication process, we have highlighted row A in ex.matrix and column B in its transpose. Directly below the matrices we show exactly how the arithmetic of the matrix multiplication proceeds. It is as simple as taking a row element of the first matrix and multiplying it by the corresponding column element from the second matrix. You then take these products and sum them. As you can see, in the resulting customer-by-customer matrix the A,B element is −1, the result of a row-by-column summation.

```
ex.mult <- ex.matrix %*% t(ex.matrix)
ex.mult
  A  B  C  D
A  2 -1 -1  1
B -1  4  0 -1
C -1  0  3 -1
D  1 -1 -1  3
```

We have also introduced some R notation in Figure 9-1, which is repeated in the preceding code block that produces the matrix multiplication. In R, you use the %*% operator to perform matrix multiplication. The interpretation of the new matrix is fairly straightforward. Because we have used the 1, −1, and 0 coding scheme, the off-diagonal values summarize their overall agreement (positive value) or disagreement (negative value) on product reviews, given those products they have both reviewed, i.e., nonzero entries. The more positive the off-diagonal element, the more agreement, and likewise, the more negative, the less agreement. Because the entries are random, there is very little divergence among the customers, with no value taking on a value greater than 1 or less than −1. The diagonal values simply represent the number of products each user reviewed.

We now have a somewhat useful summary of the differences among users. For example, customers A and D both gave product 4 a thumbs down; however, customer D liked products 1 and 3, whereas customer A did not review them. So, for the products for which we have information, we might say that they are similar, and thus have a 1 corresponding to their relationship. Unfortunately, this is very limiting because we can only say something about the overlap. We would rather have a method for extrapolating these differences into a richer representation.

To do this, we will use the concept of Euclidean distance in a multidimensional space. In one, two, or three dimensions, Euclidean distance is a formalization of our intuitions about distance. To calculate the Euclidean distance between two points in space, we measure the shortest direct path between them. For our example we want to calculate the Euclidean distance among all customers based on the measures of overall similarities and differences defined by the matrix multiplication.

To do this, we will treat each customer's ratings as a vector. To compare customer A with customer B, we can subtract the vectors, square the differences, sum them, and then take the square root. This gives us the Euclidean distance between customer A's ratings and customer B's ratings.

We can do this "by hand" in R using the base functions sum and sqrt. In the following code block we show this calculation for customers A and D, which is about 2.236. Thankfully, calculating all of the pairwise distance between the rows of a matrix is such a common operation that R has a base function called `dist` that does exactly this and returns a matrix of the distances, which we call a *distance matrix*. The `dist` function can use several different distance metrics to produce a distance matrix, but we will stick to the Euclidean distance, which is the default.

```
sqrt(sum((ex.mult[1,]-ex.mult[4,])^2))
[1] 2.236068

ex.dist <- dist(ex.mult)
ex.dist
          A        B        C
B 6.244998
C 5.477226 5.000000
D 2.236068 6.782330 6.082763
```

The `ex.dist` variable now holds our distance matrix. As you can see from this code block, this matrix is actually only the lower triangle of the entire distance matrix. It is very common to show only the lower triangle for a distance matrix because the distance matrix must be symmetric, as the distance between row X and row Y is equal to the distance between row Y and row X. Showing the upper triangle of the distance matrix is therefore redundant and generally not done. But you can override this default when calling the `dist` function by setting `upper=TRUE`.

As we can see from the values in the lower triangle of `ex.dist`, customers A and D are the closest, and customers D and B are the farthest. We now have a clearer sense of the similarities among the users based on their product reviews; however, it would be better if we could get a visual sense of these dissimilarities. This is where MDS can be used to produce a spatial layout of our customers based on the distances we just calculated.

MDS is a set of statistical techniques used to visually depict the similarities and differences from set of distances. For classical MDS, which we will use in this chapter, the process takes a distance matrix that specifies the distance between every pair of points in our data set and returns a set of coordinates for those two points that approximates those distances. The reason we need to create an approximation is that it may not be possible to find points in two dimensions that are all separated by a specific set of distances. For example, it isn't possible to find four points in two dimensions that are all at a distance of 1 from each other. (To convince yourself of this, note that three points that are all at a distance of 1 from each other are the tips of a triangle. Convince yourself that there isn't any way to find another point that's at a distance of 1 from all three points on this triangle.)

Classical MDS uses a specific approximation to the distance matrix and is therefore another example of an optimization algorithm being used for machine learning. Of course, the approximation algorithm behind classical MDS can be used in three dimensions or four, but our goal is to obtain a representation of our data that's easy to visualize.

For all cases in this chapter, we will be using MDS to scale data in two dimensions. This is the most common way of using MDS because it allows for very simple visualizations of the data on a coordinate plot. It is perfectly reasonable, however, to use MDS to scale data into higher-order dimensions. For example, a three-dimensional visualization might reveal different levels of clustering among observations as points move into the third dimension.

The classical MDS procedure is part of R's base functions as cmdscale, and its only required input is a distance matrix, such as ex.dist. By default, cmdscale will compute an MDS in two dimensions, but you can set this using the k parameter. We are only interested in scaling our distance data into two dimensions, so in the following code block we use the default settings and plot the results using R's base graphics.

```
ex.mds <- cmdscale(ex.dist)
plot(ex.mds, type='n')
text(ex.mds, c('A','B','C','D'))
```

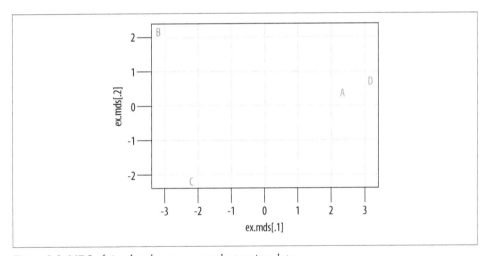

Figure 9-2. MDS of simulated customer product review data

From Figure 9-2 we can see that customers A and D do cluster together in the center-right of the plot. Customers B and C, however, do not cluster at all. From our data, then, we can see that customers A and D have somewhat similar tastes, but we would need to acquire much more data and/or customers before we could hope to understand how customers B and C cluster. It is also important to note that although we can see how A and D cluster, and likewise how B and C do not, we cannot say anything substantive about how to interpret these distances. That is, we know that A and D are more similar because of their proximity in the coordinate plane, but we cannot use the numeric distance between them to interpret *how* similar they are, nor how dissimilar they are from B or C. The exact numeric distance produced by MDS is an artifact of the MDS algorithm and allows only a very limited substantive interpretation.

In the following section we will work through a case study similar to the toy example we've just used, but now we will use real data from roll call votes from the US Senate. This data is considerably larger than the toy data set, and we will use it to show how members of the United States Senate cluster over chronological Congresses. In this case we will use these records of roll call votes in the Senate to generate our distance metric. Then we will use MDS to cluster senators in two dimensions.

How Do US Senators Cluster?

> The current Congress—the 111th—is the most ideologically polarized in modern history. In both the House and the Senate, the most conservative Democrat is more liberal than the most liberal Republican. If one defines the congressional "center" as the overlap between the two parties, the center has disappeared.
>
> —William A. Galston, The Brookings Institute (2010)

We often hear remarks like the one here from William A. Galston, a Senior Fellow in Governance Studies at the Brookings Institute, claiming that polarization in the US Congress is at an all-time high [WA10]. It is easy to understand why. Such portraits are often made in the popular press, and mainstream media outlets in the United States often work to amplify these differences. If we think of legislative morass as a by-product of this polarization, then we could look to legislative outcomes as a rough measure of polarization. In the 110th Congress nearly 14,000 pieces of legislation were introduced, but only 449 bills, or 3.3%, actually became law [PS08]. In fact, of those 449 bills, 144 simply changed the name of a federal building.

But is the US Congress actually more polarized now than ever before? Although we may believe this to be true—and we have anecdotal evidence like the quote from Professor Galston—we would prefer a more principled means of answering this question. Here our approach will be to use MDS to visualize the clustering of senators across party lines to see whether any mixing exists between members of the two parties. Before we can do this, however, we need a metric for measuring the distance among senators.

Fortunately, the US Congress is one of the most open legislative bodies in the world. We can use the public records of legislators to construct a reasonable distance metric. Here we will use legislator voting records. As in the example in the previous section, we can use roll call voting records as a means of measuring the legislators' approval or disapproval of a proposed bill. Just as the customers in the previous examples gave thumbs-up or thumbs-down votes, legislators vote with Yeas (approve) or Nays (disapprove) for bills.

For those unfamiliar with the US legislative process, a roll call vote is one of the most basic parliamentary procedures in either chamber of the US Congress. As the name suggests, it is the process by which members of the House of Representatives and Senate vote for any proposal brought before the floor. Each house has a different mechanism by which a roll call vote can be initiated, but the results are basically equivalent. A roll call vote is the record of each legislator's action on a given proposal. As mentioned earlier, this typically takes the form of a Yea or Nay, but we'll see later that the results are slightly more complicated than that.

This roll call data is a great resource for measuring similarities and differences among legislators and is an invaluable resource for political scientists who study the US Congress. The data is so valuable that two political scientists have created a unified resource for downloading it. Keith Poole (University of Georgia) and Howard Rosenthal (New York University) maintain *http://www.voteview.com/*, which is a repository for all US roll call data from the very first Congress to the most recent at the time of this writing, i.e., the 111th. There are also many other data sets available on this website, but for our purposes we will examine the roll call voting data from the US Senate for the 101st through 111th Congresses. These data files are included in the *data* directory for this chapter.

In the following sections we will work through the code used to perform MDS on this roll call data. Once the scaling has been calculated, we will visualize the results to address the question: do senators from different parties mix when clustered by roll call vote records?

Analyzing US Senator Roll Call Data (101st–111th Congresses)

As mentioned, we have collected all of the data for Senate roll call votes for the 101st through 111th Congresses and placed them in the *data* directory for this chapter. As we have done throughout this text, we will begin this case study by loading the data and inspecting it. In the process, we will use two R libraries: first, the `foreign` library, which we will discuss in a moment; and second, `ggplot2`, which we will use to visualize the results of the MDS algorithm. The files are located at *data/roll_call/*, so we use the `list.files` function to generate a character vector called `data.files` with all of the data filenames in it.

```
library(foreign)
library(ggplot2)

data.dir <- "data/roll_call/"
data.files <- list.files(data.dir)
```

When we inspect the `data.files` variable, we see that the extension for the datafiles is different from the text files we have been using for our case studies in the previous chapters. The *.dta* extension corresponds to a Stata datafile. Stata is a commercial statistical computing program that happens to be very popular among academics, particularly political scientists. Because Poole and Rosenthal decided to disseminate the data in this format, so we will need a way of loading this data into R.

```
data.files
 [1] "sen101kh.dta"      "sen102kh.dta"
 [3] "sen103kh.dta"      "sen104kh.dta"
 [5] "sen105kh.dta"      "sen106kh.dta"
 [7] "sen107kh.dta"      "sen108kh_7.dta"
 [9] "sen109kh.dta"      "sen110kh_2008.dta"
[11] "sen111kh.dta"
```

Enter the foreign package, which is designed to read a large number of exotic datafiles into R data frames, including S, SAS, SPSS, Systat, dBase, and many others. For our purposes, we will use the read.dta function, which is designed to read Stata files. For this analysis, we want to analyze the data for 10 Congresses, from the 101st to the 111th.[1] We'll store all this data in a single object that can be manipulated at once. As we'll see, these data sets are relatively small, so we do not have any concern about memory in this case. To combine our data sets, we will use the lapply function in conjunction with read.dta.

```
rollcall.data <- lapply(data.files,
    function(f) read.dta(paste(data.dir, f, sep=""), convert.factors=FALSE))
```

We now have all 10 data frames of roll call votes stored in the rollcall.data variable. When we check the dimension of the first data frame, the 101st Congress, we see that it has 103 rows and 647 columns. When we further check the head of this data frame, we can see what are in these rows and columns. There are two important things to note while inspecting the data's head. First, each row corresponds to a voter in the US Senate. Second, the first nine columns of the data frame include identification information for those voters, and the remaining columns are the actual votes. Before we can proceed, we need to make sense of this identification information.

```
dim(rollcall.data[[1]])
[1] 103 647

head(rollcall.data[[1]])
  cong     id state dist lstate party eh1 eh2       name V1 V2 V3 ... V638
1  101  99908    99    0 USA      200    0   0 BUSH        1  1  1 ...    1
2  101  14659    41    0 ALABAMA  100    0   1 SHELBY, RIC 1  1  1 ...    6
3  101  14705    41    0 ALABAMA  100    0   1 HEFLIN, HOW 1  1  1 ...    6
4  101  12109    81    0 ALASKA   200    0   1 STEVENS, TH 1  1  1 ...    1
5  101  14907    81    0 ALASKA   200    0   1 MURKOWSKI,  1  1  1 ...    6
6  101  14502    61    0 ARIZONA  100    0   1 DECONCINI,  1  1  1 ...    6
```

Some of the column are quite obvious, such as lstate and name, but what about eh1 and eh2? Thankfully, Poole and Rosenthal provide a codebook for all of the roll call data. The codebook for the 101st Congress is located at *http://www.voteview.com/sen ate101.htm* and is replicated in Example 9-1. This codebook is particularly helpful because it not only explains what is contained in each of the first nine columns, but also how each of the votes are coded, which we will need to pay attention to shortly.

---

1. There is also a specific R function for reading the *.ord* data types provided by Poole and Rosenthal called readKH. For more information, see *http://rss.acs.unt.edu/Rdoc/library/pscl/html/readKH.html*.

---

1. Congress Number
2. ICPSR ID Number: 5 digit code assigned by the ICPSR as
         corrected by Howard Rosenthal and myself.
3. State Code: 2 digit ICPSR State Code.
4. Congressional District Number (0 if Senate)
5. State Name
6. Party Code: 100 = Dem., 200 = Repub. (See PARTY3.DAT)
7. Occupancy: ICPSR Occupancy Code -- 0=only occupant; 1=1st occupant; 2=2nd occupant; etc.
8. Last Means of Attaining Office: ICPSR Attain-Office Code -- 1=general election;
      2=special election; 3=elected by state legislature; 5=appointed
9. Name
10 - to the number of roll calls + 10: Roll Call Data --
            0=not a member, 1=Yea, 2=Paired Yea, 3=Announced Yea,
                4=Announced Nay, 5=Paired Nay, 6=Nay,
            7=Present (some Congresses, also not used some Congresses),
            8=Present (some Congresses, also not used some Congresses),
            9=Not Voting

For our purposes we are only interested in the names of the voters, their party affiliations, and their actual votes. For that reason, our first step is to get the roll call vote data in a form from which we can create a reasonable distance metric from the votes. As we can see in Example 9-1, roll call votes in the Senate are not simply Yeas or Nays; there are Announced and Paired forms of Yea and Nay votes, as well as Present votes, that is, votes in which a senator abstained from voting on a specific bill but was present at the time of the vote. There are also times when the senators were simply not present to cast a vote or had not yet even been elected to the Senate. Given the variety of possible votes, how do we take this data and transform it into something we can easily use to measure distance between the senators?

One approach is to simplify the data coding by aggregating like vote types. For example, Paired voting is a procedure whereby members of Congress know they will not be present for a given roll call can have their vote "paired" with another member who is going to vote the opposite. This, along with Announced votes, are Parliamentary means for the Senate or House to a establish a quorum for a vote to be held. For our purposes, however, we are less concerned with the mechanism by which the vote occurred, but rather the intended outcome of the vote, i.e., for or against. As such, one method for aggregating would be to group all Yea and Nay types together. By the same logic, we could group all of the non-vote-casting types together.

```
rollcall.simplified <- function(df) {
    no.pres <- subset(df, state < 99)
    for(i in 10:ncol(no.pres)) {
        no.pres[,i] <- ifelse(no.pres[,i] > 6, 0, no.pres[,i])
        no.pres[,i] <- ifelse(no.pres[,i] > 0 & no.pres[,i] < 4, 1, no.pres[,i])
        no.pres[,i] <- ifelse(no.pres[,i] > 1, -1, no.pres[,i])
    }
    return(as.matrix(no.pres[,10:ncol(no.pres)]))
}

rollcall.simple <- lapply(rollcall.data, rollcall.simplified)
```

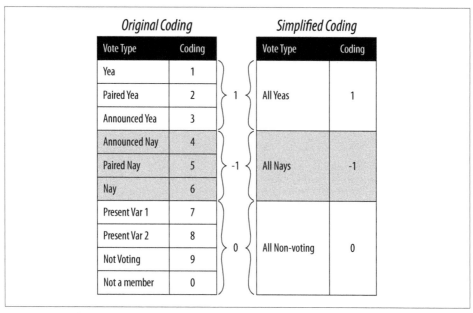

Figure 9-3. Method for simplified recoding of roll call voting data

Figure 9-3 illustrates the procedure we will use to simplify the coding from Poole and Rosenthal to be used in our analysis. As in the simulated example in the previous section, we will code all Yeas as +1, all Nays as −1, and all nonvoting observations as 0. This allows for a very straightforward application of the data coding to a distance metric. We now need to convert the data to our new coding. We also need to extract only the votes from the data frame so that we can do the necessary matrix manipulation.

To do this, we define the `rollcall.simplified` function, which takes a roll call data frame as its only argument and returns a senator-by-votes matrix with our simplified coding. You'll notice that the first step in this function removes all observations where the `state` column is equal to 99. The 99 `state` code corresponds to the Vice President of the United States, and because the Vice President very rarely votes, we remove him. We then use the `ifelse` command to perform a vectorized numeric comparison for all of the columns in the remaining matrix. Note that the order in which we do this comparison matters. We begin by setting all of the nonvotes (everything greater than 6) to zero. We can then look for votes coded greater than 0 and less than 4, the Yeas, and convert them to 1. Finally, everything greater than 4 is a Nay, so we code those as a −1.

We now have the roll call data in the same form as we started with for our simulated data from the previous section, and we can proceed with this data in exactly the same way we did with the simulated consumer review data. In the next and final section of this chapter, we will generate the MDS of this data and explore it visually.

Exploring senator MDS clustering by Congress

As before, the first step is to use the senator-by-votes matrix to create a senator-by-senator distance matrix on which we will perform MDS. We will use the `lapply` function to perform the conversion steps for each Congress separately. We begin by performing the matrix multiplication and storing the results in the `rollcall.dist` variable. We then perform MDS using the `cmdscale` function via another call to `lapply`. There are two things to notice about the MDS operation. First, by default `cmdscale` computes the MDS for two dimensions, so we are being redundant by setting `k=2`. It is useful, however, to be explicit when performing this operation when sharing code, so we add it here as a best practice. Second, notice that we are multiplying all points by −1. This is done strictly for visualization, flipping the x-axis positioning of all points, and as we will see, puts Democrats on the left side and Republicans on the right. In the American context this is a useful visual cue, as we typically think of Democrats as being ideologically left and Republicans as toward the right.

As you may have guessed, we only noticed that the Democrats would end up on the right and Republicans on the left side of the x-axis points for the MDS after we visualized it. Part of doing data analysis well is being flexible and thinking critically about how you can improve either your method or your presentation of the results after you have completed them. So, although we are presenting this linearly here, be aware that in practice the decision to flip the x-axis in the visualization came only after we had run through the exercise the first time.

```
rollcall.dist <- lapply(rollcall.simple, function(m) dist(m %*% t(m)))

rollcall.mds <- lapply(rollcall.dist,
    function(d) as.data.frame((cmdscale(d, k=2)) * -1))
```

Next, we need to add back in the appropriate identification data to the coordinate points data frames in `rollcall.mds` so that we can visualize them in the context of party affiliation. In the next code block we will do this using a simple for-loop over the `rollcall.mds` list. First, we set the names of the coordinate points columns to x and y. Next, we access the original roll call data frames in `rollcall.data` and extract the senator names column. Recall, that we must first remove the Vice President. Also, some of the senators names include first and last names, but most only the last. For consistency, we strip out the first names by splitting the `name` character vector by a comma and store that vector in the `congress.names` variable. Finally, we use the `transform` function to add in the party affiliation as a `factor` and add the Congress number.

```
congresses <- 101:111
for(i in 1:length(rollcall.mds)) {
    names(rollcall.mds[[i]]) <- c("x", "y")
    congress <- subset(rollcall.data[[i]], state < 99)
    congress.names <- sapply(as.character(congress$name),
        function(n) strsplit(n, "[, ]")[[1]][1])
```

```
    rollcall.mds[[i]] <- transform(rollcall.mds[[i]], name=congress.names,
        party=as.factor(congress$party), congress=congresses[i])
}

head(rollcall.mds[[1]])
           x         y      name party congress
2  -11.44068 293.0001    SHELBY   100      101
3  283.82580 132.4369    HEFLIN   100      101
4  885.85564 430.3451   STEVENS   200      101
5 1714.21327 185.5262 MURKOWSKI   200      101
6 -843.58421 220.1038 DECONCINI   100      101
7 1594.50998 225.8166    MCCAIN   200      101
```

By inspecting the head of the first element in `rollcall.mds` after the contextual data is added, we can see the data frame we will use for the visualization. In the R code file included for this chapter, we have a lengthy set of commands for looping over this list of data frames to create individual visualizations for all Congresses. For brevity, however, we include only a portion of this code here. The code provided will plot the data for the 110th Senate, but could easily be modified to plot any other Congress.

```
cong.110 <- rollcall.mds[[9]]
base.110 <- ggplot(cong.110, aes(x=x, y=y))+scale_size(to=c(2,2), legend=FALSE)+
    scale_alpha(legend=FALSE)+theme_bw()+
    opts(axis.ticks=theme_blank(), axis.text.x=theme_blank(),
        axis.text.y=theme_blank(),
        title="Roll Call Vote MDS Clustering for 110th U.S. Senate",
        panel.grid.major=theme_blank())+
    xlab("")+ylab("")+scale_shape(name="Party", breaks=c("100","200","328"),
        labels=c("Dem.", "Rep.", "Ind."), solid=FALSE)+
    scale_color_manual(name="Party", values=c("100"="black","200"="dimgray",
                    "328"="grey"),
        breaks=c("100","200","328"), labels=c("Dem.", "Rep.", "Ind."))


print(base.110+geom_point(aes(shape=party, alpha=0.75, size=2)))
print(base.110+geom_text(aes(color=party, alpha=0.75, label=cong.110$name, size=2)))
```

Much of what we are doing with `ggplot2` should be familiar to you by now. However, we are using one slight variation in how we are building up the graphics in this case. The typical procedure is to create a `ggplot` object and then add a `geom` or `stat` layer, but in this case, we create a base object called `case.110`, which contains all of the formatting particularities for these plots. This includes `size`, `alpha`, `shape`, `color`, and `opts` layers.

We do this because we want to make two plots: first, a plot of the points themselves where the shape corresponds to party affiliation; and second, a plot where the senators' names are used as points and the text color corresponds to party affiliation. By adding all of these formatting layers to `base.110` first, we can then simply add either `sgeom_point` or `geom_text` layer to the base to get the plot we want. Figure 9-4 shows the results of these plots.

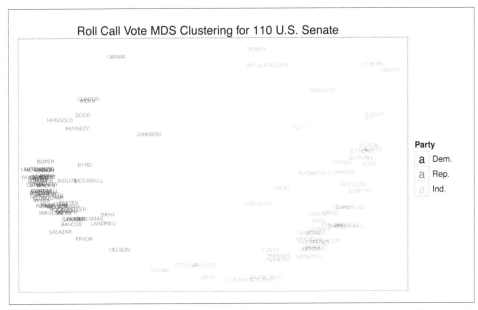

Figure 9-4. Roll call vote MDS clustering for the 110th US Senate: A) senator clustering by party; B) senator clustering with surname

We begin by addressing our initial question: do senators from different parties mix when clustered by roll call vote records? From Figure 9-4, the answer is clearly no. There appears to be quite a large gap between Democrats and Republicans. The data also confirms that those senators often thought to be most extreme are in fact outliers. We can see Senator Sanders, the Independent for Vermont, at the far left, and Senators Coburn and DeMint at the far right. Likewise, Senators Collins and Snowe are tightly clustered at the center for the 111th Congress. As you may recall, it was these moderate Republican senators who became central figures in many of the most recent large legislative battles in the US Senate.

Another interesting result of this analysis is the positioning of Senators Obama and McCain in the 110th Senate. Obama appears singled out in the upper-left quadrant of the plot, whereas McCain is clustered with Senators Wicker and Thomas, closer to the center. Although it might be tempting to interpret this as meaning the two senators had very complementary voting records, given the nature of the data's coding, it is more likely a result of the two missing many of the same votes due to campaigning. That is, when they did vote on the same bill, they may have had relatively different voting habits, although not extremely different voting records, but when they missed votes, it was often for the same piece of legislation. Of course, this begs the question: how do we interpret the position of Wicker and Thomas?

For our final visualization, we will examine the MDS plots for all Congresses in chronological time. This should give us some indication as to the overall mixing of senators by party over time, and this will give us a more principled perspective on the statement that the Senate is more polarized now than it has ever been. In the previous code block we generate a single plot from all of the data by collapsing `rollcall.mds` into a single data frame using `do.call` and `rbind`. We then build up the exact same plot we produced in the previous step, except we add a `facet_wrap` to display the MDS plots in a chronological grid by Congress. Figure 9-5 displays the results of this visualization.

```
all.mds <- do.call(rbind, rollcall.mds)
all.plot <- ggplot(all.mds, aes(x=x, y=y))+
    geom_point(aes(shape=party, alpha=0.75, size=2))+
    scale_size(to=c(2,2), legend=FALSE)+
    scale_alpha(legend=FALSE)+theme_bw()+
    opts(axis.ticks=theme_blank(), axis.text.x=theme_blank(),
        axis.text.y=theme_blank(),
        title="Roll Call Vote MDS Clustering for U.S. Senate
        (101st - 111th Congress)",
        panel.grid.major=theme_blank())+
    xlab("")+ylab("")+
    scale_shape(name="Party", breaks=c("100","200","328"),
        labels=c("Dem.", "Rep.", "Ind."),
        solid=FALSE)+facet_wrap(~ congress)
all.plot
```

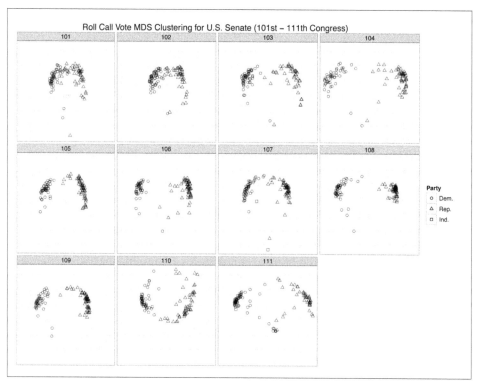

Figure 9-5. Roll call vote MDS clustering for the US Senate (101st–111th Congress)

By using roll call voting as a measure of difference among senators, it seems from these results that the US Senate is in fact just as partisan as it has ever been. By and large, we can see only large groups of triangles and circles clustered together with very few exceptions in each Congress. One might say that the 101st and 102nd Congresses were less polarized because the clusters seem closer. But this is an artifact of the axis scales. Recall that the MDS procedure is simply attempting to minimize a cost function based on the computed distance matrix among all observations. Just because the scales for the 101st and 102nd Congress are smaller than those of many of the other plots does not mean that those Congresses are less polarized. These differences can result for many reasons, such as the number of observations. However, because we have visualized them in a single plot, the scales must be uniform across all panels, which can cause some to appear squeezed or others stretched.

The important takeaway from this plot is that there is very little mixing of parties when you cluster them by roll call voting. Although there may be slight variation within parties, as we can see by the stratification of either the circles or triangle points, there is very little variation between parties. In nearly all cases, we see Democrats clustered with Democrats and Republicans with Republicans. Of course, there are many other pieces of information beyond party affiliation that would be interesting to add to this plot. For instance, we might wonder if senators from the same geographic region cluster together. Or we might wonder if committee comembership leads to clustering. These are all interesting questions, and we encourage the reader to move beyond this initial analysis to dig deeper into this data.

kNN: Recommendation Systems

The *k*-Nearest Neighbors Algorithm

In the last chapter, we saw how we could use simple correlational techniques to create a measure of similarity between the members of Congress based on their voting records. In this chapter, we're going to talk about how you can use those same sort of similarity metrics to recommend items to a website's users.

The algorithm we'll use is called *k*-nearest neighbors. It's arguably the most intuitive of all the machine learning algorithms that we present in this book. Indeed, the simplest form of *k*-nearest neighbors is the sort of algorithm most people would spontaneously invent if asked to make recommendations using similarity data: they'd recommend the song that's closest to the songs a user already likes, but not yet in that list. That intuition is essentially a 1-nearest neighbor algorithm. The full *k*-nearest neighbor algorithm amounts to a generalization of this intuition where you draw on more than one data point before making a recommendation.

The full *k*-nearest neighbors algorithm works much in the way some of us ask for recommendations from our friends. First, we start with people whose taste we feel we share, and then we ask a bunch of them to recommend something to us. If many of them recommend the same thing, we deduce that we'll like it as well.

How can we take that intuition and transform it into something algorithmic? Before we work on making recommendations based on real data, let's start with something simpler: classifying points into two categories. If you remember how we first motivated the problem of classifying spam back in Chapter 3, you'll remember a picture like the one shown in Figure 10-1.

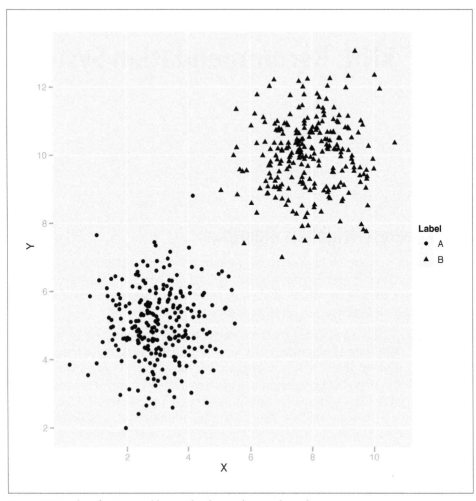

Figure 10-1. Classification problem with a linear decision boundary

As we explained, you can use logistic regression through the glm function to split those points using a single line that we called the decision boundary. At the same time that we explained how to use logistic regression, we also said that there were problems like the one shown in Figure 10-2 that can't be solved using a simple linear decision boundary.

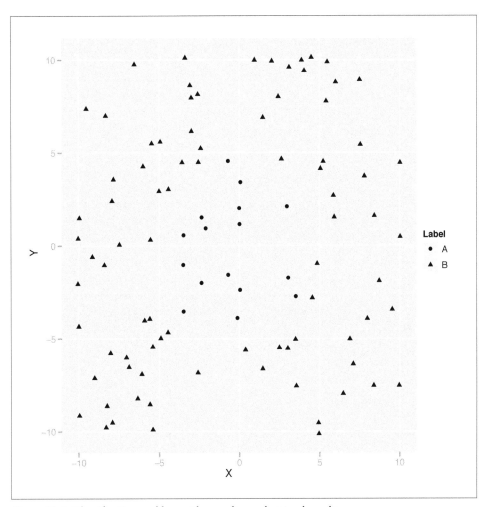

Figure 10-2. Classification problem with a nonlinear decision boundary

How could you try to build a classifier that would match a more complicated decision boundary like the one shown in Figure 10-2? You could try coming up with a nonlinear method; the kernel trick, which we'll discuss in Chapter 12, is an example of this approach.

Another approach would be to use the points nearest the point you're trying to classify to make your guess. You could, for example, draw a circle around the point you're looking at and then decide on a classification based on the points within that circle. Figure 10-3 shows just such an approach, which we'll quickly call the "Grassroots Democracy" algorithm.

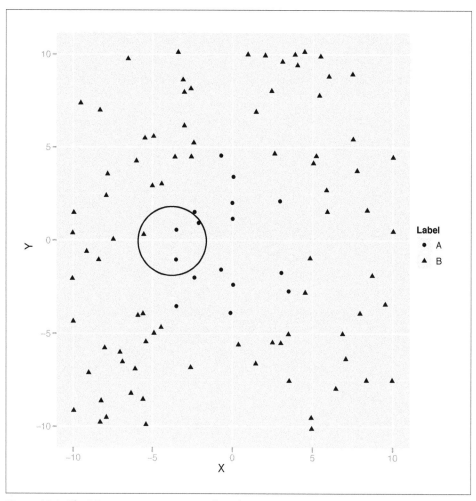

Figure 10-3. The "Grassroots Democracy" algorithm

This algorithm is actually pretty usable, but it has one noticeable flaw: we have to pick a radius for the circle we'll use to define "local" points. If all of your data points have their neighbors at roughly the same distance, this won't be a problem. But if some points have many close neighbors while others have almost none, you'll end up picking a circle that's so big it extends well past the decision boundaries for some points. What can we do to work around this problem? The obvious solution is to avoid using a circle to define a point's neighbors and instead look at the k-closest points. Those points are called the k-nearest neighbors. Once we have them, we can then look at their classifications and use majority rule to decide on a class for our new point. Let's build code to do just that now.

First, we'll read in our data set:

```
df <- read.csv('data/example_data.csv')

head(df)
#         X        Y Label
#1 2.373546 5.398106     0
#2 3.183643 4.387974     0
#3 2.164371 5.341120     0
#4 4.595281 3.870637     0
#5 3.329508 6.433024     0
#6 2.179532 6.980400     0
```

Then we need to compute the distance between each of the points in our data set. We'll store this information in a distance matrix, which is a simple 2D array in which the distance between point i and point j is found at the array entry distance.matrix[i, j]. The following code produces this distance matrix using the Euclidean distance formula:

```
distance.matrix <- function(df)
{
  distance <- matrix(rep(NA, nrow(df) ^ 2), nrow = nrow(df))

  for (i in 1:nrow(df))
  {
    for (j in 1:nrow(df))
    {
      distance[i, j] <- sqrt((df[i, 'X'] - df[j, 'X']) ^ 2 + (df[i, 'Y'] - df[j, 'Y'])
                        ^ 2)
    }
  }

  return(distance)
}
```

Once we have the distance matrix, we need a function that will return the k-nearest neighbors for a point. It's actually easy to implement this in R because you can simply look at the ith row of the distance matrix to find how far all the other points are from your input point. Once you sort this row, you have a list of the neighbors ordered by their distance from the input point. Just select the first k entries after ignoring the input point (which should always be the very first point in the distance matrix), and you'll have the k-nearest neighbors of your input point.

```
k.nearest.neighbors <- function(i, distance, k = 5)
{
  return(order(distance[i, ])[2:(k + 1)])
}
```

Once you've done that, we'll build a knn function that takes a data frame and a value for k and then produces predictions for each point in the data frame. Our function isn't very general, because we're assuming that the class labels are found in a column called Label, but this is just a quick exercise to see how the algorithm works. There are already implementations of *k*-nearest neighbors in R that you can use for practical work, and we'll discuss one in just a moment.

```
knn <- function(df, k = 5)
{
  distance <- distance.matrix(df)

  predictions <- rep(NA, nrow(df))

  for (i in 1:nrow(df))
  {
    indices <- k.nearest.neighbors(i, distance, k = k)
    predictions[i] <- ifelse(mean(df[indices, 'Label']) > 0.5, 1, 0)
  }

  return(predictions)
}
```

As you can see, we've used majority rules voting to make our predictions by taking the mean label and then thresholding at 0.5. Calling this function returns a vector of predictions, so we append those to our data frame and then assess our performance:

```
df <- transform(df, kNNPredictions = knn(df))

sum(with(df, Label != kNNPredictions))
#[1] 7

nrow(df)
#[1] 100
```

We've incorrectly predicted the labels for 7 points out of 100, so we're correct 93% of the time. That's not bad performance for such a simple algorithm. Now that we've explained how the *k*-nearest neighbors (kNN) algorithm works, we'll apply kNN to some real data about the usage of R packages.

But before we do that, let's quickly show you how to use a black-box implementation of kNN for your own projects:

```
rm('knn') # In case you still have our implementation in memory.
library('class')

df <- read.csv('data/example_data.csv')

n <- nrow(df)

set.seed(1)
indices <- sort(sample(1:n, n * (1 / 2)))

training.x <- df[indices, 1:2]
test.x <- df[-indices, 1:2]
training.y <- df[indices, 3]
test.y <- df[-indices, 3]

predicted.y <- knn(training.x, test.x, training.y, k = 5)
sum(predicted.y != test.y)
```

```
#[1] 7

length(test.y)
#[1] 50
```

Here we've tested the knn function from the **class** package using cross-validation. Amazingly, we get exactly 7 labels wrong here as well, but the test set has only 50 examples, so we're only achieving 86% accuracy. That's still pretty good, though. Let's just show you how a logistic model would have worked to give you a point of comparison:

```
logit.model <- glm(Label ~ X + Y, data = df[indices, ])

predictions <- as.numeric(predict(logit.model, newdata = df[-indices, ]) > 0)

sum(predictions != test.y)
#[1] 16
```

As you can see, the best logistic classifier mispredicts 16 data points, which gives it an accuracy of 68%. When your problem is far from being linear, kNN will work out of the box much better than other methods.

R Package Installation Data

Now that we have an understanding of how to use kNN, let's go through the logic of making recommendations. One way we could start to make recommendations is to find items that are similar to the items our users already like and then apply kNN, which we'll call the item-based approach. Another approach is to find items that are popular with users who are similar to the user we're trying to build recommendations for and then apply kNN, which we'll call the user-based approach.

Both approaches are reasonable, but one is almost always better than the other one in practice. If you have many more users than items (just like Netflix has many more users than movies), you'll save on computation and storage costs by using the item-based approach because you only need to compute the similarities between all pairs of items. If you have many more items than users (which often happens when you're just starting to collect data), then you probably want to try the user-based approach. For this chapter, we'll go with the item-based approach.

But before we discuss algorithms for making recommendations in any more detail, let's look at the data we're going to work with. The data set we'll use is the data that was available to participants in the R package recommendation contest on Kaggle. In this contest, we provided contestants with the complete package installation record for approximately 50 R programmers. This is quite a small data set, but it was sufficient to start learning things about the popularity of different packages and their degree of similarity.

The winning entries for the contest all used kNN as part of their recommendation algorithm, though it was generally only one part of many for the winning algorithms. The other important algorithm that was incorporated into most of the winning solutions is called matrix factorization. We won't describe the algorithm in detail, but anyone building a production-level recommendation system should consider combining recommendations from both kNN and matrix factorization models. In fact, the best systems often combine kNN, matrix factorization, and other classifiers together into a super-model. The tricks for combining many classifiers together are usually called ensemble methods. We'll discuss them briefly in Chapter 12.

In the R contest, participants were supposed to predict whether a user would install a package for which we had withheld the installation data by exploiting the fact that you knew which other R packages the user had installed. When making predictions about a new package, you could look at the packages that were most similar to it and check whether they were installed. In other words, it was natural to use an item-based kNN approach for the contest.

So let's load the data set and inspect it a bit. After that, we'll construct a similarity measure between packages. The raw data for the contest is not ideally suited for this purpose, so we've prepared a simpler data set in which each row describes a user-item pair and a third column states whether that user has the package installed or not.

```
installations <- read.csv('data/installations.csv')
head(installations)

#              Package User Installed
#1              abind    1         1
#2 AcceptanceSampling    1         0
#3             ACCLMA    1         0
#4           accuracy    1         1
#5            acepack    1         0
#6         aCGH.Spline    1         0
```

As you can see, user 1 for the contest had installed the abind package, but not the AcceptanceSampling package. This raw information will give us a measure of similarity between packages after we transform it into a different form. What we're going to do is convert this "long form" data into a "wide form" of data in which each row corresponds to a user and each column corresponds to a package. We can do that using the cast function from the reshape package:

```
library('reshape')
user.package.matrix <- cast(installations, User ~ Package, value = 'Installed')

user.package.matrix[, 1]
# [1]  1  3  4  5  6  7  8  9 11 13 14 15 16 19 21 23 25 26 27 28 29 30 31 33 34
#[26] 35 36 37 40 41 42 43 44 45 46 47 48 49 50 51 54 55 56 57 58 59 60 61 62 63
#[51] 64 65
user.package.matrix[, 2]
```

```
# [1] 1 1 0 1 1 1 1 1 1 1 1 0 0 1 1 1 1 1 0 0 1 1 1 1 1 1 1 0 1 0 1 0 1 1 1 1 1 1
#[39] 1 1 1 1 1 1 1 1 0 1 1 1 1 1

row.names(user.package.matrix) <- user.package.matrix[, 1]
user.package.matrix <- user.package.matrix[, -1]
```

First, we've used cast to make our user-package matrix. Once we inspect the first column, we realize that it just stores the user IDs, so we remove it after storing that information in the row.names of our matrix. Now we have a proper user-package matrix that makes it trivial to compute similarity measures. For simplicity, we'll use the correlation between columns as our measure of similarity. To compute that, we can simply call the cor function from R:

```
similarities <- cor(user.package.matrix)

nrow(similarities)
#[1] 2487
ncol(similarities)
#[1] 2487

similarities[1, 1]
#[1] 1
similarities[1, 2]
#[1] -0.04822428
```

Now we have the similarity between all pairs of packages. As you can see, package 1 is perfectly similar to package 1 and somewhat dissimilar from package 2. But kNN doesn't use similarities; it uses distances. So we need to translate similarities into distances. Our approach here is to use some clever algebra so that a similarity of 1 becomes a distance of 0 and a similarity of −1 becomes an infinite distance. The code we've written here does this. If it's not intuitively clear why it works, try to spend some time thinking about how the algebra moves points around.

```
distances <- -log((similarities / 2) + 0.5)
```

With that computation run, we have our distance measure and can start implementing kNN. We'll use k = 25 for example purposes, but you'd want to try multiple values of k in production to see which works best.

To make our recommendations, we'll estimate how likely a package is to be installed by simply counting how many of its neighbors are installed. Then we'll sort packages by this count value and suggest packages with the highest score.

So let's rewrite our k.nearest.neighbors function from earlier:

```
k.nearest.neighbors <- function(i, distances, k = 25)
{
  return(order(distances[i, ])[2:(k + 1)])
}
```

Using the nearest neighbors, we'll predict the probability of installation by simply counting how many of the neighbors are installed:

```
installation.probability <- function(user, package, user.package.matrix, distances,
                                     k = 25)
{
  neighbors <- k.nearest.neighbors(package, distances, k = k)

  return(mean(sapply(neighbors, function (neighbor) {user.package.matrix[user,
          neighbor]})))
}

installation.probability(1, 1, user.package.matrix, distances)
#[1] 0.76
```

Here we see that for user 1, package 1 has probability 0.76 of being installed. So what we'd like to do is find the packages that are most likely to be installed and recommend those. We do that by looping over all of the packages, finding their installation probabilities, and displaying the most probable:

```
most.probable.packages <- function(user, user.package.matrix, distances, k = 25)
{
  return(order(sapply(1:ncol(user.package.matrix),
                      function (package)
                      {
                        installation.probability(user,
                                                 package,
                                                 user.package.matrix,
                                                 distances,
                                                 k = k)
                      }),
               decreasing = TRUE))
}

user <- 1
listing <- most.probable.packages(user, user.package.matrix, distances)
colnames(user.package.matrix)[listing[1:10]]
#[1] "adegenet"    "AIGIS"     "ConvergenceConcepts"
#[4] "corcounts"   "DBI"       "DSpat"
#[7] "ecodist"     "eiPack"    "envelope"
#[10]"fBasics"
```

One of the things that's nice about this approach is that we can easily justify our predictions to end users. We can say that we recommended package P to a user because he had already installed packages X, Y, and Z. This transparency can be a real virtue in some applications.

Now that we've built a recommendation system using only similarity measures, it's time to move on to building an engine in which we use social information in the form of network structures to make recommendations.

## CHAPTER 11

Analyzing Social Graphs

Social Network Analysis

Social networks are everywhere. According to Wikipedia, there are over 200 active social networking websites on the Internet, excluding dating sites. As you can see from Figure 11-1, according to Google Trends there has been a steady and constant rise in global interest in "social networks" since 2005. This is perfectly reasonable: the desire for social interaction is a fundamental part of human nature, and it should come as no surprise that this innate social nature would manifest in our technologies. But the mapping and modeling of social networks is by no means news.

In the mathematics community, an example of social network analysis at work is the calculation of a person's Erdős number, which measures her distance from the prolific mathematician Paul Erdős. Erdős was arguably the most prolific mathematician of the 20th century and published over 1,500 papers during his career. Many of these papers were coauthored, and Erdős numbers measure a mathematician's distance from the circle of coauthors that Erdős enlisted. If a mathematician coauthored with Erdős on a paper, then she would have an Erdős number of one, i.e., her distance to Erdős in the network of 20th-century mathematics is one. If another author collaborated with one of Erdős' coauthors but not with Erdős directly, then that author would have an Erdős number of two, and so on. This metric has been used, though rarely seriously, as a crude measure of a person's prominence in mathematics. Erdős numbers allow us to quickly summarize the massive network of mathematicians orbiting around Paul Erdős.

Erving Goffman, one of the most celebrated intellectuals of the 20th century and very much the equivalent of Paul Erdős in the social sciences based on the overwhelming breadth of his contributions, provides one of the best statements on the nature of human interaction:

[W]hen persons are present to one another they can function not merely as physical instruments but also as communicative ones. This possibility, no less than the physical one, is fateful for everyone concerned and in every society appears to come under strict normative regulation, giving rise to a kind of communication traffic order.

—Erving Goffman, from *Behavior in public places: notes on the social organization of gatherings (1966)*

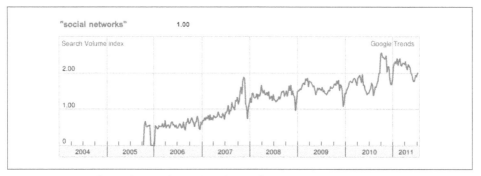

Figure 11-1. Rise of "social networks" in Google searches

The "traffic order" that Goffman was referring to is exactly a social network. The by-product of our desire to interact and socialize with each other are highly structured graphs, which provide a sort of "map" of our identities and histories. Social networking services such as Facebook, Twitter, and LinkedIn simply provide highly stylized templates for engaging in this very natural behavior. The innovation of these services is not in their function, but rather the way in which they provide insight into the social cartography of a very large portion of humanity. To hackers like us, the data that social networking sites expose is a veritable geyser of awesome.

But the value of social graphs goes beyond social networking sites. There are several types of relationships that can be modeled as a network, and many of those are also captured by various Internet services. For example, we could map the relationships among movie watchers based on the movies they have watched on Netflix. Likewise, we could show how various music genres relate to one another based on the patterns of listeners using services such as Last.fm or Spotify. In a more basic way, we may also model the structure of a local computer network—or even the entire Internet—as a massive series of nodes and edges.

Although the study of social networks is very popular now, in large part due to the proliferation of social networking sites, what's commonly referred to as "social network analysis" is a set of tools that has been used and developed over the past several decades. At its core, the study of networks relies on the language of graph theory to describe interconnected objects. As early as 1736, Leonhard Euler used the concept of nodes and edges to formalize the Königsberg Bridge problem.

The Königsberg Bridge problem is an early variant of the Traveling Salesman Problem, in which you must devise a path through the city of Königsberg, Prussia (now Kaliningrad, Russia) by traversing each of its seven bridges exactly once. Euler solved the problem by converting a map of the city to a simple graph with four nodes (city sections) and seven edges (the bridges).

In the 1920s, famed psychologist Jacob L. Moreno developed a method for studying human relationships called "sociometry." Moreno was interested in how people's social interactions affected their well-being, so he asked people who their friends were and began mapping this structure. In 1937, anthropologist Joan Criswell used Moreno's sociometric methods to study racial cleavages between black and white elementary school children [JC37].

Most of what we consider to be contemporary social network analysis is a conglomeration of theory and methods from a wide array of disciplines. A large portion comes from sociology, including prominent scholars such as Linton Freeman, Harrison White, Mark Granovetter, and many others. Likewise, many contributions have also come from physics, economics, computer science, political science, psychology, and countless other disciplines and scholars. There are far too many authors and citations to list here, and tomes have been written that review the methods in this large area of study. Some of the most comprehensive include *Social Network Analysis*, by Stanley Wasserman and Katherine Faust [WF94]; *Social and Economic Networks*, by Matthew O. Jackson [MJ10]; and *Networks, Crowds, and Markets*, by David Easley and Jon Kleinberg [EK10]. In this brief introduction to social network analysis we will cover only a tiny portion of this topic. For those interested in learning more, we highly recommend any of the texts just mentioned.

That said, what will we cover in this chapter? As we have throughout this book, we will focus on a case study in social networks that takes us through the entire data-hacking cycle of acquiring social network data, cleaning and structuring it, and finally analyzing it. In this case we will focus on the preeminent "open" social network of the day: Twitter. The word "open" is in scare quotes because Twitter is not really open in the sense that we can freely access all of its data. Like many social networking sites, it has an API with a strict rate limit. For that reason, we will build a system for extracting data from Twitter without running into this rate limit and without violating Twitter's terms of service. In fact, we won't ever access Twitter's API directly during this chapter.

Our project begins by building a local network, or ego-network, and snowballing from there in the same way that an Erdős number is calculated. For our first analysis, we will explore methods of community detection that attempt to partition social networks into cohesive subgroups. Within the context of Twitter, this can give us information about the different social groups that a given user belongs to. Finally, because this book is about machine learning, we will build our own "who to follow" recommendation engine using the structure of Twitter's social graph.

We will try to avoid using jargon or niche academic terms to describe what we are doing here. There are, however, some terms that are worth using and learning for the purposes of this chapter. We have just introduced the term *ego-network* to describe a type of graph. As we will be referring to ego-networks many more times going forward, it will be useful to define this term. An ego-network always refers to the structure of a social graph immediately surrounding a single node in a network. Specifically, an ego-network is the subset of a network induced by a seed (or ego) and its neighbors, i.e., those nodes directly connected to the seed. Put another way, the ego-network for a given node includes that node's neighbors, the connections between the seed and those neighbors, and the connections among the neighbors.

Thinking Graphically

Before we can dive head first into hacking the Twitter social graph, it will be useful to take a step back and define a network. Mathematically, a network—or graph—is simply a set of nodes and edges. These sets have no context; they only serve the purpose of representing some world in which the edges connect the nodes to one another. In the most abstract formulation, these edges contain no information other than the fact that they connect two nodes. We can, however, see how this general vessel of organizing data can quickly become more complex. Consider the three graphs in Figure 11-2.

In the top panel of Figure 11-2 is an example of an *undirected graph*. In this case, the edges of the graph have no direction. Another way to think about it is that a connection between nodes in this case implies mutuality of the tie. For example, Dick and Harry share a connection, and because this graph is undirected, we can think of this as meaning they can exchange information, goods, etc. with one another over this tie. Also, because this is a very basic network setup, it is easy to overlook the fact that even in the undirected case we have increased the complexity of the graph beyond the most general case we mentioned earlier. In all the graphs in Figure 11-2, we have added labels to the nodes. This is additional information, which is quite useful here, but is important to consider when thinking about how we move from a network abstraction to one that describes real data.

Moving to the middle panel of Figure 11-2, we see a *directed graph*. In this visualization, the edges have arrows that denote the directionality of an edge. Now, edges are not mutual, but indicate instead a one-way tie. For example, Dick and Drew have ties to John, but John only has a tie to Harry. In the final panel of Figure 11-2, we have added *edge labels* to the graph. Specifically, we have added a positive or negative sign to each label. This could indicate a "like" or "dislike" relationship among the members of this network or some level of access. Just as node labels add information and context to a network, so too do edge labels. These labels can also be much more complex than a simple binary relationship. These labels could be weights indicating the strength or type of a relationship.

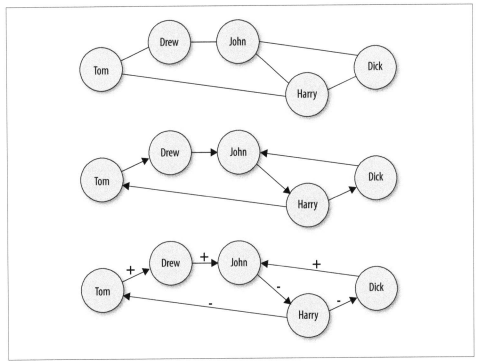

Figure 11-2. Different types of networks: A) undirected network; B) directed network; C) directed network with labeled edges

It is important to consider the differences among these different graph types because the social graph data we will encounter online comes in many different forms. Variation in how the graphs are structured can affect how people use the service and, consequently, how we might analyze the data. Consider two popular social networking sites that vary in the class of graphs they use: Facebook and Twitter. Facebook is a massive, undirected social graph. Because "friending" requires approval, all edges imply a mutual friendship. This has caused Facebook to evolve as a relatively more closed network with dense local network structures rather than the massive central hubs of a more open service. On the other hand, Twitter is a very large directed graph. The following dynamics on Twitter do not require mutuality, and therefore the service allows for large asymmetries in the directed graph in which celebrities, news outlets, and other high-profile users acts as major broadcast points for tweets.

Although the differences in how connections are made between the services may seem subtle, the resulting differences are very large. By changing the dynamic slightly, Twitter has created an entirely different kind of social graph and one that people use in a very different way than they use Facebook. Of course, the reasons for this difference go beyond the graph structures, including Twitter's 140-character limit and the completely public nature of most Twitter accounts, but the graph structure powerfully affects how the entire network operates. We will focus on Twitter for the case study in this chapter, and we will therefore have to consider its directed graph structures during all aspects of the analysis. We begin with the challenge of collecting Twitter's relationship data without exceeding the API rate limit or violating the terms of service.

Hacking Twitter Social Graph Data

At the time of this writing, Twitter provides two different kinds of access to its API. The first is unauthenticated, which allows for 150 requests per hour before getting cut off. Alternatively, OAuth authenticated calls to the API are limited to 350 per hour. Being limited to 150 API calls per hour is far too few to scrape the data we need in a reasonable amount of time. The second limit of 350 is also too few, and furthermore, we are not interested in building a Twitter application that requires authentication. We want to get the data quickly to build the networks so we can begin hacking the data.

 If you are not familiar with RESTful APIs or have never heard of OAuth, don't worry. For the purposes of this exercise we will not worry about those details. If you are interested in learning more about any of them, we suggest reading the documentation for the specific service you are attempting to access. In the case of Twitter, the best reference is the API FAQ: *https://dev.twitter.com/docs/api-faq*.

Unfortunately, we won't be able to do this if we use the API provided by Twitter. To get the data we want, we will have to use another source of Twitter's social graph data: Google's SocialGraph API (also called the SGA). Google introduced the SGA back in 2008 with the intention of creating a single online identity used across all social networking sites. For example, you may have accounts with several online services, all of which resolve to a single email address. The idea with SGA is to use that single bit of information to collate your entire social graph across multiple services. If you're curious about how long your trail of digital exhaust is in Google, type the following in your favorite web browser:

```
https://socialgraph.googleapis.com/lookup?q=@EMAIL_ADDRESS&fme=1&pretty=1
```

If you replace the *EMAIL_ADDRESS* with a proper address, the API will return raw JSON to the browser window, which you can explore to see how much of your social graph Google is already storing! If you have a Twitter account registered to the email address you entered, you will likely also notice that your Twitter page's URL shows up as one of the social graph services that resolves to the email address. Twitter is one of the many social networking sites the SGA crawls to store public social graph data. Therefore, we can use the SGA to query the social network of a specific user and then build out the network.

The primary advantage of using the SGA is that unlike the pittance of hourly queries that Twitter provides, the SGA allows *50,000 queries per day*. Even at Twitter's scale, this will be more than enough queries to build the social graph for the vast majority of users. Of course, if you are Ashton Kutcher or Tim O'Reilly, the method described in this case study will not work. That said, if you are a celebrity and still interested in following along with this exercise, you are welcome to use either of our Twitter usernames: @johnmyleswhite or @drewconway.

```
https://socialgraph.googleapis.com/lookup?q=http://twitter.com/
        drewconway&edo=1&edi=1&pretty=1
```

For example, let's use Drew's Twitter page to explore how SGA structures the data. Type the preceding API query into your web browser of choice. If you would like, you are welcome to query the SGA with your own Twitter username. As before, the SGA will return raw JSON describing Drew's Twitter relationships. From the API query itself, we see three important parameters: edo, edi, and pretty. The pretty parameter is useful only in this browser view because it returns formatted JSON. When we are actually parsing this JSON into a network, we will drop this parameter. edi and edo, however, correspond to the direction of the Twitter relationships. The edo parameter stands for "edges out," i.e., Twitter friends, and edi means "edges in," i.e., Twitter followers.

In Example 11-1 we see an abbreviated version of the formatted raw JSON returned for @drewconway. The JSON object we are most interested is nodes. This contains some descriptive information about the Twitter user—but more importantly, the in- and outbound relationships. The nodes_referenced object contains all of the Twitter friends for the node being queried. These are the other users the node is following (out-degree). Likewise, the nodes_referenced_by object contains the Twitter users following the queried node (in-degree).

Example 11-1. Structure of Google SocialGraph data in raw JSON

```
{
 "canonical_mapping": {
  "http://twitter.com/drewconway": "http://twitter.com/drewconway"
 },
 "nodes": {
  "http://twitter.com/drewconway": {
   "attributes": {
    "exists": "1",
    "bio": "Hopeful academic, data nerd, average hacker, student of conflict.",
    "profile": "http://twitter.com/drewconway",
    "rss": "http://twitter.com/statuses/user_timeline/drewconway.rss",
    "atom": "http://twitter.com/statuses/user_timeline/drewconway.atom",
    "url": "http://twitter.com/drewconway"
   },
   "nodes_referenced": {
     ...
   },
   "nodes_referenced_by": {
     ...
   }
  }
 }
}
```

The SGA crawler simply scans Twitter for public links among users and stores the relationships in its database. Private Twitter accounts are therefore absent from the data. If you are examining your own SGA data, you may notice that it does not reflect your exact current Twitter relationships. Specifically, the `nodes_referenced` object may contain users that you no longer follow. This is because SGA only periodically crawls the active links, so its cached data does not always reflect the most up-to-date data.

Of course, we do not want to work with SGA through the browser. This API is meant to be accessed programmatically, and the returned JSON needs to be parsed into a graph object so that we can build and analyze these Twitter networks. To build these graph objects, our strategy will be to use a single Twitter user as a seed (recall the Erdős number) and build out the network from that seed. We will use a method called snowball sampling, which begins with a single seed and then finds all in- and out-degree connections to that seed. Then we will use those connections as new seeds and repeat the process for a fixed number of rounds.

For this case study, we will perform only two rounds of sampling, which we do for two reasons. First, we are interested in mapping and analyzing the seed user's local network structure to make recommendations about who the seed user should follow. Second, because of the scale of Twitter's social graph, we might quickly exceed the SGA rate limit and our hard drive's storage capacity if we used more rounds. With this limitation in mind, in the next section we begin by developing the foundational functions for working with the SGA and parsing the data.

Working with the Google SocialGraph API

A Major Change in the Google SocialGraph API

As this book went to print, it came to our attention that the Google SocialGraph API no longer stored the same amount of Twitter data as it had when this chapter and code were first written. As such, if you run the code exactly as it appears in this section, the resulting data will differ dramatically from what is required to complete the case study in this chapter. Unfortunately there is nothing we can do to fix this data problem. We decided to leave this section because we believe having exposure to working with APIs is extremely important, and we did not want to deprive the reader of this exposition. We have included several example data sets in the supplemental files of the book that were generated by this code before the SocialGraph API occurred. You can use this data to work through the rest of the case study.

We begin by loading the R packages we will need to generate the Twitter graphs. We will be using three R packages for building these graphs from the SGA. The `RCurl` package provides an interface to the `libcurl` library, which we will use for making

HTTP requests to the SGA. Next, we will use RJSONIO to parse the JSON returned by the SGA in the R lists. As it happens, both of these packages are developed by Duncan Temple Lang, who has developed many indispensable R packages (see *http://www.ome gahat.org/*). Finally, we will use igraph to construct and store the network objects. The igraph package is a powerful R package for creating and manipulating graph objects, and its flexibility will be very valuable to us as we begin to work with our network data.

```
library(RCurl)
library(RJSONIO)
library(igraph)
```

The first function we will write works with the SGA at the highest level. We will call the function twitter.network to query the SGA for a given seed user, parse the JSON, and return a representation of that user's ego-network. This function takes a single parameter, user, which is a string corresponding to a seed Twitter user. It then constructs the corresponding SGA GET request URL and uses the getURL function in RCurl to make an HTTP request. Because the snowball search will require many HTTP requests at once, we build in a while-loop that checks to make sure that the page returned is not indicating a service outage. Without this, the script would inadvertently skip those nodes in the snowball search, but with this check it will just go back and attempt a new request until the data is gathered. Once we know the API request has returned JSON, we use the fromJSON function in the RJSONIO package to parse the JSON.

```
twitter.network <- function(user) {
    api.url <-
    paste("https://socialgraph.googleapis.com/lookup?q=http://twitter.com/",
              user, "&edo=1&edi=1", sep="")
    api.get <- getURL(api.url)
    # To guard against web-request issues, we create this loop
    # to ensure we actually get something back from getURL.
    while(grepl("Service Unavailable. Please try again later.", api.get)) {
        api.get <- getURL(api.url)
    }
    api.json <- fromJSON(api.get)
    return(build.ego(api.json))
}
```

With the JSON parsed, we need to build the network from that data. Recall that the data contains two types of relationships: nodes_referenced (out-degree) and nodes_referenced_by (in-degree). So we will need to make two passes through the data to include both types of edges. To do so, we will write the function build.ego, which takes parsed SGA JSON as a list and builds the network. Before we can begin, however, we have to clean the relational data returned by the SGA. If you inspect carefully all of the nodes returned by the API request, you will notice that some of the entries are not proper Twitter users. Included in the results are relationships extraneous to this exercise. For example, there are many Twitter lists as well as URLs that refer to "account" redirects. Though all of these are part of the Twitter social graph, we are not interested in including these nodes in our graph, so we need to write a helper function to remove them.

```
find.twitter <- function(node.vector) {
    twitter.nodes <- node.vector[grepl("http://twitter.com/", node.vector,
                                        fixed=TRUE)]
    if(length(twitter.nodes) > 0) {
        twitter.users <- strsplit(twitter.nodes, "/")
        user.vec <- sapply(1:length(twitter.users),
                        function(i) (ifelse(twitter.users[[i]][4]=="account",
                                        NA, twitter.users[[i]][4])))
        return(user.vec[which(!is.na(user.vec))])
    }
    else {
        return(character(0))
    }
}
```

The find.twitter function does this by exploiting the structure of the URLs returned
by the SGA to verify that they are in fact Twitter users, rather than some other part of
the social graph. The first thing this function does is check which nodes returned by
the SGA are actually from Twitter by using the grepl function to check for the pattern
http://twitter.com/. For those URLs that match, we need to find out which ones correspond to actual accounts, rather than lists or redirects. One way to do this is to split
the URLs by a backslash and then check for the word "account," which indicates a
non-Twitter-user URL. Once we identify the indices that match this non-Twitter pattern, we simply return those URLs that don't match this pattern. This will inform the
build.ego function which nodes should be added to the network.

```
build.ego <- function(json) {
    # Find the Twitter user associated with the seed user
    ego <- find.twitter(names(json$nodes))
    # Build the in- and out-degree edgelist for the user
    nodes.out <- names(json$nodes[[1]]$nodes_referenced)
    if(length(nodes.out) > 0) {
        # No connections, at all
        twitter.friends <- find.twitter(nodes.out)
        if(length(twitter.friends) > 0) {
            # No twitter connections
            friends <- cbind(ego, twitter.friends)
        }
        else {
            friends <- c(integer(0), integer(0))
        }
    }
    else {
        friends <- c(integer(0), integer(0))
    }
    nodes.in <- names(json$nodes[[1]]$nodes_referenced_by)
    if(length(nodes.in) > 0) {
        twitter.followers <- find.twitter(nodes.in)
        if(length(twitter.followers) > 0) {
            followers <- cbind(twitter.followers, ego)
        }
        else {
            followers <- c(integer(0), integer(0))
```

```
        }
    }
    else {
        followers <- c(integer(0), integer(0))
    }
    ego.el <- rbind(friends, followers)
    return(ego.el)
}
```

With the proper nodes identified in the list, we can now begin building the network. To do so, we will use the `build.ego` to create an "edge list" to describe the in- and out-degree relationships of our seed user. An edge list is simply a two-column matrix representing the relationships in a directional graph. The first column contains the sources of edges, and the second column contains the targets. You can think of this as nodes in the first column linking to those in the second. Most often, edge lists will contain either integer or string labels for the nodes. In this case, we will use the the Twitter username string.

Though the `build.ego` function is long in line-count, its functionality is actually quite simple. Most of the code is used to organize and error-check the building of the edge lists. As you can see, we first check that the API calls for both `nodes_referenced` and `nodes_referenced_by` returned at least some relationships. And then we check which nodes actually refer to Twitter users. If either of these checks returns nothing, we will return a special vector as the output of our function: `c(integer(0), integer(0))`. Through this process we create two edge-list matrices, aptly named `friends` and `followers`. In the final step, we use `rbind` to bind these two matrices into a single edge list, called `ego.el`. We used the special vector `c(integer(0), integer(0))` in the cases where there is no data because the `rbind` will effectively ignore it and our results will not be affected. You can see this for yourself by typing the following at the R console:

```
rbind(c(1,2), c(integer(0), integer(0)))
     [,1] [,2]
[1,]   1    2
```

 You may be wondering why we are building up only an edge list of relationships rather than building the graph directly with `igraph`. Because of the way `igraph` stores graphs in memory, it can be difficult to iteratively build graphs in the way that a snowball sample requires. As such, it is much easier to build out the entire relational data set first (in this case as an edge list) and then convert that data to a graph later.

We have now written the core of our graph-building script. The `build.ego` function does the difficult work of taking parsed JSON from the SGA and turning it into something that `igraph` can turn into a network. The final bit of functionality we will need to build is to pull everything together in order to generate the snowball sample. We will create the `twitter.snowball` function to generate this sample and one small helper function, `get.seeds`, to generate the list of new seeds to visit. As in `build.ego`, the primary purpose of `twitter.snowball` is to generate an edge list of the network relationships. In this case, however, we will be binding together the results of many calls to `build.ego` and returning an `igraph` graph object. For simplicity, we begin with the `get.seeds` function, though it will refer to things generated in `twitter.snowball`.

```
get.seeds <- function(snowball.el, seed) {
    new.seeds <- unique(c(snowball.el[,1],snowball.el[,2]))
    return(new.seeds[which(new.seeds!=seed)])
}
```

The purpose of `get.seeds` is to find the unique set of nodes from a edge list that are *not* the seed nodes. This is done very easily by reducing the two-column matrix into a single vector and then finding the unique elements of that vector. This clean vector is called `new.seeds`, and from this, only those elements that are not the seed are returned. This is a simple and effective method, but there is one thing we must consider when using this method.

The `get.seeds` function only checks that the new seeds are not the same as the current seed. We would like to include something to ensure that during our snowball sample we do not revisit nodes in the network for which structure has already been regenerated. From a technical perspective this is not necessarily important, as we could very easily remove duplicate rows in the final edge list. It is important, however, from a practical perspective. By removing nodes that have already been visited from the list of potential new seeds before building new structure, we cut down on the the number of API calls that we must make. This in turn reduces the likelihood of hitting up against the SGA's rate limit and shortens our script's running time. Rather than having the `get.seeds` function handle this, we add this functionality to `twitter.snowball`, where the entire network edge list is already stored in memory. This ensures that there are not multiple copies of the entire edge list in memory as we are building out the entire snowball. Remember, at these scales, we need to be very conscious of memory, especially in a language like R.

```
twitter.snowball <- function(seed, k=2) {
    # Get the ego-net for the seed user. We will build onto
    # this network to create the full snowball search.
    snowball.el <- twitter.network(seed)

    # Use neighbors as seeds in the next round of the snowball
    new.seeds <- get.seeds(snowball.el, seed)
    rounds <- 1  # We have now completed the first round of the snowball!

    # A record of all nodes hit, this is done to reduce the amount of
    # API calls done.
    all.nodes <- seed

    # Begin the snowball search...
    while(rounds < k) {
        next.seeds <- c()
        for(user in new.seeds) {
            # Only get network data if we haven't already visited this node
            if(!user %in% all.nodes) {
```

```
                    user.el <- twitter.network(user)
                    if(dim(user.el)[2] > 0) {
                        snowball.el <- rbind(snowball.el, user.el)
                        next.seeds <- c(next.seeds, get.seeds(user.el, user))
                        all.nodes <- c(all.nodes, user)
                    }
                }
            }
        new.seeds <- unique(next.seeds)
        new.seeds <- new.seeds[!which(new.seeds %in% all.nodes)]
        rounds <- rounds + 1
    }
    # It is likely that this process has created duplicate rows.
    # As a matter of housekeeping we will remove them because
    # the true Twitter social graph does not contain parallel edges.
    snowball.el <- snowball.el[!duplicated(snowball.el),]
    return(graph.edgelist(snowball.el))
}
```

The functionality of the `twitter.snowball` function is as you might expect. The function takes two parameters: `seed` and k. The first is a character string for a Twitter user, and in our case, this could be "drewconway" or "johnmyleswhite." The k is an integer greater than or equal to two and determines the number of rounds for the snowball search. In network parlance, the *k* value generally refers to a degree or distance within a graph. In this case, it corresponds to the distance from the seed in the network the snowball sample will reach. Our first step is to build the initial ego-network from the seed; from this, we will get the new seeds for the next round.

We do this with calls to `twitter.network` and `get.seeds`. Now the iterative work of the snowball sample can begin. The entire sampling occurs inside the while-loop of `twitter.snowball`. The basic logical structure of the loop is as follows. First, check that we haven't reached the end of our sample distance. If not, then proceed to build another layer of the snowball. We do so by iteratively building the ego-networks of each of our new seed users. The `all.nodes` object is used to keep track of nodes that have already been visited; in other words, before we build a node's ego-network, we first check that it is not already in `all.nodes`. If it is not, then we add this user's relationships to `snowball.el`, `next.seeds`, and `all.nodes`. Before we proceed to the next round of the snowball, we check that the new `new.seeds` vector does not contain any duplicates. Again, this is done to prevent revisiting nodes. Finally, we increment the `rounds` counter.

In the final step, we take the matrix `snowball.el`, which represents the edge list of the entire snowball sample, and convert it into an `igraph` graph object using the `graph.edge list` function. There is one final bit of housekeeping we must do, however, before the conversion. Because the data in the SGA is imperfect, occasionally there will be duplicate relationships between the sample edges. Graphing theoretically, we could leave these relationships in and use a special class of graph called a "multi-graph" as our Twitter network. A multi-graph is simply a graph with multiple edges between the same nodes. Although this paradigm may be useful in some contexts, there are very few social network analysis metrics that are valid for such a model. Also, because in this case the extra edges are the result of errors, we will remove those duplicated edges before converting to a graph object.

We now have all the functionality we need to build out Twitter networks. In the next section we will build supplemental scripts that make it easy to quickly generate network structure from a given seed user and perform some basic structural analysis on these graphs to discover the local community structure in them.

Analyzing Twitter Networks

It's time to start building Twitter networks. By way of introducing an alternative approach to building and running R scripts, in this case we will build the code as a shell script to be run at the command line. Up to this point we have been writing code to be run inside the R console, which will likely be the dominant way in which you will use the language. Occasionally, however, you may have a task or program that you wish to perform many times with different inputs. In this case, it can be easier to write a program that runs at the command line and takes inputs from standard input. To do this we will use the `Rscript` command-line program that comes with your R installation. Rather than run the code now, let's first go through it so we understand what it is doing before we fire up the program.

 Recall that due to a change in Google SocialGraph API that became apparent to us at the time of this writing, we can no longer generate new Twitter network data. As such, for the remainder of this chapter we will be using the Twitter network data for John (@johnmyleswhite) as it stood at the time we first collected it.

Because we may want to build Twitter networks for many different users, our program should be able to take different usernames and input and generate the data as needed. Once we have built the network object in memory, we will perform some basic network analysis on it to determine the underlying community structure, add this information to the graph object, and then export the networks as files to the disk. We begin by loading the igraph library as well as the functions built in the previous section, which we have placed in the *google_sg.R* file.

```
library(igraph)

source('google_sg.R')

user <- 'johnmyleswhite'

user.net <- read.graph(paste("data/",user, "/", user, "_net.graphml", sep =
""), format = "graphml")
```

We will again be using the `igraph` library to build and manipulate the Twitter graph objects. We use the `source` function to load in the functions written in the previous section. Because we are not going to be generating new data for this case study, we load data previously scraped for John's Twitter network by loading the data in the *johnmyleswhite* folder.

 A note to Windows users: you may not be able to run this script from the DOS shell. In this case, you should just set the user variable to whatever Twitter user you would like to build the network for and run this script as you have done before. This is noted again in the *twitter_net.R* file as well.

After having built all of the necessary support functions in the previous section, we need only pass our seed user to the `twitter.snowball` function. Also, because in this example we are interested in building the seed user's ego-network, we will have used only two rounds for the snowball sample. Later in this chapter we will load the network files into the graph visualization software Gephi, which will allow us to build beautiful visualizations of our data. Gephi has some reserved variable names that it uses for visualization. One of those is the `Label` variable, which is used to label nodes in the graph. By default, `igraph` stores label information as the `name` vertex attribute, so we need to create a new vertex attribute called `Label` that duplicates this information. We use the `set.vertex.attribute` function to do this, which takes the `user.net` graph object created in the previous step, a new attribute, and a vector of data to assign to that attribute.

```
user.net <- set.vertex.attribute(user.net, "Label",
    value = get.vertex.attribute(user.net, "name"))
```

 Gephi is an open source, multiplatform graph visualization and manipulation platform. The built-in network visualization tools in R and igraph are useful, but insufficient for our needs. Gephi is specifically designed for network visualizations and includes many useful features for creating high-quality network graphics. If you do not have Gephi installed or have an old version, we highly recommend installing the latest version, available at *http://gephi.org/*.

With the graph object now built, we will perform some basic network analysis on it to both reduce its complexity and uncover some of its local community structure.

Local Community Structure

Our first step in the analytical process is extracting the core elements of the graph. There are two useful subgraphs of the full `user.net` object that we will want to extract. First, we will perform a *k-core* analysis to extract the graph's 2-core. By definition, a k-core analysis will decompose a graph by node connectivity. To find the "coreness" of a graph, we want to know how many nodes have a certain degree. The k in k-core describes the degree of the decomposition. So, a graph's 2-core is a subgraph of the nodes that have a degree of two or more. We are interested in extracting the 2-core because a natural by-product of doing a snowball search is having many pendant nodes at the exterior of the network. These pendants contribute very little, if any, useful information about the network's structure, so we want to remove them.

Recall, however, that the Twitter graph is directed, which means that nodes have both an in- and out-degree. To find those nodes that are more relevant to this analysis, we will use the `graph.coreness` function to calculate the coreness of each node by its in-degree by setting the `mode="in"` parameter. We do this because we want to keep those nodes that receive at least two edges, rather than those that give two edges. Those pendants swept up in the snowball sample will likely have connectivity into the network, but not from it; therefore, we use in-degree to find them.

```
user.cores <- graph.coreness(user.net, mode="in")
user.clean <- subgraph(user.net, which(user.cores>1)-1)
```

The `subgraph` function takes a graph object and a set of nodes as inputs and returns the subgraph induced by those nodes on the passed graph. To extract the 2-core of the `user.net` graph, we use the base R `which` function to find those nodes with an in-degree coreness greater than one.

```
user.ego <- subgraph(user.net, c(0, neighbors(user.net, user, mode = "out")))
```

 One of the most frustrating "gotchas" of working with `igraph` is that `igraph` uses zero-indexing for nodes, whereas R begins indexing at one. In the 2-core example you'll notice that we subtract one from the vector returned by the `which` function, lest we run into the dreaded "off by one" error.

The second key subgraph we will extract is the seed's ego-network. Recall that this is the subgraph induced by the seed's neighbors. Thankfully, `igraph` has a useful `neighbors` convenience function for identifying these nodes. Again, however, we must be cognizant of Twitter's directed graph structure. A node's neighbors be can either in- or outbound, so we must tell the `neighbors` function which we would like. For this example, we will examine the ego-network induced by the out-degree neighbors, or those Twitter users that the seed follows, rather than those that follow the seed. From an analytical perspective it may be more interesting to examine those users someone follows, particularly if you are examining your own data. That said, the alternative may be interesting as well, and we welcome the reader to rerun this code and look at the in-degree neighbors instead.

For the rest of this chapter we will focus on the ego-network, but the 2-core is very useful for other network analyses, so we will save it as part of our data pull. Now we are ready to analyze the ego-network to find local community structure. For this exercise we will be using one of the most basic methods for determining community membership: hierarchical clustering of node distances. This is a mouthful, but the concept is quite simple. We assume that nodes, in this case Twitter users, that are more closely connected, i.e., have less hops between them, are more similar. This make sense practically because we may believe that people with shared interests follow each other on Twitter and therefore have shorter distances between them. What is interesting is to see what that community structure looks like for a given user, as people may have several different communities within their ego-network.

```
user.sp <- shortest.paths(user.ego)
user.hc <- hclust(dist(user.sp))
```

The first step in performing such an analysis is to measure the distances among all of the nodes in our graph. We use `shortest.paths`, which returns an N-by-N matrix, where N is the number of nodes in the graph and the shortest distance between each pair of nodes is the entry for each position in the matrix. We will use these distances to calculate node partitions based on the proximity of nodes to one another. As the name suggests, "hierarchical" clustering has many levels. The process creates these levels, or cuts, by attempting to keep the closest nodes in the same partitions as the number of partitions increases. For each layer further down the hierarchy, we increase the number of partitions, or groups of nodes, by one. Using this method, we can iteratively decompose a graph into more granular node groupings, starting with all nodes in the same group and moving down the hierarchy until all the nodes are in their own group.

R comes with many useful functions for doing clustering. For this work we will use a combination of the `dist` and `hclust` functions. The `dist` function will create a distance matrix from a matrix of observation. In our case, we have already calculated the distances with the `shortest.path` function, so the `dist` function is there simply to convert that matrix into something `hclust` can work with. The `hclust` function does the clustering and returns a special object that contains all of the clustering information we need.

One useful thing to do once you have clustered something hierarchically is to view the *dendrogram* of the partition. A dendrogram produces a tree-like diagram that shows how the clusters separate as you move further down the hierarchy. This will give us our first peek into the community structure of our ego-network. As an example, let's inspect the dendrogram for John's Twitter ego-network, which is included in the *data/* directory for this chapter. To view his dendrogram, we will load his ego-network data, perform the clustering, and then pass the `hclust` object to the `plot` function, which knows to draw the dendrogram.

```
user.ego <- read.graph('data/johnmyleswhite/johnmyleswhite_ego.graphml', format =
                       'graphml')

user.sp <- shortest.paths(user.ego)
user.hc <- hclust(dist(user.sp))

plot(user.hc)
```

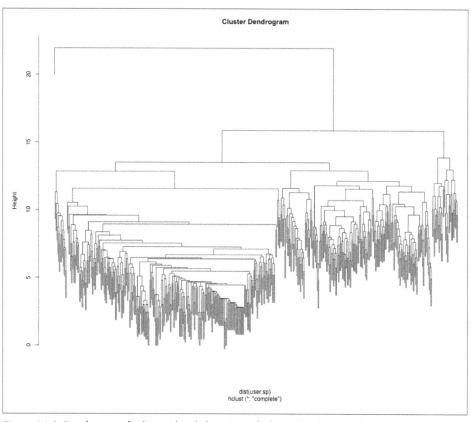

Figure 11-3. Dendrogram for hierarchical clustering of johnmyleswhite's Twitter ego-network, with partitions of hierarchy along the y-axis.

Looking at Figure 11-3, we can already see some really interesting community structure emerging from John's Twitter network. There appears to be a relatively clean split between two high-level communities, and then within those are many smaller tightly knit subgroups. Of course, everyone's data will be different, and the number of communities you see will be largely dependent on the size and density of your Twitter ego-network.

Although it is interesting from an academic standpoint to inspect the clusters using the dendrogram, we would really like to see them on the network. To do this, we will need to add the clustering partition data to the nodes, which we will do by using a simple loop to add the first 10 nontrivial partitions to our network. By nontrivial we mean we are skipping the first partition, because that partition assigns all of the nodes to the same group. Though important in terms of the overall hierarchy, it gives us no local community structure.

```
for(i in 2:10) {
    user.cluster <- as.character(cutree(user.hc, k=i))
```

```
    user.cluster[1] <- "0"
    user.ego <- set.vertex.attribute(user.ego, name=paste("HC",i,sep=""),
        value=user.cluster)
}
```

The cutree function returns the partition assignment for each element in the hierarchy at a given level, i.e., it "cuts the tree." The clustering algorithm doesn't know that we have given it an ego-network where a single node is the focal point, so it has grouped our seed in with other nodes at every level of clustering. To make it easier to identify the seed user later during visualization, we assign it to its own cluster: "0". Finally, we use the set.vertex.attributes function again to add this information to our graph object. We now have a graph object that contains the Twitter names and the first 10 clustering partitions from our analysis.

Before we can fire up Gephi and visualize the results, we need to save the graph object to a file. We will use the write.graph function to export this data as GraphML files. GraphML is one of many network file formats and is XML-based. It is useful for our purposes because our graph object contains a lot of metadata, such as node labels and cluster partitions. As with most XML-based formats, GraphML files can get large fast and are not ideal for simply storing relational data. For more information on GraphML, see *http://graphml.graphdrawing.org/*.

```
write.graph(user.net, paste("data/", user, "/", user, "_net.graphml", sep=""),
    format="graphml")
write.graph(user.clean, paste("data/", user, "/", user, "_clean.graphml", sep=""),
    format="graphml")
write.graph(user.ego, paste("data/", user, "/", user, "_ego.graphml", sep=""),
    format="graphml")
```

We save all three graph objects generated during this process. In the next section we will visualize these results with Gephi using the example data included with this book.

Visualizing the Clustered Twitter Network with Gephi

As mentioned earlier, we will be using the Gephi program to visually explore our network data. If you have already downloaded and installed Gephi, the first thing to do is to open the application and load the Twitter data. For this example, we will be using Drew's Twitter ego-network, which is located in the *code/data/drewconway/* directory for this chapter. If, however, you have generated your own Twitter data, you are welcome to use that instead.

This is by no means a complete or exhaustive introduction to visualizing networks in Gephi. This section will explain how to visually explore the local community structures of the Twitter ego-network data only. Gephi is a robust program for network visualization that includes many options for analyzing the data. We will use very few of these capabilities in this section, but we highly encourage you to play with the program and explore its many options. One great place to start is Gephi's own Quick Start Tutorial, which is available online here: *http://gephi.org/ 2010/quick-start-tutorial/*.

With Gephi open, you will load the the ego-network at the menu bar with File→Open. Navigate to the *drewconway* directory, and open the *drewconway_ego.graphml* file, as shown in the top panel of Figure 11-4. Once you have loaded the graph, Gephi will report back some basic information about the network file you have just loaded. The bottom panel of Figure 11-4 shows this report, which includes the number of nodes (263) and edges (6,945). If you click the Report tab in this window, you will also see all of the attribute data we have added to this network. Of particular interest are the node attributes HC*, which are the hierarchical clustering partition labels for the first 10 nontrivial partitions.

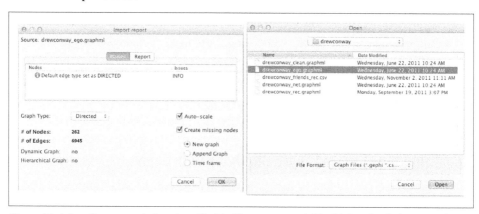

Figure 11-4. Loading network data into Gephi: A) open network file; B) data loaded into Gephi

The first thing you'll notice is that Gephi loads the network as a large mess of randomly placed nodes, the dreaded "network hairball." Much of the community structure information in the network can be expressed by a more deliberate placement of these nodes. Methods and algorithms for node placement in large, complex networks are something of a cottage industry; as such, there are a tremendous number of ways in which we can rearrange the nodes. For our purposes, we want nodes with more shared connections to be placed closer together. Recall that our clustering method was based on placing nodes in groups based on their distance from each other. Nodes with shorter distances would be grouped together, and we want our visualization technique to mirror this.

One group of popular methods for placing nodes consists of "force-directed" algorithms. As the name suggests, these algorithms attempt to simulate how the nodes would be placed if a force of attraction and repulsion were placed on the network. Imagine that the garbled mess of edges among nodes that Gephi is currently displaying are actually elastic bands, and the nodes are ball bearings that could hold a magnetic charge. A force-directed algorithm attempts to calculate how the ball bearing nodes would repel away from each other as a result of the charge, but then be pulled back by the elastic edges. The result is a visualization that neatly places nodes together depending on their local community structure.

Gephi comes with many examples of force-directed layouts. In the Layout panel, the pull-down menu contains many different options, some of which are force-directed. For our purposes we will choose the Yifan Hu Proportional algorithm and use the default settings. After selecting this algorithm, click the Run button, and you will see Gephi rearranging the nodes in this force-directed manner. Depending on the size of your network and the particular hardware you are running, this may take some time. Once the nodes have stopped moving, the algorithm has optimized the placement of the nodes, and we are ready to move on.

To more easily identify the local communities in the network and their members, we will resize and color the nodes. Because the network is a directed ego-network, we will set the node size as a function of the nodes' in-degrees. This will make the seed node the largest because nearly every member of the network is following the seed, and it will also increase the size of other prominent users in the ego-network. In the Rankings panel, click the Nodes tab and select InDegree from the pull-down. Click the red diamond icon to set the size; you can set the min and max sizes to whatever you like. As you can see in the bottom half of Figure 11-5, we have chosen 2 and 16 respectively for Drew's network, but other settings may work better for you. Once you have the values set, click the Apply button to resize the nodes.

The final step is to color the nodes by their community partitions. In the Partition panel, located above the Rankings panel, you will see an icon with two opposing arrows. Click this to refresh the list of partitions for this graph. After you've done that, the pull-down will include the node attribute data we included for these partitions. As shown in the top half of Figure 11-5, we have chosen HC8, or the eighth partition, which includes a partition for Drew (drewconway) and seven other nodes in his ego-network. Again, click the Apply button, and the nodes will be colored by their partition.

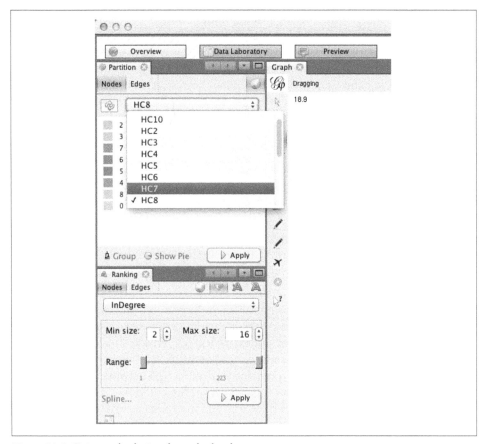

Figure 11-5. Sizing and coloring the nodes by cluster

Immediately, you will see the underlying structure! One excellent way to see how a particular network begins to fracture into smaller subcommunities is to step through the partitions of a hierarchical cluster. As an exercise, we suggest doing that in Gephi by iteratively recoloring the nodes by increasingly granular partitions. Begin with HC2 and work your way to HC10, each time recoloring the nodes to see how larger groups begin to split. This will tell you a lot about the underlying structure of the network. Figure 11-6 shows Drew's ego-network colored by HC8, which highlights beautifully the local community structure of his Twitter network.

Drew appears to have essentially four primary subcommunities. With Drew himself colored in teal at the center, we can see two tightly connected groups colored red and violet to his left; and two other less tightly connected subgroups to his right are in blue and green. There are, of course, other groups colored in orange, pink, and light green, but we will focus on the four primary groups.

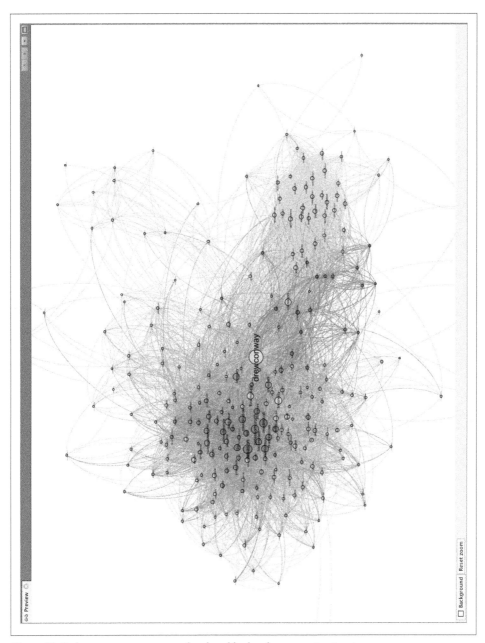

Figure 11-6. drewconway ego-network colored by local community structure

In Figure 11-7 we have focused on the left side of the network and removed the edges to make it easier to view the node labels. Quickly looking over the Twitter names in this cluster, it is clear that this side of Drew's network contains the data nerds Drew follows on Twitter. First, we see very high-profile data nerds, such as Tim O'Reilly (timoreilly) and Nathan Yau (flowingdata) colored in light green because they are somewhat in a "league of their own." The purple and red groups are interesting as well, as they both contain data hackers, but are split by one key factor: Drew's friends who are colored purple are prominent members of the data community, such as Hilary Mason (hmason), Pete Skomoroch (peteskomoroch), and Jake Hofman (jakehofman), but none of them are vocal members of the R community. On the other hand, the nodes colored in red are vocal members of the R community, including Hadley Wickham (hadleywickham), David Smith (revodavid), and Gary King (kinggary).

Moreover, the force-directed algorithm has succeed in placing these members close to each other and placed those that sit between these two communities at the edges. We can see John (johnmyleswhite) colored in purple, but placed in with many other red nodes. This is because John is prominent in both communities, and the data reflects this. Other examples of this include JD Long (cmastication) and Josh Reich (i2pi).

Although Drew spends a lot of time interacting with members of the data community —both R and non-R users alike—Drew also uses Twitter to interact with communities that satisfy his other interests. One interest in particular is his academic career, which focuses on national security technology and policy. In Figure 11-8 we highlight the right side of Drew's network, which includes members from these communities. Similarly to the data nerds group, this includes two subgroups, one colored blue and the other green. As with the previous example, the partition color and placement of the node can illustrate much about their role in the network.

Twitter users in the blue partition are spread out: some are closer to Drew and the left side of the network, whereas others are farther to the right and near the green group. Those farther to the left are people who work or speak about the role of technology in national security, including Sean Gourley (sgourley), Lewis Shepherd (lewisshepherd), and Jeffrey Carr (Jeffrey Carr). Those closer to the green are more focused on national security policy, like the other members of the green group. In green, we see many high-profile members of the national security community on Twitter, including Andrew Exum (abumuqawama), Joshua Foust (joshua Foust), and Daveed Gartenstein-Ross (daveedgr). Interestingly, just as before, people who sit between these groups are placed close to the edges, such as Chris Albon (chrisalbon), who is prominent in both.

If you are exploring your own data, what local community structure do you see emerging? Perhaps the structure is quite obvious, as is the case with Drew's network, or maybe the communities are more subtle. It can be quite interesting and informative to explore these structures in detail, and we encourage you to do so. In the next and final section, we will use these community structures to build our own "who to follow" recommendation engine for Twitter.

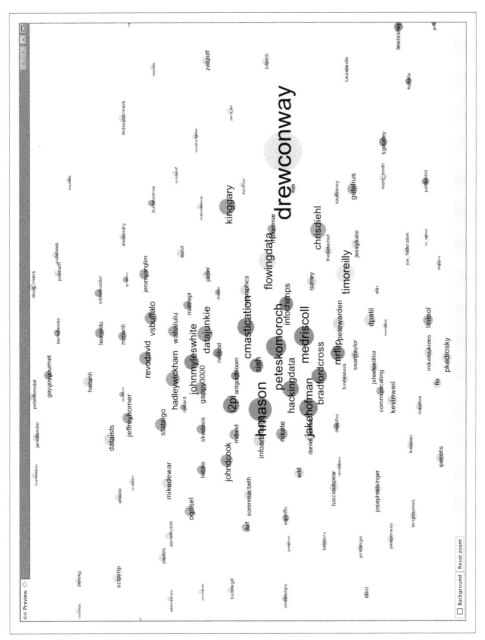

Figure 11-7. Drew's data nerd friends

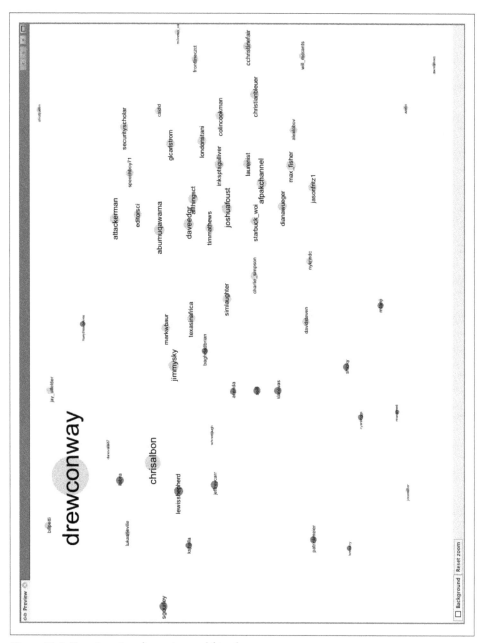

Figure 11-8. Drew's national security nerd friends

Building Your Own "Who to Follow" Engine

There are many ways that we might think about building our own friend recommendation engine for Twitter. Twitter has many dimensions of data in it, so we could think about recommending people based on what they "tweet" about. This would be an exercise in text mining and would require matching people based on some common set of words or topics within their corpus of tweets. Likewise, many tweets contain geo-location data, so we might recommend users who are active and in close proximity to you. Or we could combine these two approaches by taking the intersection of the top 100 recommendations from each. This, however, is a chapter on networks, so we will focus on building an engine based only on people's relationships.

A good place to begin is with a simple theory about how useful relations evolve in a large social network. In his seminal work from 1958, Fritz Heider introduced the idea of "social balance theory."

> my friend's friend is my friend
>
> my friend's enemy is my enemy
>
> my enemy's friend is my enemy
>
> my enemy's enemy is my friend

> —Fritz Heider, *The Psychology of Interpersonal Relations*

The idea is quite simple and can be described in terms of closing and breaking up triangles in a social graph. One thing that Heider's theory requires is the presence of signed relationships, i.e., my friend (positive) or my enemy (negative). Knowing that we do not have this information, how can we use his theory to build a recommendation engine for Twitter relationships? First, a successful recommendation Twitter engine might work to close open triangles, that is, finding my friends' friends and making them my friends. Although we do not have fully signed relationships, we do know all of the positive relationships if we assume that enemies do not follow each other on Twitter.

When we did our initial data pull, we did a two-round snowball search. This data contains our friends and our friends' friends. So we can use this data to identify triangles that need closing. The question then is: which of the many potential triangles should I recommend closing first? Again, we can look to social balance theory. By looking for those nodes in our initial snowball search that the seed is not following, but which many of their friends are following, we may have good candidates for recommendations. This extends Heider's theory to the following: the friend of many of my friends is likely to be a good friend for me. In essence, we want to close the most obvious triangle in the set of the seed's Twitter relationships.

From a technical perspective, this solution is also much easier than attempting to do text mining or geospatial analysis to recommend friends. Here, we simply need to count who of our friends' friends the majority of our friends are following. To do this, we begin by loading in the full network data we collected earlier. As before, we will use

Drew's data in this example, but we encourage you to follow along with your own data if you have it.

```
user <- "drewconway"

user.graph <- read.graph(paste("data/", user, "/", user, "_net.graphml",sep=""),
    format="graphml")
```

Our first step is to get the Twitter names of all of the seed's friends. We can use the neighbors function to get the indices of the neighbors, but recall that because of igraph's different indexing defaults in relation to R's, we need to add one to all of these values. Then we pass those values to the special V function, which will return a node attribute for the graph, which in this case is name. Next, we will generate the full edge list of the graph as a large N-by-2 matrix with the get.edgelist function.

```
friends <- V(user.graph)$name[neighbors(user.graph, user, mode="out")+1]
user.el <- get.edgelist(user.graph)
```

We now have all the data we will need to count the number of my friends that are following all users who are not currently being followed by the seed. First, we need to identify the rows in the user.el that contain links from the seed's friends to users that the seed is currently not following. As we have in previous chapters, we will use the vectorized sapply function to run a function that contains a fairly complex logical test over each row of the matrix. We want to generate a vector of TRUE and FALSE values to determine which rows contain the seed's friends' friends who the seed is not following.

We use the ifelse function to set up the test, which itself is vectorized. The initial test asks if any element of the row is the user and if the first element (the source) is not one of the seed's friends. We use the any function to test whether either of these statements is true. If so, we will want to ignore that row. The other test checks that the second element of the row (the target) is not one of the seed's friends. We care about who our friends' friends are, not who follows our friends, so we also ignore these. This process can take a minute or two, depending on the number of rows, but once it is done we extract the appropriate rows into non.friends.el and create a count of the names using the table function.

```
non.friends <- sapply(1:nrow(user.el), function(i) ifelse(any(user.el[i,]==user |
    !user.el[i,1] %in% friends) | user.el[i,2] %in% friends, FALSE, TRUE))

non.friends.el <- user.el[which(non.friends==TRUE),]
friends.count <- table(non.friends.el[,2])
```

Next, we want to report the results. We want to find the most "obvious" triangle to close, so we want to find the users in this data that show up the most. We create a data frame from the vector created by the table function. We will also add a normalized measure of the best users to recommend for following by calculating the percentage of the seed's friends that follow each potential recommendation. In the final step, we can sort the data frame in descending order by highest percentage of friends following each user.

```
friends.followers <- data.frame(list(Twitter.Users=names(friends.count),
    Friends.Following=as.numeric(friends.count)), stringsAsFactors=FALSE)

friends.followers$Friends.Norm <- friends.followers$Friends.Following/length(friends)
friends.followers <- friends.followers[with(friends.followers, order(-Friends.Norm)),]
```

To report the results, we can inspect the first 10 rows, or our top 10 best recommendations for whom to follow, by running `friends.followers[1:10,]`. In Drew's case, the results are in Table 11-1.

Table 11-1. Social graph

Twitter user	# of friends following	% of friends following
cshirky	80	0.3053435
bigdata	57	0.2175573
fredwilson	57	0.2175573
dangerroom	56	0.2137405
shitmydadsays	55	0.2099237
al3x	53	0.2022901
fivethirtyeight	52	0.1984733
theeconomist	52	0.1984733
zephoria	52	0.1984733
cdixon	51	0.1946565

If you know Drew, these names will make a lot of sense. Drew's best recommendation is to follow Clay Shirky (cshirky), a professor at NYU who studies and writes on the role of technology and the Internet in society. Given what we have already learned about Drew's bifurcated brain, this seems like a good match. Keeping this in mind, the rest of the recommendations fit one or both of Drew's general interests. There is Danger Room (dangerroom); Wired's National Security blog; Big Data (bigdata); and 538 (fivethirtyeight), the *New York Times'* election forecasting blog by Nate Silver. And, of course, shitmydadsays.

Although these recommendations are good—and since the writing of the first draft of this book, Drew has enjoyed following the names this engine presented—perhaps there is a better way to recommend people. Because we already know that a given seed user's network has a lot of emergent structure, it might be useful to use this structure to recommend users that fit into those groups. Rather than recommending the best friends of friends, we can recommend friends of friends who are like the seed on a given dimension. In Drew's case, we could recommend triangles to close in his national security and policy community or in the data or R communities.

```
user.ego <- read.graph(paste("data/", user, "/", user, "_ego.graphml", sep=""),
    format="graphml")
friends.partitions <- cbind(V(user.ego)$HC8, V(user.ego)$name)
```

The first thing we'll need to do is load back in our ego-network that contains the partition data. Because we have already explored the HC8 partition, we'll stick to that one for this final tweak of the recommendation engine. Once the network is loaded, we'll create the `friends.partitions` matrix, which now has the partition number in the first column and the username in the second. For Drew's data, it looks like this:

```
> head(friends.partitions)
     [,1] [,2]
[1,] "0"  "drewconway"
[2,] "2"  "311nyc"
[3,] "2"  "aaronkoblin"
[4,] "3"  "abumuqawama"
[5,] "2"  "acroll"
[6,] "2"  "adamlaiacano"
```

Now all we have to do is calculate the most obvious triangles to close within each subcommunity. So we build the function `partition.follows` that takes a partition number and finds those users. All of the data has already been calculated, so the function simply looks up the users in each partition and then returns the one with the most followers among the seed's friends. The only bit of error checking in this function that may stick out is the if-statement to check that the number of rows in a given subset is less than two. We do this because we know one partition will have only one user, the seed, and we do not want to make recommendations out of that hand-coded partition.

```
partition.follows <- function(i) {
    friends.in <- friends.partitions[which(friends.partitions[,1]==i),2]
    partition.non.follow <- non.friends.el[which(!is.na(match(non.friends.el[,1],
        friends.in))),]
    if(nrow(partition.non.follow) < 2) {
        return(c(i, NA))
    }
    else {
        partition.favorite <- table(partition.non.follow[,2])
        partition.favorite <- partition.favorite[order(-partition.favorite)]
        return(c(i,names(partition.favorite)[1]))
    }
}

partition.recs <- t(sapply(unique(friends.partitions[,1]), partition.follows))
partition.recs <- partition.recs[!is.na(partition.recs[,2]) &
    !duplicated(partition.recs[,2]),]
```

We can now look at those recommendations by partition. As we mentioned, the "0" partition for the seed has no recommendations, but the others do. What's interesting is that for some partitions we see some of the same names from the previous step, but for many we do not.

```
> partition.recs
  [,1] [,2]
0 "0"  NA
2 "2"  "cshirky"
3 "3"  "jeremyscahill"
4 "4"  "nealrichter"
```

```
5 "5"  "jasonmorton"
6 "6"  "dangerroom"
7 "7"  "brendan642"
8 "8"  "adrianholovaty"
```

Of course, it is much more satisfying to see these recommendations inside the network. This will make it easier to see who is recommended for which subcommunity. The code included in this chapter will add these recommendations to a new graph file that includes these nodes and the partition numbers. We have excluded the code here because it is primarily an exercise in housekeeping, but we encourage you to look through it within the code available through O'Reilly for this book. As a final step, we will visualize this data for Drew's recommendations. See Figure 11-9 for the results.

These results are quite good! Recall that the blue nodes are those Twitter users in Drew's network that sit between his interest in technology and national security. The engine has recommended the Danger Room blog, which covers both of these things exactly. And the green nodes are those people tweeting about national security policy; among them, our engine has recommended Jeremy Scahill (jeremyscahill). Jeremy is the national security reporter for *The Nation* magazine, which fits in perfectly with this group and perhaps informs us a bit about Drew's own political perspectives.

On the other side, the red nodes are those in the R community. The recommender suggests Brendan O'Connor (brendan642), a PhD student in machine learning at Carnegie Mellon. He is also someone who tweets and blogs about R. Finally, the violet group contains others from the data community. Here, the suggestion is Jason Morton (jasonmorton), an assistant professor of mathematics and statistics at Pennsylvania State. All of these recommendations match Drew's interests, but are perhaps more useful because we now know precisely how they fit into his interest.

There are many more ways to hack the recommendation engine, and we hope that you will play with the code and tweak it to get better recommendations for your own data.

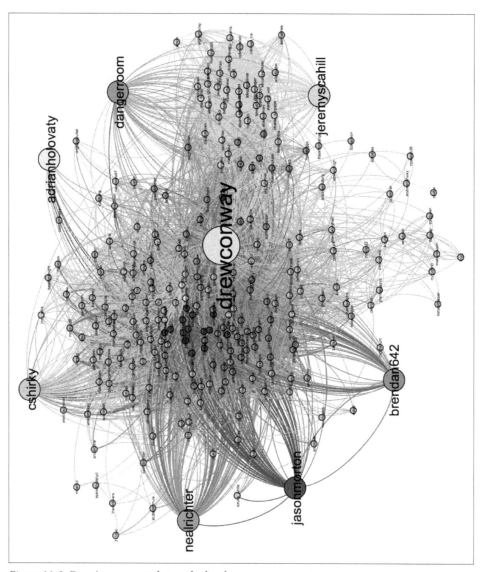

Figure 11-9. Drew's recommendations by local community structure

## CHAPTER 12

Model Comparison

SVMs: The Support Vector Machine

In Chapter 3, we introduced the idea of decision boundaries and noted that problems in which the decision boundary isn't linear pose a problem for simple classification algorithms. In Chapter 6, we showed you how to perform logistic regression, a classification algorithm that works by constructing a linear decision boundary. And in both chapters, we promised to describe a technique called the kernel trick that could be used to solve problems with nonlinear decision boundaries. Let's deliver on that promise by introducing a new classification algorithm called the support vector machine (SVM for short), which allows you to use multiple different kernels to find nonlinear decision boundaries. We'll use an SVM to classify points from a data set with a nonlinear decision boundary. Specifically, we'll work with the data set shown in Figure 12-1.

Looking at this data set, it should be clear that the points from Class 0 are on the periphery, whereas points from Class 1 are in the center of the plot. This sort of nonlinear decision boundary can't be discovered using a simple classification algorithm like the logistic regression algorithm we described in Chapter 6. Let's demonstrate that by trying to use logistic regression through the `glm` function. We'll then look into the reason why logistic regression fails.

```
df <- read.csv('data/df.csv')

logit.fit <- glm(Label ~ X + Y,
                 family = binomial(link = 'logit'),
                 data = df)

logit.predictions <- ifelse(predict(logit.fit) > 0, 1, 0)

mean(with(df, logit.predictions == Label))
#[1] 0.5156
```

As you can see, we've correctly predicted the class of only 52% of the data. But we could do exactly this well by predicting that every data point belongs to Class 0:

```
mean(with(df, 0 == Label))
#[1] 0.5156
```

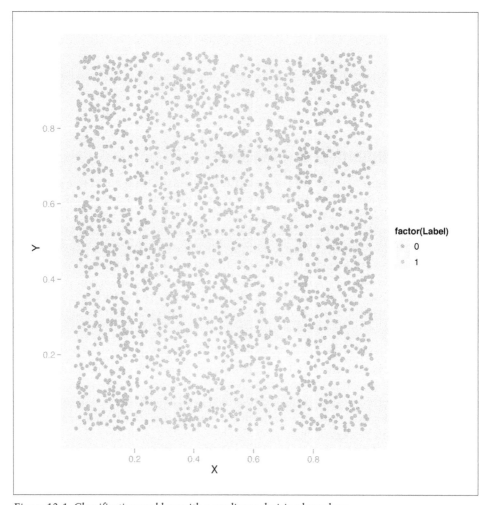

Figure 12-1. Classification problem with a nonlinear decision boundary

In short, the logistic regression model (and the linear decision boundary it finds) is completely useless. It makes the same predictions as a model with no information beyond the fact that Class 0 occurs more often than Class 1, and so should be used as a prediction in the absence of all other information.

So how can we do better? As you'll see in a moment, the SVM provides a trivial way to outperform logistic regression. Before we describe how it does this, let's just show you that it works as a black-box algorithm that produces useful answers. To do so, we'll use the e1071 package, which provides a function svm that is just as easy to use as glm:

```
library('e1071')

svm.fit <- svm(Label ~ X + Y, data = df)
svm.predictions <- ifelse(predict(svm.fit) > 0, 1, 0)
mean(with(df, svm.predictions == Label))
#[1] 0.7204
```

Here we've clearly done better than logistic regression just by switching to SVMs. How is the SVM doing this?

The first way to gain insight into the superior performance of the SVM is to plot its predictions versus those from a logistic regression:

```
df <- cbind(df,
            data.frame(Logit = ifelse(predict(logit.fit) > 0, 1, 0),
                       SVM = ifelse(predict(svm.fit) > 0, 1, 0)))

predictions <- melt(df, id.vars = c('X', 'Y'))

ggplot(predictions, aes(x = X, y = Y, color = factor(value))) +
  geom_point() +
  facet_grid(variable ~ .)
```

Here we've added the logistic regression predictions and the SVM predictions to the raw data set. Then we use the melt function to build up a data set that's easier to work with for plotting purposes, and we store this new data set in a data frame called predictions. We then plot the ground truth labels along with the logit and SVM predictions in the faceted plot shown in Figure 12-2.

Once we've done this, it becomes obvious that the logistic regression is useless because it puts the decision boundary outside of the data set, while the ground truth data in the top row clearly has a band of entries for Class 1 in the center. The SVM is able to capture this band structure, even though it makes odd predictions near the furthest boundaries of the data set.

So now we've seen that the SVM produces, as promised, a nonlinear decision boundary. But how does it do that? The answer is that the SVM uses the kernel trick. Using a mathematical transformation, it moves the original data set into a new mathematical space in which the decision boundary is easy to describe. Because this transformation depends only on a simple computation involving "kernels," this technique is called the kernel trick.

Describing the mathematics of the kernel trick is nontrivial, but it's easy to gain some intuition by testing out different kernels. This is easy because the SVM function has a parameter called kernel that can be set to one of four values: linear, polynomial, radial, and sigmoid. To get a feel for how these kernels work, let's try using all of them to generate predictions and then plot the predictions:

```
df <- df[, c('X', 'Y', 'Label')]

linear.svm.fit <- svm(Label ~ X + Y, data = df, kernel = 'linear')
with(df, mean(Label == ifelse(predict(linear.svm.fit) > 0, 1, 0)))

polynomial.svm.fit <- svm(Label ~ X + Y, data = df, kernel = 'polynomial')
with(df, mean(Label == ifelse(predict(polynomial.svm.fit) > 0, 1, 0)))

radial.svm.fit <- svm(Label ~ X + Y, data = df, kernel = 'radial')
with(df, mean(Label == ifelse(predict(radial.svm.fit) > 0, 1, 0)))

sigmoid.svm.fit <- svm(Label ~ X + Y, data = df, kernel = 'sigmoid')
with(df, mean(Label == ifelse(predict(sigmoid.svm.fit) > 0, 1, 0)))

df <- cbind(df,
            data.frame(LinearSVM = ifelse(predict(linear.svm.fit) > 0, 1, 0),
                       PolynomialSVM = ifelse(predict(polynomial.svm.fit) > 0, 1, 0),
                       RadialSVM = ifelse(predict(radial.svm.fit) > 0, 1, 0),
                       SigmoidSVM = ifelse(predict(sigmoid.svm.fit) > 0, 1, 0)))

predictions <- melt(df, id.vars = c('X', 'Y'))

ggplot(predictions, aes(x = X, y = Y, color = factor(value))) +
  geom_point() +
  facet_grid(variable ~ .)
```

As you can see from Figure 12-3, the linear and polynomial kernels look more or less like logistic regression. In contrast, the radial kernel gives us a decision boundary somewhat like the ground truth boundary. And the sigmoid kernel gives us a very complex and strange decision boundary.

You should generate some of your own data sets and play around with these four kernels to build up your intuition for how they work. After you've done that, you may suspect that the SVM could make much better predictions than it seems to do out of the box. This is true. The SVM comes with a set of hyperparameters that are not set to useful values by default, and getting the best predictions from the model requires tuning these hyperparameters. Let's describe the major hyperparameters and see how tuning them improves our model's performance.

The first hyperparameter you can work with is the degree of the polynomial used by the polynomial kernel. You can change this by setting the value of **degree** when calling svm. Let's see how this hyperparameter works with four simple examples:

```
polynomial.degree3.svm.fit <- svm(Label ~ X + Y,
                                  data = df,
                                  kernel = 'polynomial',
                                  degree = 3)
with(df, mean(Label != ifelse(predict(polynomial.degree3.svm.fit) > 0, 1, 0)))
#[1] 0.5156

polynomial.degree5.svm.fit <- svm(Label ~ X + Y,
                                  data = df,
                                  kernel = 'polynomial',
```

```
                          degree = 5)
with(df, mean(Label != ifelse(predict(polynomial.degree5.svm.fit) > 0, 1, 0)))
#[1] 0.5156

polynomial.degree10.svm.fit <- svm(Label ~ X + Y,
                                data = df,
                                kernel = 'polynomial',
                                degree = 10)
with(df, mean(Label != ifelse(predict(polynomial.degree10.svm.fit) > 0, 1, 0)))
#[1] 0.4388

polynomial.degree12.svm.fit <- svm(Label ~ X + Y,
                                data = df,
                                kernel = 'polynomial',
                                degree = 12)
with(df, mean(Label != ifelse(predict(polynomial.degree12.svm.fit) > 0, 1, 0)))
#[1] 0.4464
```

Here we can see that setting **degree** to 3 or 5 doesn't have any effect on the quality of the model's predictions. (It's worth noting that the default value of **degree** is 3.) But setting **degree** to 10 or 12 does have an effect. To see what's happening, let's plot out the decision boundaries again:

```
df <- df[, c('X', 'Y', 'Label')]

df <- cbind(df,
            data.frame(Degree3SVM = ifelse(predict(polynomial.degree3.svm.fit) > 0,
                                            1,
                                            0),
                       Degree5SVM = ifelse(predict(polynomial.degree5.svm.fit) > 0,
                                            1,
                                            0),
                       Degree10SVM = ifelse(predict(polynomial.degree10.svm.fit) > 0,
                                            1,
                                            0),
                       Degree12SVM = ifelse(predict(polynomial.degree12.svm.fit) > 0,
                                            1,
                                            0)))

predictions <- melt(df, id.vars = c('X', 'Y'))

ggplot(predictions, aes(x = X, y = Y, color = factor(value))) +
  geom_point() +
  facet_grid(variable ~ .)
```

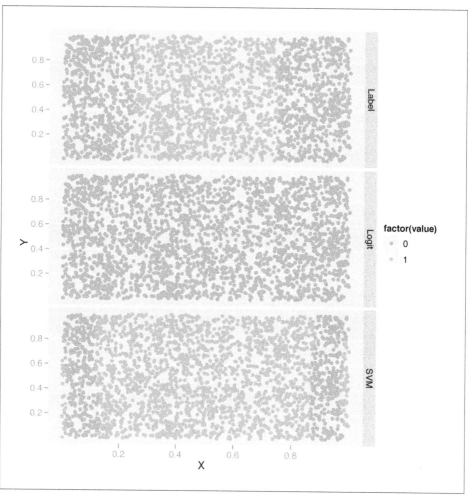

Figure 12-2. Comparing the predictions from a logistic regression and an SVM

Looking at the predictions shown in Figure 12-4, it's clear that using a larger degree improves the quality of the predictions, though it does so in a hackish way that's not really mimicking the structure of the data. And, as you'll notice, the model-fitting step becomes slower and slower as the degree increases. And finally, the same overfitting problems we saw in Chapter 6 with polynomial regression will creep up. For that reason, you should always use cross-validation to experiment with setting the **degree** hyperparameter in applications that use SVMs with polynomial kernels. Although there's no doubt that SVMs with polynomial kernels are a valuable tool to have in your toolkit, they can't be guaranteed to work well without some effort and thinking on your part.

After playing with the **degree** hyperparameter for the polynomial kernel, let's try out the **cost** hyperparameter, which is used with all of the possible SVM kernels. To see

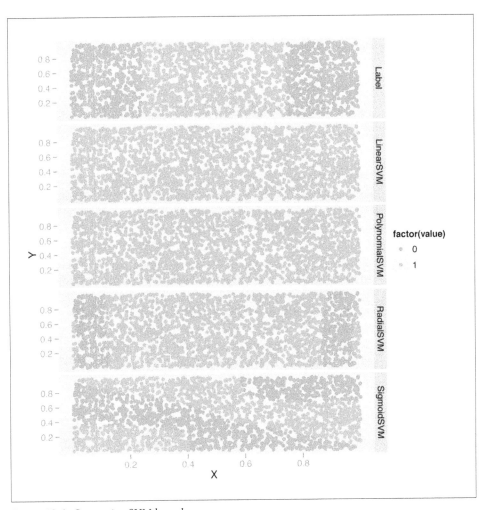

Figure 12-3. Comparing SVM kernels

the effect of changing cost, we'll use a radial kernel and try four different cost settings. To change things up, we'll also stop counting errors and start seeing how many data points we predict correctly, as we're ultimately interested in seeing how good the best model is and not how bad the worst model is. The following shows the code for this exploration of the cost parameter:

```
radial.cost1.svm.fit <- svm(Label ~ X + Y,
                            data = df,
                            kernel = 'radial',
                            cost = 1)
with(df, mean(Label == ifelse(predict(radial.cost1.svm.fit) > 0, 1, 0)))
#[1] 0.7204

radial.cost2.svm.fit <- svm(Label ~ X + Y,
                            data = df,
```

```
                                    kernel = 'radial',
                                    cost = 2)
with(df, mean(Label == ifelse(predict(radial.cost2.svm.fit) > 0, 1, 0)))
#[1] 0.7052

radial.cost3.svm.fit <- svm(Label ~ X + Y,
                                    data = df,
                                    kernel = 'radial',
                                    cost = 3)
with(df, mean(Label == ifelse(predict(radial.cost3.svm.fit) > 0, 1, 0)))
#[1] 0.6996

radial.cost4.svm.fit <- svm(Label ~ X + Y,
                                    data = df,
                                    kernel = 'radial',
                                    cost = 4)
with(df, mean(Label == ifelse(predict(radial.cost4.svm.fit) > 0, 1, 0)))
#[1] 0.694
```

As you can see, increasing the cost parameter makes the model progressively fit more and more poorly. That's because the cost is a regularization hyperparameter like the lambda parameter we described in Chapter 6, and increasing it will always make the model fit the training data less tightly. Of course, this increase in regularization can improve your model's performance on test data, so you should always see what value of cost most improves your test performance using cross-validation.

To get some insight into what's happening in terms of the fitted model, let's look at the predictions graphically in Figure 12-5:

```
df <- df[, c('X', 'Y', 'Label')]

df <- cbind(df,
               data.frame(Cost1SVM = ifelse(predict(radial.cost1.svm.fit) > 0, 1, 0),
                          Cost2SVM = ifelse(predict(radial.cost2.svm.fit) > 0, 1, 0),
                          Cost3SVM = ifelse(predict(radial.cost3.svm.fit) > 0, 1, 0),
                          Cost4SVM = ifelse(predict(radial.cost4.svm.fit) > 0, 1, 0)))

predictions <- melt(df, id.vars = c('X', 'Y'))

ggplot(predictions, aes(x = X, y = Y, color = factor(value))) +
  geom_point() +
  facet_grid(variable ~ .)
```

The changes induced by the cost parameter are quite subtle, but can be seen on the periphery of the data set shown in Figure 12-5. As the cost goes up, the boundaries created by the radial kernel become more and more linear.

Figure 12-4. Setting the polynomial kernel SVM's degree hyperparameter

Having looked at the cost parameter, we'll conclude our SVM hyperparameter experiments by playing around with the gamma hyperparameter. For testing purposes, we'll observe its effects on a sigmoid kernel by testing out four different gamma values:

```
sigmoid.gamma1.svm.fit <- svm(Label ~ X + Y,
                               data = df,
                               kernel = 'sigmoid',
                               gamma = 1)
with(df, mean(Label == ifelse(predict(sigmoid.gamma1.svm.fit) > 0, 1, 0)))
#[1] 0.478

sigmoid.gamma2.svm.fit <- svm(Label ~ X + Y,
                               data = df,
                               kernel = 'sigmoid',
```

```
                                        gamma = 2)
     with(df, mean(Label == ifelse(predict(sigmoid.gamma2.svm.fit) > 0, 1, 0)))
     #[1] 0.4824

     sigmoid.gamma3.svm.fit <- svm(Label ~ X + Y,
                                   data = df,
                                   kernel = 'sigmoid',
                                   gamma = 3)
     with(df, mean(Label == ifelse(predict(sigmoid.gamma3.svm.fit) > 0, 1, 0)))
     #[1] 0.4816

     sigmoid.gamma4.svm.fit <- svm(Label ~ X + Y,
                                   data = df,
                                   kernel = 'sigmoid',
                                   gamma = 4)
     with(df, mean(Label == ifelse(predict(sigmoid.gamma4.svm.fit) > 0, 1, 0)))
     #[1] 0.4824
```

Every time we increase gamma, the model does a little better. To get a sense for the source of that improvement, let's turn to graphical diagnostics of the predictions:

```
     df <- df[, c('X', 'Y', 'Label')]

     df <- cbind(df,
                 data.frame(Gamma1SVM = ifelse(predict(sigmoid.gamma1.svm.fit) > 0, 1, 0),
                            Gamma2SVM = ifelse(predict(sigmoid.gamma2.svm.fit) > 0, 1, 0),
                            Gamma3SVM = ifelse(predict(sigmoid.gamma3.svm.fit) > 0, 1, 0),
                            Gamma4SVM = ifelse(predict(sigmoid.gamma4.svm.fit) > 0, 1, 0)))

     predictions <- melt(df, id.vars = c('X', 'Y'))

     ggplot(predictions, aes(x = X, y = Y, color = factor(value))) +
       geom_point() +
       facet_grid(variable ~ .)
```

As you can see from looking at Figure 12-6, the rather complicated decision boundary chosen by the sigmoid kernel warps around as we change the value of gamma. To really get a better intuition for what's happening, we recommend that you experiment with many more values of gamma than the four we've just shown you.

That ends our introduction to the SVM. We think it's a valuable algorithm to have in your toolkit, but it's time to stop building up your toolkit and instead start focusing on thinking critically about which tool is best for any given job. To do that, we'll explore multiple models simultaneously on a single data set.

Comparing Algorithms

Since we know how to use to SVMs, logistic regression, and kNN, let's compare their performance on the SpamAssassin data set we worked with in Chapters 3 and 4. Experimenting with multiple algorithms is a good habit to develop when working with real-world data because often you won't be able to know in advance which algorithm will work best with your data set. Also, one of the major skills that separates the most

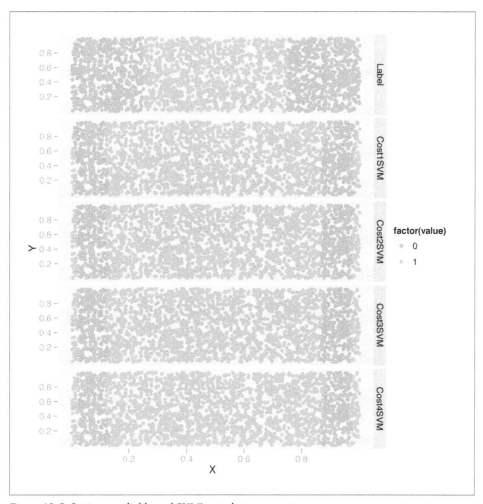

Figure 12-5. Setting a radial kernel SVM's cost hyperparameter

experienced people in machine learning from those just starting to use it is the ability to know from the structure of a problem when a certain algorithm won't work well. The best way to build up this intuition is to apply all of the standard algorithms to every problem you come across until you have a sense of when they'll fail.

The first step is simply to load our data and preprocess it appropriately. Because this was done in detail before, we're going to skip several steps and simply load a document-term matrix from disk using the `load` function in R, which reads in a binary format that can be used to write R objects to disk for long-term storage. Then we'll do a training set/test set split and discard the raw data set using the `rm` function, which allows us to delete an object from memory:

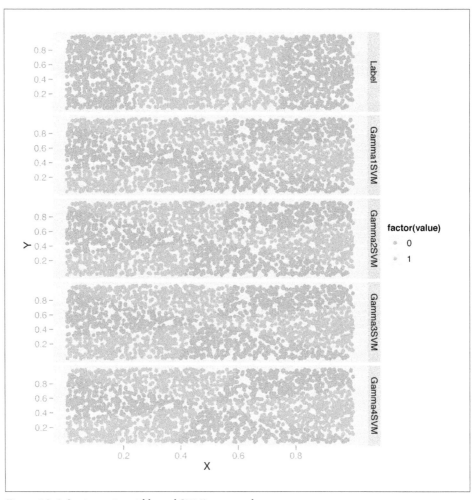

Figure 12-6. Setting a sigmoid kernel SVM's gamma hyperparameter

```
load('data/dtm.RData')

set.seed(1)

training.indices <- sort(sample(1:nrow(dtm), round(0.5 * nrow(dtm))))
test.indices <- which(! 1:nrow(dtm) %in% training.indices)
train.x <- dtm[training.indices, 3:ncol(dtm)]
train.y <- dtm[training.indices, 1]
test.x <- dtm[test.indices, 3:ncol(dtm)]
test.y <- dtm[test.indices, 1]

rm(dtm)
```

Now that we have a data set in memory, we can immediately move forward and fit a regularized logistic regression using glmnet:

```
library('glmnet')
regularized.logit.fit <- glmnet(train.x, train.y, family = c('binomial'))
```

Of course, that still leaves us with a great deal of flexibility, so we'd like to compare various settings for the lambda hyperparameter to see which gives us the best performance. To push through this example quickly, we'll cheat a bit and test the hyperparameter settings on the test set rather than do repeated splits of the training data. If you're rigorously testing models, you shouldn't make this sort of simplification, but we'll leave the clean tuning of lambda as an exercise for you to do on your own. For now, we'll just try all of the values that glmnet proposed and see which performs best on the test set:

```
lambdas <- regularized.logit.fit$lambda
performance <- data.frame()

for (lambda in lambdas)
{
  predictions <- predict(regularized.logit.fit, test.x, s = lambda)
  predictions <- as.numeric(predictions > 0)
  mse <- mean(predictions != test.y)

  performance <- rbind(performance, data.frame(Lambda = lambda, MSE = mse))
}

ggplot(performance, aes(x = Lambda, y = MSE)) +
  geom_point() +
  scale_x_log10()
```

Looking at Figure 12-7, we see a pretty clear region of values for lambda that gives the lowest possible error rate. To find the best value for our final analysis, we can then use simple indexing and the min function:

```
best.lambda <- with(performance, max(Lambda[which(MSE == min(MSE))]))
```

In this case, there are actually two different values of lambda that give identical performance, so we extract the larger of the two using the max function. We choose the larger value because it is the one with greater regularization applied. We can then calculate the MSE for our logistic model using this best value for lambda:

```
mse <- with(subset(performance, Lambda == best.lambda), MSE)
mse
#[1] 0.06830769
```

We can see that using regularized logistic regression, which requires only a trivial amount of hyperparameter tuning to implement, misclassifies only 6% of all emails in our test set. But we'd like to see how other methods do with similar amounts of work so that we can decide whether we should be using logistic regression, SVMs, or kNN.

For that reason, let's start by fitting a linear kernel SVM to see how it compares with logistic regression:

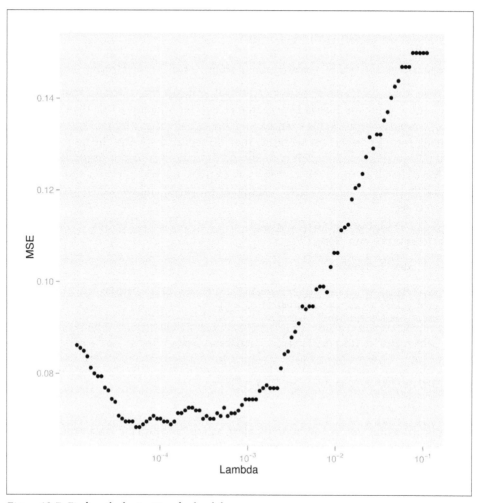

Figure 12-7. Finding the best setting for lambda

```
library('e1071')
linear.svm.fit <- svm(train.x, train.y, kernel = 'linear')
```

Fitting the linear kernel SVM is a little bit slow with this large data set. For that reason, we're going to be somewhat unfair to the SVM and simply use the default settings for the hyperparameters. As was the case with picking the ideal hyperparameter for logistic regression by assessing performance on our test set, this use of default hyperparameter values isn't ideal, but it's also a regular occurrence in the machine learning literature. When you compare models, you need to keep in mind that one of the things you see in your results is simply a measure of how hard you've worked to make each model fit the data. If you spend more time tuning one model than another, the differences in their performance can be partly attributable not to their differing structure, but to the different levels of effort you invested in them.

Knowing that, we'll blindly forge ahead and assess the linear kernel SVM's performance on our test data:

```
predictions <- predict(linear.svm.fit, test.x)
predictions <- as.numeric(predictions > 0)
mse <- mean(predictions != test.y)
mse
#0.128
```

We can see that we get a 12% error rate, which is double that of the logistic regression model. To get a better sense of the real limits of the linear kernel SVM, you should experiment with manipulating the cost hyperparameter to find its ideal value before estimating the error rate for the linear kernel SVM.

But for now we'll just stick with the results we already have for the linear kernel SVM and move on to a radial kernel SVM to see how much the kernel changes the results we get in this practical problem that we can't visualize in the same way we could visualize the toy problem at the start of this chapter:

```
radial.svm.fit <- svm(train.x, train.y, kernel = 'radial')

predictions <- predict(radial.svm.fit, test.x)
predictions <- as.numeric(predictions > 0)
mse <- mean(predictions != test.y)
mse
#[1] 0.1421538
```

Somewhat surprisingly, the radial kernel does a little worse on this data set than the linear kernel, which is the opposite of what we saw from our example of nonlinear data. And that's an example of a broader lesson you'll absorb with more experience working with data: the ideal model for your problem depends on the structure of your data. In this case, the inferior performance of the radial kernel SVM suggests that the ideal decision boundary for this problem might really be linear. That's also supported by the fact that we've already seen that logistic regression is beating both the linear and the radial kernel SVMs. These sorts of observations are the most interesting ones we can make while comparing algorithms on a fixed data set because we learn something about the true structure of the data from the misfit of our models.

But before we stop fitting models and decide to stick with logistic regression, let's try the method that works best with nonlinear data: kNN. Here we fit kNN using 50 neighbors for each prediction:

```
library('class')
knn.fit <- knn(train.x, test.x, train.y, k = 50)

predictions <- as.numeric(as.character(knn.fit))
mse <- mean(predictions != test.y)
mse
#[1] 0.1396923
```

As we can see, we get a 14% error from kNN, which is further evidence that linear models are better for classifying spam than nonlinear models. And because kNN doesn't take so long to fit on this data set, we'll also try several values for k to see which performs best:

```
performance <- data.frame()

for (k in seq(5, 50, by = 5))
{
  knn.fit <- knn(train.x, test.x, train.y, k = k)

  predictions <- as.numeric(as.character(knn.fit))
  mse <- mean(predictions != test.y)

  performance <- rbind(performance, data.frame(K = k, MSE = mse))
}

best.k <- with(performance, K[which(MSE == min(MSE))])
best.mse <- with(subset(performance, K == best.k), MSE)
best.mse
#[1] 0.09169231
```

With tuning, we see that we can get a 9% error rate from kNN. This is halfway between the performance we've seen for SVMs and logistic regression, as you can confirm by looking at Table 12-1, which collates the error rates we obtained with each of the four algorithms we've used on this spam data set.

Table 12-1. Model comparison results

Model	MSE
Regularized logistic regression	0.06830769
Linear kernel SVM	0.128
Radial kernel SVM	0.1421538
kNN	0.09169231

In the end, it seems that the best approach for this problem is to use logistic regression with a tuned hyperparameter for regularization. And that's actually a reasonable conclusion because industrial-strength spam filters have all switched over to logistic regression and left the Naive Bayes approach we described in Chapter 3 behind. For reasons that aren't entirely clear to us, logistic regression simply works better for this sort of problem.

What broader lessons should you take away from this example? We hope you'll walk away with several lessons in mind: (1) you should always try multiple algorithms on any practical data set, especially because they're so easy to experiment with in R; (2) the types of algorithms that work best are problem-specific; and (3) the quality of the results you get from a model are influenced by the structure of the data and also by the amount of work you're willing to put into setting hyperparameters, so don't shirk the hyperparameter tuning step if you want to get strong results.

To hammer those lessons home, we encourage you to go back through the four models we've fit in this chapter and set the hyperparameters systematically using repeated splits of the training data. After that, we encourage you to try the polynomial and sigmoid kernels that we neglected while working with the spam data. If you do both of these things, you'll get a lot of experience with the nuts and bolts of fitting complicated models to real-world data, and you'll learn to appreciate how differently the models we've shown you in this book can perform on a fixed data set.

On that note, we've come to the end of our final chapter and the book as a whole. We hope you've discovered the beauty of machine learning and gained an appreciation for the broad ideas that come up again and again when trying to build predictive models of data. We hope you'll go on to study machine learning from the classic mathematical textbooks such as Hastie et al. [HTF09] or Bishop [Bis06], which cover the material we've described in a practical fashion from a theoretical bent. The best machine learning practitioners are those with both practical and theoretical experience, so we encourage you to go out and develop both.

Along the way, have fun hacking data. You have a lot of powerful tools, so go apply them to questions you're interested in!

Works Cited

Books

[Adl10] Adler, Joseph. *R in a Nutshell*. O'Reilly Media, 2010.

[Abb92] Abbot, Edwin A. *Flatland: A Romance of Many Dimensions*. Dover Publications, 1992.

[Bis06] Bishop, Christopher M. *Pattern Recognition and Machine Learning*. Springer; 1st ed. 2006. Corr.; 2nd printing ed. 2007.

[GH06] Gelman, Andrew, and Jennifer Hill. *Data Analysis Using Regression and Multilevel/Hierarchical Models*. Cambridge University Press, 2006.

[HTF09] Hastie, Trevor, Robert Tibshirani, and Jerome Friedman. *The Elements of Statistical Learning*. Springer, 2009.

[JMR09] Jones, Owen, Robert Maillardet, and Andrew Robinson. *Introduction to Scientific Programming and Simulation Using R*. Chapman and Hall, 2009.

[Seg07] Segaran, Toby. *Programming Collective Intelligence: Building Smart Web 2.0 Applications*. O'Reilly Media, 2007.

[Spe08] Spector, Phil. *Data Manipulation with R*. Springer, 2008.

[Wic09] Wickham, Hadley. *ggplot2: Elegant Graphics for Data Analysis*. Springer, 2009.

[Wil05] Wilkinson, Leland. *The Grammar of Graphics*. Springer, 2005.

[Pea09] Pearl, Judea. *Causality*. Cambridge University Press, 2009.

[WF94] Wasserman, Stanley, and Katherine Faust. *Social Network Analysis: Methods and Applications*. Cambridge University Press, 1994.

[MJ10] Jackson, Matthew O. *Social and Economic Networks*. Princeton University Press, 2010.

[EK10] Easley, David, and Jon Kleinberg. *Networks, Crowds, and Markets: Reasoning About a Highly Connected World*. Cambridge University Press, 2010.

[Wa03] Wasserman, Larry. *All of Statistics*. Springer, 2003.

Articles

[LF08] Ligges, Uwe, and John Fox. "R help desk: How can I avoid this loop or make it faster?" *http://www.r-project.org/doc/Rnews/Rnews_2008-1.pdf*. May 2008.

[DA10] Aberdeen, Douglas, Ondrej Pacovsky, and Andrew Slater. "The Learning Behind Gmail Priority Inbox." LCCC: NIPS 2010 Workshop on Learning on Cores, Clusters and Clouds. *http://research.google.com/pubs/archive/36955.pdf*. 2010.

[HW11] Wickham, Hadley. "The Split-Apply-Combine Strategy for Data Analysis." *Journal of Statistical Software*, April 2011, 40 (1).

[SR08] Stross, Randall. "What Has Driven Women Out of Computer Science?" *The New York Times*, November 15, 2008.

[JC37] Criswell, Joan H.. "Racial Cleavage in Negro-White Groups." *Sociometry*, Jul.-Oct. 1937, 1 (1/2).

[WA10] Galston, William A.. "Can a Polarized American Party System Be 'Healthy'?" *Brookings Institute - Issues in Governance Studies*, April 2010 (34).

[PS08] Singer, Paul. "Members Offered Many Bills but Passed Few." *Roll Call*, December 1, 2008.

Index

Symbols

%*% (percent, asterisk, percent), for matrix multiplication, 219
? (question mark) syntax, for R help, 13
?? (question mark, double) syntax, for R help, 13

A

additivity assumption, 133–141
aggregating data (see data, aggregating)
analyzing data (see data analysis)
apply functions
    lapply function, 17, 22, 106, 224, 227
    sapply function, 81, 83, 188
as.Date function, 14
as.factor function, 14
as.matrix function, 83

B

baseline model, for linear regression, 127–131
Bayesian classifier (see Naive Bayes classifier)
bell curve, 44–60
    modes in, 52–54
    types of, 53–60
    verifying with density plots, 45–51
    verifying with different binwidths, 44–45
bimodal, 53
binary classification, 73–77, 178–181
    (see also spam detection case study)
book popularity prediction case study, 174–181
books and publications
    bibliography of, 293–294
    machine learning, viii

    R language, 27
    social network analysis, 245
boot package, 179

C

Caesar cipher, 195
case studies
    book popularity prediction, 174–181
    code breaking, 193–204
    list of, viii–x
    priority inbox, 93–125
        feature generation, 95–99, 100–107
        testing, 123–125
        training, 117–120
        weighting scheme for, 108–117
    R package installation, 239–242
    spam detection, 74–92
        improving results of classifier, 90–92
        testing classifier, 87–90
        training classifier, 80–84
        writing classifier, 78–87
    stock market index, 205–213
    Twitter follower recommendations, 269–273
    Twitter network analysis, 245–266
        building networks, 256–257
        data for, obtaining, 248–256
        ego-network analysis, 258–261
        k-core analysis, 257–258
        visualizations for, 261–266
    UFO sightings, 12–27
        aggregating data, 19–23
        analyzing data, 24–27
        cleaning data, 16–18
        loading data, 13–15

We'd like to hear your suggestions for improving our indexes. Send email to *index@oreilly.com*.

malformed data, handling, 15–16
US Senate clustering, 222–231
web traffic predictions, 141–152
cast function, 206, 240, 241
categorical variables, 13
Cauchy distribution, 54–57
class function, 239
classification
    binary classification, 73–77, 178–181
    ranking classes, 93–95
        (see also priority inbox case study)
        feature generation, 95–99, 100–107
        testing, 123–125
        training, 117–120
        weighting scheme for, 108–117
    SVM (support vector machine) for, 275–284
    text classification, 74–78
        (see also spam detection case study)
classification picture, 66–69
cleaning data (see data, cleaning)
clustering, 215–216
    hierarchical clustering of node distances, 258–266
    MDS (multidimensional scaling) for, 216–222
    of US Senate, 222–231
cmdscale function, 221, 227
code breaking case study, 193–204
code examples, using, xi
coef function, 137–138, 173
columns
    meaning of, 36
    names for, assigning, 14
    relationships between, visualizations for, 61–70
    types of data in, determining, 34–36
Comprehensive R Archive Network (CRAN), x
computer hacker (see hacker)
conditional probability, 77–78
confirmatory data analysis, 29–30
Congress, US (see US Senate clustering case study)
contact information for this book, xii
content features, of email, 96
control list, 82
conventions used in this book, x
convergence, 187

cor function, 153, 241
Corpus function, 82
correlation, 33, 152–154
Cowgill, Bo (Google, Inc.)
    regarding R language, 2, 3
CRAN (Comprehensive R Archive Network), x
Criswell, Joan (anthropologist)
    sociometry used by, 245
cross-validation, 166–168
curve function, 187, 191–192
curve, in scatterplot, 133
cutree function, 261

D

data, 30–34
    aggregating, 19–23
    cleaning, 16–18
    columns in
        meaning of, 36
        names for, assigning, 14
        relationships between, visualizations for, 61–70
        types of data in, determining, 34–36
    loading, 13–15
    malformed, handling, 15–16
    "as rectangles" model of, 31
    source of, 30
data analysis
    confirmatory, 29–30
    correlation, 33, 152–154
    dimensionality reduction, 33
    exploratory, 29–30
    numeric summary, 31, 37
    visualizations, 32–34, 44–60
        density plot (see density plot)
        histogram, 19–23, 44–46
        line plot, 24–27
        network graphs, 261–266
        relationships between columns, 61–70
        scatterplot (see scatterplot)
data dictionary, 34
data frame structure, 3, 13
data types and structures
    data frame structure, 3, 13
    dates
        conversions to, 14–16
        sequence of, creating, 22
    determining for data columns, 34–36

factor data type, 13
list structure, 17
vector data type, 3
data.frame function, 83
database, data set compared to, 31
    (see also matrices)
dates
    conversions to, 14–16
    sequence of, creating, 22
ddply function, 22, 108
decision boundary
    linear, 73
    nonlinear, handling, 155–158, 275–284
dendrogram, 259
density plot, 45–60, 128–129, 143, 207–209
dimensionality reduction, 33
dir function, 81
directed graph, 246
dist function, 219, 259
distance matrix, 220
distance metrics, 219–222, 237–239
distributions, 44
    bell curve (normal distribution), 44–60
        modes in, 52–53
        verifying with density plots, 45–51
        verifying with different binwidths, 44–
            45
    Cauchy distribution, 54–57
    exponential distribution, 57–60
    gamma distribution, 57–59
    heavy-tailed distribution, 54–57
    skewed distribution, 53–54
    symmetric distribution, 53–54
    thin-tailed distribution, 54–57
do.call function, 17, 22, 106
.dta file extension, 223
dummy coding, 35
dummy variables, regression using, 132–133

E

e1071 package, 277
ego-network, 246, 258–261
email
    detecting spam in (see spam detection case
        study)
    prioritizing messages in (see priority inbox
        case study)
encoding schemes, 35–36
enumerations, compared to factors, 34

Erdős number, 243
error handling, 16
Euclidean distance, 219, 237
Euler, Leonhard (mathematician)
    regarding Königsberg Bridge problem, 244
exploratory data analysis, 29–30
exponential distribution, 57–60

F

F-statistic, 150
facet_wrap function, 24, 230
factor data type, 13, 34
feature generation, 74, 95–99
first quartile, 37, 38
fonts used in this book, x
force-directed algorithms, 263
foreign package, 223, 224
fromJSON function, 251

G

Galston, William A. (Senior Fellow, Brookings
        Institute)
    regarding polarization in US Congress, 222
gamma distribution, 57–59
Gaussian distribution (see bell curve)
geom_density function, 46
    (see also density plot)
geom_histogram function, 19, 44
    (see also histogram)
geom_line function, 24
geom_point function, 64
    (see also scatterplot)
geom_smooth function, 65, 135, 144, 153, 155,
        160
geom_text function, 228
Gephi software, 257, 261–266
get.edgelist function, 270
getURL function, 251
ggplot object, 19
ggplot2 package, 11, 12, 19, 24
    (see also specific functions)
    MDS results using, 223
    plotting themes of, 24
    resources for, 28
    two plots using, 228
ggsave function, 19, 25
glm function, 275–276
glmnet function, 170–173, 175, 178, 287

glmnet package, 11, 170
global optimum, 188
Goffman, Erving (social scientist)
    regarding nature of human interaction, 243
Google
    priority inbox by, 95–96
    SocialGraph API (see SGA)
gradient, 187
graph.coreness function, 258
GraphML files, 261
grepl function, 102, 103, 105, 252
grid search, 185–186
gsub function, 16, 105

H

hacker, vii
hclust function, 259
head function, 14
heavy-tailed distribution, 54–57
Heider, Fritz (psychologist)
    social balance theory by, 269
help, for R language, 13
help.search function, 13
hierarchical clustering of node distances, 258–266
histogram, 19–23, 44–46

I

IDEs, for R, 8
ifelse function, 15
igraph library, 256
igraph package, 11, 251, 258
install.packages function, 9
inv.logit function, 179
is.character function, 34
is.factor function, 34
is.na function, 18, 23
is.numeric function, 34

J

jittering, 75

K

k-core analysis, 257–258
k-nearest neighbors algorithm (see kNN algorithm)
KDE (kernel density estimate) (see density plot)

kernel trick (see SVM (support vector machine))
kNN (k-nearest neighbors) algorithm, 233–242
    comparing to other algorithms, 284
    R package installation case study using, 239–242
knn function, 239
Königsberg Bridge problem, 244

L

L1 norm, 170
L2 norm, 170
label features, of email, 96
labels, compared to factors, 35
Lambda, for regularization, 171–173, 176, 190
lapply function, 17, 22, 106, 224, 227
length function, 16
library function, 9
line plot, 24
line, in scatterplot, 133
linear kernel SVM, 277, 287
linear regression, 127–141
    adapting for nonlinear relationships, 155–158
    assumptions in, 133–141
    baseline model for, 127–131
    correlation as indicator of, 152–154
    dummy variables for, 132–133
    lm function for, 2, 137, 145, 153, 183
    optimizing, 183
    web traffic predictions case study using, 141–152
linearity assumption, 133–141
Linux, installing R language on, 8
list structure, 17
list.files function, 223
lm function, 2, 137, 145, 153, 183
load function, 285
loading data (see data, loading)
log base-10 transformation, 110
log function, 112
log-transformations, 110
log-weighting scheme, 109–112
log1p function, 112
logarithms, 110
logistic regression, 178–181
    comparing to other algorithms, 284

glm function for, 275–276
  when not to use, 234, 275–276
lubridate package, 206

M

Mac OS X, installing R language on, 6
machine learning, vii, viii
  compared to statistics, 1
  as pattern recognition algorithms, 1
  resources for, viii, 293–294
malformed data, 15–16
match function, 18
matrices
  conversions to, 83
  data as, 31
  multiplication of, 217–219
  transposition of, 217
max function, 40
maximum value, 37, 40
MDS (multidimensional scaling), 216–222
  cmdscale function for, 221
  dimensions of, 221
  for US Senate clustering, 222–231
mean, 37–39
mean function, 38
mean squared error (MSE), 130–131, 140
median, 37–39
median function, 38
melt function, 211, 277
merge function, 23
Metropolis method, 194–204
min function, 40
minimum value, 37, 40
mode, 39, 52–54
monotonicity, 133
Moreno, Jacob L. (psychologist)
  sociometry developed by, 245
MSE (mean squared error), 130–131, 140
multidimensional scaling (see MDS)
multimodal, 53

N

Naive Bayes classifier, 77–78
  improving results of, 90–92
  testing, 87–90
  training, 80–84
  writing, 78–87
names function, 14

natural log, 110
nchar function, 15
neighbors function, 258, 270
Netflix
  recommendation system used by, 93
network graphs, 246–248, 261–266
network hairball, 262
noise (see jittering)
normal distribution (see bell curve)
nrow function, 22
numbers, determining whether column
    contains, 34
numeric summary, 31, 37

O

objective function, 185
online resources (see website resources)
optim function, 186–190–192
optimization, 183–190
  code breaking case study using, 193–204
  grid search for, 185–186
  Metropolis method for, 194–204
  optim function for, 186–190
  ridge regression for, 190–193
  stochastic optimization, 194
optimum, 183, 188
opts function, 25
orthogonal polynomials, 163
overfitting, 164–173
  cross-validation preventing, 166–168
  regularization preventing, 169–173

P

p-value, 149, 150
packages for R, 9–12
  (see also specific packages)
  case study involving, 239–242
  installing, 9–12
  list of, 11
  loading, 9
paste function, 80
pattern matching, in expressions (see regular
    expressions)
patterns in data, 1
  (see also classification; distributions;
  regression)
  confirming, 29–30
  pattern recognition algorithms for, 1

PCA (principal components analysis), 206–213

percent, asterisk, percent (%*%), for matrix multiplication, 219

plot function, 3, 259

plotting results (see visualizations of data)

plyr package, 13, 22, 108

poly function, 158–164

polynomial kernel SVM, 277, 278–280

polynomial regression, 158–164
    overfitting with, preventing, 164–173
    underfitting with, 168

Poole, Keith (political scientist)
    roll call data repository by, 223

predict function, 138, 179, 210

predictions, improving (see optimization)

principle components analysis (PCA), 206–213

princomp function, 207

print function, 9

priority inbox case study, 93–125
    feature generation, 95–99, 100–107
    testing, 123–125
    training, 117–120
    weighting scheme for, 108–117

Q

quantile function, 40, 42, 148

quantiles, 37, 40–41

question mark (?) syntax, for R help, 13

question mark, double (??) syntax, for R help, 13

R

R console
    Linux, 8
    Mac OS X, 6
    Windows, 5

R programming language, x, 1–2–5
    data types and structures
        data frame structure, 3, 13
        dates, 14–16, 22
        factor data type, 13
        list structure, 17
        vector data type, 3
    disadvantages of, 3–4
    downloading, 5
    help for, 13
    IDEs for, 8
    installing, 5–8
    packages for
        case study involving, 239–242
        checking for, 11
        installing, 9–12
        list of, 11
        loading, 9
    resources for, 27, 293–294
    text editors for, 8

R Project for Statistical Computing, 2

R-Bloggers website, 4

R2 (R squared), 141, 150, 151, 158

radial kernel SVM, 277, 280–282, 289

random number generation, 202, 216

range function, 40, 41

ranking classes, 93–95
    feature generation, 95–99, 100–107
    testing, 123–125
    training, 117–120
    weighting scheme for, 108–117

rbind function, 17, 106, 168

RCurl package, 11, 250

read.* functions, 13

read.delim function, 13

read.dta function, 224

readKH function, 224

readLines function, 80, 101

recommendation system, 93
    (see also ranking classes)
    k-nearest neighbors algorithm for, 233–242
    R package installation case study using, 239–242
    of Twitter followers, 269–273

rectangles, data as, 31
    (see also matrices)

regression, 127
    linear regression, 127–141
        adapting for nonlinear relationships, 155–158
        assumptions in, 133–141
        baseline model for, 127–131
        correlation as indicator of, 152–154
        dummy variables for, 132–133
        lm function for, 2, 137, 145, 153, 183
        optimizing, 183
    logistic regression, 178–181
        comparing to other algorithms, 284
        glm function for, 275–276

when not to use, 234, 275–276
polynomial regression, 158–164
  overfitting with, preventing, 164–173
  underfitting with, 168
ridge regression, 190–193
text regression, 174–181
regression picture, 63–66
regular expressions
grepl function for, 102, 105
gsub function for, 16
regularization
logistic regression using, 178–181, 287,
    290
preventing overfitting using, 169–173
ridge regression using, 190
SVM using, 282
text regression using, 174–177
rep function, 23
require function, 9
reshape package, 11, 13, 206, 240
residuals function, 138–141
resources (see books and publications; website
    resources)
RGui and R Console, 5
ridge regression, 190–193
RJSONIO package, 11, 250
rm function, 285
RMSE (root mean squared error), 132–133,
    140, 150, 167
root mean squared error (RMSE), 132–133,
    140, 150, 167
Rosenthal, Howard (political scientist)
  roll call data repository by, 223
ROT13 cipher, 195
rowSums function, 83
Rscript utility, 256
RSeek website, 4
RSiteSearch function, 13
#rstats Twitter community, 4

S

sample function, 167, 216
sapply function, 81, 83, 188
scale function, 211
scale_color_manual function, 25
scale_x_date function, 19, 25
scale_x_log function, 144
scale_y_log function, 144

scatterplot, 63–70, 89, 133–137, 143, 144,
    155
second quartile, 37, 38
seed (see ego-network; random number
    generation)
Senators, US (see US Senate clustering case
    study)
separability, 133
separating hyperplane, 68, 73
  (see also decision boundary)
seq function, 41
seq.Date function, 22
set.seed function, 216
set.vertex.attributes function, 261
setwd function, 11
SGA (SocialGraph API), 248–256
sgeom_point function, 228
shortest.paths function, 259
sigmoid kernel SVM, 277, 283–284
simulated annealing, 204
singularity, 162
skewed distribution, 53–54
social balance theory, 269
social features, of email, 96
social network analysis, 243–248
  (see also Twitter network analysis case
  study)
SocialGraph API (see SGA)
sociometry, 245
source function, 12, 256
spam detection case study, 74–92
  improving results of classifier, 90–92
  testing classifier, 87–90
  training classifier, 80–84
  writing classifier, 78–87
SpamAssassin public corpus, 74, 96
spread, 41–42
squared error, 130–131, 139, 184–185
StackOverflow website, 4
standard deviation, 43
statistics
  compared to machine learning, 1
  R language for (see R programming
    language)
  resources for, viii, 293–294
stochastic optimization, 194
stock market index case study, 205–213
strftime function, 21

strings, determining whether column contains, 34
strptime function, 106
strsplit function, 16, 102
subgraph function, 258
subset function, 18, 20
substitution cipher, 195
summary function, 19, 37, 145–151
summary, numeric (see numeric summary)
supervised learning, 94
SVM (support vector machine), 275–284
svm function, 277
symmetric distribution, 53–54

T

t function, 217
t value, 149
tab-delimited files, 13
table function, 270
tables (see matrices)
tail function, 14
TDM (term document matrix), 81
Temple, Duncan (developer)
    packages developed by, 251
term document matrix (TDM), 81
text classification, 74–78
    (see also spam detection case study)
text editors, for R, 8
text mining package (see tm package)
text regression, 174–181
thin-tailed distribution, 54–57
third quartile, 37
thread features, for email, 96
tm package, 10, 11, 80–82, 175
tolower function, 17
traffic order, 244
    (see also social network analysis)
training set, 1, 84, 166
transform function, 17, 83, 227
Traveling Salesman problem, 245
tryCatch function, 16
.tsv file extension, 13
    (see also tab-delimited files)
Tukey, John (statistician)
    regarding data not always having an answer, 177
    regarding exploratory data analysis, 29
Twitter follower recommendations case study, 269–273

Twitter network analysis case study, 245–266
    building networks, 256–257
    data for, obtaining, 248–256
    ego-network analysis, 258–261
    k-core analysis, 257–258
    visualizations for, 261–266

U

UFO sightings, case study of, 12–27
    aggregating data, 19–23
    analyzing data, 24–27
    cleaning data, 16–18
    loading data, 13–15
    malformed data, handling, 15–16
underfitting, 168
undirected graph, 246
unimodal, 53
unsupervised learning, 94, 205–213
US Senate clustering case study, 222–231

V

var function, 42
variables
    categorical, 13
    dummy, for linear regression, 132–133
variance, 42–43
vector data type, 3
VectorSource function, 82
Video Rchive website, 4
visualizations of data, 32–34, 44–60
    density plot (see density plot)
    histogram, 19–23, 44–46
    line plot, 24–27
    network graphs, 261–266
    relationships between columns, 61–70
    scatterplot (see scatterplot)

W

wave, in scatterplot, 133
web traffic predictions case study, 141–152
website resources
    codebook for US Congress data, 224
    for this book, xii
    Google Priority Inbox paper, 95
    R language, x, 28
    R language communities, 4
    R language downloads, 5
    R language packages, 11

R Project for Statistical Computing, 2
roll call data repository for US Congress,
223
SpamAssassin public corpus, 74, 96
Twitter API, 248
which function, 16
Windows, installing R language on, 5
write.graph function, 261

X

xlab function, 25
XML package, for R, 11
XML-based file formats (see GraphML files)

Y

ylab function, 25
ymd function, 206

About the Authors

Drew Conway is a PhD candidate in Politics at NYU. He studies international relations, conflict, and terrorism using the tools of mathematics, statistics, and computer science in an attempt to gain a deeper understanding of these phenomena. His academic curiosity is informed by his years as an analyst in the U.S. intelligence and defense communities.

John Myles White is a PhD student in the Princeton Psychology Department, where he studies how humans make decisions both theoretically and experimentally. Outside of academia, John has been heavily involved in the data science movement, which has pushed for an open source software approach to data analysis. He is also the lead maintainer for several popular R packages, including ProjectTemplate and log4r.

Colophon

The animal on the cover of *Machine Learning for Hackers* is a griffon vulture (family accipitridae). These considerably large birds hail from the warmer areas of the Old World, namely around the Mediterranean.

These birds hatch naked with a white head, broad wings, and short tail feathers. Adult griffon vultures—ranging in size from 37–43 inches long with an average wingspan of 7.5–9.2 feet—are generally a yellowish-brown with variations of black quill feathers and white down surrounding the neck. The griffon vulture is a scavenger, feeding only on prey that is already deceased.

The oldest recorded griffon vulture lived to be 41.4 years in captivity. They breed in the mountains of southern Europe, northern Africa, and Asia, laying one egg at a time.

The cover image is from Wood's Animate Creation. The cover font is Adobe ITC Garamond. The text font is Linotype Birka; the heading font is Adobe Myriad Condensed; and the code font is LucasFont's TheSansMonoCondensed.

Get even more for your money.

Join the O'Reilly Community, and register the O'Reilly books you own. It's free, and you'll get:

- $4.99 ebook upgrade offer
- 40% upgrade offer on O'Reilly print books
- Membership discounts on books and events
- Free lifetime updates to ebooks and videos
- Multiple ebook formats, DRM FREE
- Participation in the O'Reilly community
- Newsletters
- Account management
- 100% Satisfaction Guarantee

Signing up is easy:

1. **Go to: oreilly.com/go/register**
2. **Create an O'Reilly login.**
3. **Provide your address.**
4. **Register your books.**

Note: English-language books only

To order books online:
oreilly.com/store

For questions about products or an order:
orders@oreilly.com

To sign up to get topic-specific email announcements and/or news about upcoming books, conferences, special offers, and new technologies:
elists@oreilly.com

For technical questions about book content:
booktech@oreilly.com

To submit new book proposals to our editors:
proposals@oreilly.com

O'Reilly books are available in multiple DRM-free ebook formats. For more information:
oreilly.com/ebooks

Spreading the knowledge of innovators   oreilly.com

Have it your way.

Milton Keynes UK
Ingram Content Group UK Ltd.
UKHW032142211223
R3475900001B/R34759PG434674UKX00005B/11